T0319812

HENRY FORD'S PLAN FOR THE AMERICAN SUBURB

HENRY FORD'S PLAN
FOR THE AMERICAN SUBURB

DEARBORN AND DETROIT

HEATHER B. BARROW

NIU PRESS / DEKALB

Northern Illinois University Press, DeKalb 60115
© 2015 by Northern Illinois University Press
All rights reserved

24 23 22 21 20 19 18 17 16 15   1 2 3 4 5
978-0-87580-490-3 (cloth)
ISBN: 978-0-875-80795-9

Book and cover design by Shaun Allshouse

Library of Congress Cataloging-in-Publication Data
Barrow, Heather B.
Henry Ford's plan for the American suburb : Dearborn and Detroit /
Heather B. Barrow.
    pages   cm
Includes bibliographical references and index.
ISBN 978-0-87580-490-3 (hardback) —
ISBN 978-1-60909-180-4 (ebook)
1. Ford, Henry, 1863–1947. 2. Suburbs—Michigan—Detroit—
History—20th century. 3. Suburbs—Michigan—Dearborn—History—
20th century. 4. Cities and towns—Michigan—Growth—History—
20th century. 5. Detroit (Mich.)—Economic conditions—20th century.
6. Dearborn (Mich.)—Economic conditions—20th century.
7. Automobile industry and trade—Social aspects—Michigan—History
—20th century. 8. Fordism—United States—History—20th century. 9.
United States—Economic conditions—20th century. I. Title.
HT352.U62D4833 2015
307.7609774'340904—dc23
2015006809

"I will build a motor car for the multitude . . . for the unskilled individual to operate easily . . . built of honest materials . . . after the simplest designs. . . . It shall be so low in price that the man of moderate means may own one—and enjoy with his family the blessings of happy hours spent in God's great open spaces."

—Henry Ford, "An Ideal Realized," *Ford Times*

Table of Contents

Illustrations

Figures

Tables

Timeline for Henry Ford, Detroit, and Dearborn

2001   Anniversary of 300 years since Detroit was incorporated as a city

2003   Anniversary of 100 years since the Ford Motor Company was founded

2004   Anniversary of 75 years since the City of Dearborn was consolidated

2008   Anniversary of 100 years since the Model T was introduced

2013   Anniversary of 150 years since the birth of Henry Ford

2014   Anniversary of 100 years since the five-dollar day was offered

2015   Anniversary of 70 years since Henry Ford II became president of the Ford Motor Company

Preface

"Detroit always comes back," declared President Barack Obama in a speech to the citizens of Michigan, in the days running up to his 2015 State of the Union address. Taking Detroit as a symbol of the "middle-class economics" that would become the centerpiece of his address to the nation, Obama emphasized the city's ability to experience a turnaround in spite of a drastic and desperate decline. Detroit's public finances were in shambles, placing it into state receivership, and the city's recent exit from bankruptcy—the largest of its kind in the history of the country—pointed to a stability that was temporary, at best.

Its private-sector economy, concentrated in the automobile industry, was doing only a little better. The Big Three car makers had been reliant upon government help during the worst of the Great Recession. General Motors and Chrysler benefited from $80 billion in taxpayer money to rescue them from closing their companies. As a side effect of the deal, though, Chrysler was no longer a US-headquartered company, having merged with Europe-based Fiat. Meanwhile, Ford Motor Company avoided taking so-called "bail-out" money, which the government offered through the Troubled Asset Relief Program (TARP), but it relied instead upon other federal aid during this time, using a $5.9 billion loan from the Department of Energy for environmental mitigation.

Detroit barely scraped along throughout the economic downturn, but in the end, government intervention proved to be effective. Ultimately, jobs totaling one million were saved and the assistance package was eventually paid back. By 2015 Detroit's automobile industry was experiencing improved sales, the best since 2006, and auto workers were also over the worst of it, netting 164,000 jobs since 2009.

Whether Detroit and its automobile-based economy are on an upswing remains debatable, with many uncertainties still ahead for a recovery from devastation. Yet, few would disagree with the president's conclusion to the Michigan speech that "America is rooting for Detroit." After all, what city could be more American than Detroit? Also known as "Motor City" or "Motown," it long-ago embodied all the best qualities that made the United States so exceptional: the ingenuity to invent a new machine, the work ethic of the assembly line, the immigrants who thronged the factories needing jobs, the improved quality of life attained through high wages, and the aspirations of residents who spread to suburbs in search of a middle-class lifestyle. These suburbs included the iconic Dearborn, home to the Ford Motor Company since 1918. In this way, Detroit suburbs became the point of origin for "middle-class economics" that became prevalent during the twentieth century and remain a touchstone in a presidential address from our current century. It was Henry Ford and the new political economy he started, referred to as "Fordism," that created an American middle class, who could afford to become home-owners, car-owners, and suburbanites. No wonder Barack Obama referred to the auto industry as a "good bet" and the "bedrock" of the economy.

Surely, the prevalent headlines about the comeback of Detroit and its most famous industry would be sufficient evidence that this topic remains eternally relevant to anyone interested in American history. But should more evidence be needed, it is worthwhile to dwell a moment on some recent historical milestones that have been passed by during the last decade or so. The year 2001 was an anniversary for the City of Detroit, celebrating three hundred years of history and its origins as a settlement by the French and the British. This was a rare event for the region of the Midwest, which is usually considered to be a newer part of the nation, mistakenly believed to be without colonial roots. The year 2004 was memorable for Detroit's most influential suburb, Dearborn, which marked seventy-five years for its status as a consolidated city. A spate of one hundred-year anniversaries was reached by Ford Motor Company in recent years: 2003 was the centenary of the company's founding, 2008 was the centenary for the introduction of the Model T, and 2014 was the centenary of the five-dollar day. Bringing us up to the year 2013 was the sesquicentennial of the birth of Henry Ford. This was followed in 2015 with the seventy-year anniversary of Henry Ford II's take-over of the company as president, only a few years before the death of his ailing grandfather. Henry Ford II was able to transform the Ford Motor Company, turning it into a corporation that resembles companies of the present day and readying it to enter the post-war period.

These landmarks in time outline the journey taken by Henry Ford and his company and their impact on one of the country's major cities, creating a movement for suburbanization that eventually swept the nation. It is the story of how Detroit rose through the ranks to become the fourth-largest city in the country, and how Dearborn, its most sizeable suburb, grew within the space of a single decade from an agrarian village to a modern community containing the world's greatest manufacturing complex. It was a time of phenomenal change, still generating discussion today of how the future might return to the past.

HENRY FORD'S PLAN FOR THE AMERICAN SUBURB

Introduction

IN THE DETROIT AREA, suburbanization was led mostly by Henry Ford, who not only located an entire manufacturing complex over the city's border in Dearborn, but was first among the Big Three to make the automobile a mass-consumer item. The city's suburbanization, in other words, was spurred simultaneously by the migration of the automobile industry and the mobility of automobile users, and Ford was involved with both. A welfare capitalist, Henry Ford was a leader on many fronts—he was the first to raise wages, increase leisure time, and transform workers into consumers, and he was the most effective at making suburbs an intrinsic part of American life.[1] Certainly, the tens of thousands of people who moved to Dearborn were amenable to this idea. Suburbanization, however, was never a simple matter of growth in the fringe paralleling growth in the center. Instead, it was a matter of resources being lost from the city as they were transferred to the suburbs. Almost immediately, discrepancies between Detroit's central city and suburbs became apparent: its suburbs were more likely to be home to white-collar workers than blue-collar; to skilled industrial workers than less skilled; to whites than blacks; to native-borns than immigrants. Meanwhile, the central city witnessed the arrival of a crushing number of job seekers attracted by the promise of factory work, the rise of an inner-city residential slum, growing economic depression in neighborhoods left behind by industry, the diversion of industrial wealth from its tax base, an increase in welfare cases as wage earners adjusted to the cyclical nature of industrial production, and an increasing reliance on municipal debt— even during periods of prosperity—for the needed expansion of services and infrastructure.

Henry Ford's relocation of his company to Dearborn was the second and final step in his pilgrimage from the downtown, following a 1910 move from his Detroit factory at Piquette Avenue to the Highland Park site.[2] By the late 1910s, the Highland Park plant—famous for its assembly line—was curtailed in its growth by the city of Detroit, which now enveloped it. In comparison, a suburban site offered a number of advantages.[3] Although land for relocation could still be found in Detroit, particularly in neighborhoods recently added to the city, the tax rate was comparatively high. Besides, the suburbs would provide a good place for Ford's workers to live, accommodating thousands of employees within commuting distance. Plus, turning workers into suburbanites would make them less likely to unionize: they would be dependent upon a single major employer, tied down by a mortgage, and cut off from labor organizing in the city. Finally, Ford needed autonomy in operating his company, a fiefdom guaranteed only in a suburban locale, where he—as the single largest taxpayer and among the richest men in the nation—would soon have the local council in his vest pocket. Altogether, frustration with urban politics, taxation, labor, and logistics conspired to point Ford toward the suburbs, prompting him to construct his last and largest plant, the River Rouge facility, in the community that would become Dearborn.

It is possible as well that Henry Ford just preferred the suburbs, regardless of circumstances. In developing Dearborn, he expressed a wish for it to become "an ideal home section away from the congestion of the city, with all the advantages of city life incorporated in suburban dwellings."[4] To him, suburbs were "quieter, cleaner, sunnier, airier and in every way more healthful for children and adults the whole year round," and he emphasized their bounty, noting "you can work farther from home where living conditions are better and expenses are not so high."[5] Ford realized, of course, it was the automobile that made suburbs more feasible than ever before, and he commented, "Now it is effecting a spreading out of cities and populations." He believed relocation to the suburbs would provide better opportunities for workers: abundant and affordable land made homeownership more accessible; lack of congestion made car ownership more appealing; and low taxes meant the money earned by wage earners would go farther. "One of the most hopeful facts," he observed, "is that, whereas only the well-to-do once found it possible to get away from the city, now the workingman finds it not only possible but advantageous to live in the country, and thousands of them are doing it even while they work in the City."[6] In fact, Ford called moving workers out of the city a return to the "early American idea."[7] Indeed, Dearborn was benefiting from a phase of growth in which wages were high, taxes were low, government was small, and consumer goods affordable—what, after all, could be more American than this kind of community?

Spurred by the presence of gargantuan industry, the suburb of Dearborn experienced phenomenal growth. Over the decade of the 1920s, Dearborn doubled its physical size and multiplied its population ten times over, increasing from five to fifty thousand. An initial group of Ford Motor Company workers was induced to live in Dearborn, attracted by a company-sponsored subdivision called Ford Homes, consisting of about three hundred houses and a school. Within ten years, automobile industry wage earners comprised half the employed residents throughout the expanding municipality. Dearborn's citizens enjoyed a relatively high standard of living, with rates of home- and car ownership equal to or exceeding the national average. The suburb, however, was far from truly inclusive, as the vast majority of those employed at the River Rouge plant did not live in Dearborn. Lower-skilled workers probably could not afford to live there; African Americans were excluded by de facto and de jure segregation.[8] Nonetheless, Dearborn shifted the paradigm for a worker community, surpassing the conventions of a company town by its large scale, proximity to a metropolis, and ability to attract residents other than employees. Dearborn is better understood as a working-class suburb.[9]

Ultimately, Dearborn provided a model that was repeated throughout the nation in the 1920s, as newly affordable automobiles enabled people of all classes to relocate to suburbs and a major demographic shift took place away from central cities. "Suburban communities burgeoned from New York to Los Angeles," states historian Joseph Arnold in regard to this time. "Growth rates of four or five hundred percent were not uncommon." He continues:

> During the same period the number of wage earners in some central core areas began to decline. By the end of the decade, 5,176,000 persons had moved to suburban homes. The automobile and concrete highway opened thousands of heretofore inaccessible acres of land around the cities, and the increase of motor vehicle registrations from 9.2 million in 1920 to 26.5 million in 1930 gives a rough picture of the number of Americans who were able to live beyond the end of the streetcar line.[10]

Net growth in central cities continued at this time: the 1920 census was the first of a series that revealed a majority of people living in urban places. Yet the rate of growth in suburbs began outpacing that of cities. This settlement pattern was characteristic of the 97 metropolitan districts defined by the 1930 census as any city with a population of 50,000 or more that contained within a contiguous territory an aggregate of at least 100,000 people.[11] Simply put, metropolitan districts were central cities and their suburbs. They existed throughout the country, in the Northeast, Midwest, South, and West. They were also diverse, including obvious choices such as Chicago, New York, Philadelphia, Boston, Los Angeles, and Detroit—as well as Altoona and Atlanta, Baltimore and Birmingham, Rockford and Rochester, San Francisco and Salt Lake, to name just a few. Between 1920 and 1930, the suburban population within metropolitan districts grew by a third, while the population of central cities increased by only a quarter. This was a remarkable reversal of the situation two decades earlier when central cities grew by 37 percent and their suburbs by 26 percent.[12]

Suburbanization in the interwar period had many causes. Cities overflowed from a growing urban population due to migration within the nation, pressure from immigration in previous decades, and natural increase. Meanwhile, people lived and worked farther apart due to improvements in the technologies of transportation (the automobile), communication (the telephone), and energy (electricity), all of which became more widespread. New settlement patterns emerged because of the dual economic forces of concentration and dispersion: commercial and professional activities were attracted to the downtown, while other functions that required a lower density such as large-scale manufacturing and residential development spun out toward the fringes. Cultural changes also motivated outward migration, through campaigns to "own your own home" and the "Garden City" movements. The rise of political opposition to urban annexation contributed to this trend as well. While in previous decades, suburbs were incorporated into the cities, they now remained separate entities. Even so, they fell under the influence of the central city, economically, socially, and culturally.[13]

Crucial in bringing about this suburban trend were Henry Ford and the welfare capitalists who copied him. They transformed workers into consumers by paying high wages and providing increased leisure.[14] Workers in turn were better able to buy houses and cars and move to the suburbs, pioneering the "crabgrass frontier."[15] Additionally, these industrialists often situated their manufacturing facilities in the suburbs, providing further incentive for workers to relocate their residences away from central cities. The decade of the 1920s was predominated by this new political economy—also known as "Fordism"—linking mass production with mass consumption through high wages.[16] The rise of Dearborn and numerous communities like it demonstrated that Fordism was connected with mass suburbanization as well.[17] Eventually, this system laid the foundation for suburban stability and growth in the postwar period, causing the spread of communities like Long Island–based Levittown, a place that, because of its affordability, attracted a broad middle class. Thus, the mass suburbanization of the Baby Boom era can be seen as a continuation of the trend from the 1920s, merely interrupted by the Great Depression.[18] A critical difference in the pre- and postwar periods, however, was that while cities were still growing during the first phase of suburbanization, by the second they were in decline.[19]

Mass suburbanization was a national phenomenon. Yet the example of Detroit is an important baseline since the trend was more discernible there than elsewhere.[20] Until this point, Detroit's suburbs remained small and were of little consequence economically, containing at the turn of the century only 7 percent of the metropolitan area's manufacturing and population. This was one-third the average for all major metropolises. Detroit varied from comparable cities like Boston, Pittsburgh, Providence, Cincinnati, and New York, where substantial manufacturing and population had located to industrial satellites decades earlier, during the nineteenth century. In contrast, Detroit's trend of decentralization appeared rather suddenly in 1910.[21] From then until 1940, the geographic district outside Detroit expanded close to seven times, increasing from 110 square miles to 718. The suburban population swelled, notably between 1920 and 1930, when it little more than doubled, going from a population of 256,588 to 536,102.[22] By 1939, more than half of the Detroit-area employment in automobile manufacturing was outside the city.[23] A year later, Detroit's suburbs had the most manufacturing and the second-highest population.[24] Eventually, Dearborn was transformed into one of Detroit's largest suburbs in terms of population, and it gained the highest number of manufacturing jobs, constituting close to a quarter of such jobs in the entire metropolis.[25] Growth within the central city was also decentralized because, even there, the settlement pattern was determined by a high rate of automobile ownership and a preponderance of one- and two-family homes.[26] In fact, by 1940, Detroit's population density was slightly lower than average compared to other cities, a notable change from previous decades between 1900 and 1920, when it was relatively high.[27]

At the beginning of Dearborn's growth spurt, the giant scale of the River Rouge plant was formative in creating a suburb for the masses, offering untold employment opportunities for workers looking for an excuse to leave the central city. Much more than a single factory, the River Rouge plant was a manufacturing complex linking several facilities in order to achieve what became known as vertical integration.[28] Within one site, this complex had the unprecedented ability to process raw materials into value-added products that could be assembled into one final consumer item. Vertical integration, or any kind of monopoly for that matter, was not entirely new.

In the era that led to trust-busting Progressivism, vertical integration was first attempted by late nineteenth-century robber barons. Henry Ford simply took this process and scaled it up by an exponential degree. Construction of the River Rouge plant began in 1917, but automotive production was delayed until after the end of World War I, when it created an output of 800 car bodies a day. By 1921, a new coke oven, sawmill, and blast furnace went into operation, and tractor manufacturing began, with a combined production of cars and tractors totaling 36,000 by the end of the year. In 1925, construction of the steel complex started—which meant building additional coke ovens, open-hearth furnaces, a blooming mill, and a rolling mill, which all went into operation in mid-1926. In 1927, the assembly line was transferred from Highland Park, finally establishing the River Rouge plant as Ford Motor Company's main assembly plant and gradually rendering the Highland Park plant obsolete. At its peak in 1929, the River Rouge plant employed 98,300 hourly workers, a significant increase from the beginning of car production ten years earlier when it employed only 8,800. By now, iron ore could enter the plant at one end and be transformed into a finished automobile within a time span of a little over twenty-four hours.[29]

Moreover, Henry Ford's version of vertical integration was an important concept at the time because it was a business practice that set apart his company from its biggest rival of the day, General Motors. Upon completion of the River Rouge plant and the demotion of the Highland Park plant, Ford Motor Company centralized both its production and its administration headquarters in Dearborn. General Motors, in contrast, took a different approach, choosing to build a series of assembly plants in Flint, Detroit, Lansing, and Pontiac, siting a corporate headquarters in Detroit, and relying on a host of small suppliers located throughout the metropolitan region. In other words, General Motors chose to decentralize rather than concentrate its operations. In comparison, Chrysler's approach fell in between those of its competitors: its largest plant, the Dodge Main, was located in Hamtramck, but its administrative headquarters and an additional plant, the former Maxwell plant, were in Highland Park. During this time, the Big Three (Ford Motor Company, General Motors, and Chrysler) were just emerging as leaders in the automotive field, following a consolidation that eliminated dozens of smaller companies. So the race to see which business approach became hegemonic—concentration or decentralization—took on particular drama. At stake, after all, was the future of the automobile industry.[30]

More relevant to urban development was the way in which different locational approaches of the Big Three impacted workers and the communities they chose as home. It might seem intuitive that the decentralized approach of General Motors and Chrysler would spur the greatest degree of suburbanization. While this would happen eventually, at the time it was decades away. Plants sited by General Motors in Flint, Detroit, Lansing, and Pontiac were all in areas that could be considered relatively urban, a mixture of cities ranging in size and density. Chrysler, meanwhile, was located in Hamtramck and Highland Park, two independent communities that, through a fluke of history, became surrounded by Detroit as the central city grew. In other words, these were two essentially urban communities, floating like islands in the sea of Detroit. Chrysler workers tended to live in either Hamtramck, Highland Park, or Detroit, and so they were unlikely to relocate to the suburbs as this would mean a lengthy reverse commute. Only in the example of Ford Motor Company did the siting choice of a plant create an immediate motive for workers to become suburbanites.

However, in the postwar period, the vertical integration once championed by Henry Ford was gradually abandoned as its weaknesses were revealed. One limitation was the difficulty in accommodating year-to-year style changes or in producing more than one model within a year. By the late 1920s, the Ford Motor Company market share was threatened by the ability of General Motors to offer a variety of automobiles through a flexible mode of production based upon multiple assembly plants.[31] Wartime conversion of the automobile industry to defense purposes also facilitated decentralized production methods as greenfield sites located in outlying regions along interstate highways were sought to build large factories quickly and cheaply. Additionally, since the centralization of manufacturing lent itself to labor organizing, manufacturers began spreading out their facilities with the intention of isolating workers as well as drawing upon less mobilized labor pools found in rural settings.

The decline of vertical integration held consequences for urban development, just as its rise had done. Metropolitan centers like Detroit descended into political chaos and economic impoverishment as deindustrialization took its toll.[32] Earlier in its history, Detroit had attracted job seekers in such droves that its population increased from a quarter million in 1900 to nearly a million in 1920, and by 1940, it had reached more than a million and a half.[33] As early as 1914, autoworkers comprised 40 percent of the city's factory employees, ten times as many as in 1900.[34] Automobile plants leapfrogged across the city, with obsolescent facilities abandoned and newer, bigger ones built in a series of rings progressing from the center, totaling thirty-seven major plants and 250 accessory plants by 1925.[35] Detroit maintained its status as the country's fourth-largest city throughout the 1920s and 1930s.

Following World War II, though, the number of inhabitants in Detroit started to drop, and the decline continued with every subsequent decade. Detroit, which had been the country's fourth-largest city since 1920, began to slip behind in national rankings of size, dropping in 1940 from fourth to fifth place. Then, it fell again in 1980 and 1990, coming in sixth and then seventh. Employment decreased as well: between 1950 and 1970, the central city lost 100,000 automotive jobs alone, while its suburbs gained 40,000.[36] With the 2000 census, Detroit gained the dubious honor of being the first city among those with a population of over a million to fall below that mark. This drop occurred despite a trend that year in which most major US cities, even those in the Rustbelt, showed an increase, however modest.

All the while, suburbanized areas often flourished, benefiting not just by the flight from cities of residents but also by the flight of jobs. For example, Dearborn continued to thrive, even after the River Rouge plant passed its high point of employment and began reducing its workforce. From 1940 to 1950, Dearborn's population doubled, rising to a total of 95,000 residents, almost entirely white. In 1950, Ford Motor Company employed 65,000 workers at the River Rouge plant, of which 20,000 lived in Dearborn. Between 1940 and 1950, more than 11,000 houses were built, and the homeownership rate was higher than ever, reaching 73 percent by the end of the decade. Also in this period, automobile registrations grew by 60 percent, and by 1950, the car ownership rate stood at close to two automobiles per household. The overall fiscal health of the community was indicated by an assessed valuation that rose from $215 million in 1940 to $376 million ten years later, an increase of 45 percent, as well as by bank deposits totaling $80,000,000 in 1950. Finally, of the 200 largest communities in the country, Dearborn ranked only 121st, yet its effective buying power based on income per family placed it at eleventh.[37]

By the postwar period, Dearborn and suburbs throughout the Detroit metropolitan area reflected a solid economy underpinned by the industrial wealth that was relocated out of the central city through a process going on for decades. In developing their sites of production outside Detroit, the Big Three drained the central city of its tax revenue and opportunities for jobs and housing. Although comprehensive metropolitan plans to rebuild the region holistically were repeatedly proposed by citizens' groups, never was anything implemented other than in piecemeal fashion. On the other hand, too much intervention by policy makers can also be blamed—witness the redlining by the Federal Housing Administration, which promoted racial discrimination in housing; government subsidization of wartime factories in the suburbs, which accelerated decentralization; and postwar urban renewal and highway development, which destroyed entire neighborhoods and displaced an unjustified number of residents. Thus, the fate of Detroit and suburbs like Dearborn was determined by a complex relationship between the automobile industry and various urban-development policies, including those of Henry Ford. The example of the Detroit metropolis raises the question as to whether the mass suburbanization originating in the 1920s—and revived in the postwar period—can be said to represent an achievement of the "American dream"—and if so, by whom and at what cost.[38]

Henry Ford, motor-car magnate, is not an easy subject for historical inquiry—he is so full of contradictions. Among serious scholars, he is a figure who has been vilified many times over for his anti-Semitic and anti-labor biases. At the same time, many of the public view him as an American folk hero, to be celebrated for his ingenuity and rags-to-riches rise. His personality was mercurial and capricious, even enigmatic—qualities to be expected in a rich, powerful man who was used to giving orders without the need for explaining motives. But he could also be quixotic, taking on hopelessly idealistic causes and then quickly abandoning them. Thus, his seemingly rigid ideology could suddenly bend in an opposite direction.[39] Although he left us with many famous quotations, he was not always verbose in person; most of the time, he was pithy to the point of being cryptic, and never did he reveal a sense of irony or introspection about himself.[40] Reconciling the different facets of his complicated personality is likely impossible, yet this somehow fails to put off readers drawn to the abundant literature about him.[41] In addition, the company he founded, which still bears his name, continues to thrive, despite many setbacks typical of heavy industry in the United States.[42] And as long as Ford Motor Company still generates headlines, attention to Henry Ford the man will likely never flag. Yet, with so much written about him already, what more of any value could be added to his story?

The existing literature about Henry Ford falls into a few major categories. There are biographies galore, some intended for an academic audience, others for a popular one.[43] Given that Ford had a rather long life span, stretching from 1863 to 1947, he witnessed a time of immense change for America, living from the time of the Civil War to World War II. He survived into his eighties when that was an uncommon achievement, and it seems symbolic that about half his life was spent in the nineteenth century and the other in the twentieth, with his middle age pivoting on the turn of the century. As such, he was able to experience directly some of the most important phases of the Industrial Revolution, even before he began influencing this movement himself through the promotion and perfecting of mass production. The time frame for his life may explain one of the more paradoxical qualities of his character—that someone so visionary could also be so nostalgic for the very past he was instrumental in destroying. So even while he was commissioning the creation of the River Rouge factory (the largest manufacturing complex of its time anywhere in the world), he was also acquiring historical artifacts of agrarian living for his museum, Greenfield Village.[44] Perhaps only someone whose life straddled two centuries would be motivated to act this way. In any case, these dimensions of his personality have proved ever fascinating to the audience of his biographies.

Works about Henry Ford usually fall into the area of business history.[45] This scholarship focuses upon Ford's many enterprises both before and after the creation of Ford Motor Company. Fleeing the drudgery of farmwork, as a young man he sought employment as a machinist in Detroit, and eventually he became an engineer with the Edison Illuminating Company. On his own time, he began experimenting with gasoline engines to propel primitive automobiles, on frames adapted from bicycle models. In 1896, he finally came up with a viable prototype, which encouraged him to found his first company, the short-lived Detroit Automobile Company (1899–1901). By late 1901, he had developed a new firm, the Henry Ford Company, and had attracted the attention of prospective stockholders through his participation in automobile racing. Following a lawsuit brought by parts suppliers the Dodge Brothers, Henry Ford was compelled to reinvent his business persona once more, and he founded the Ford Motor Company in 1903.[46]

By now he was forty years old—yet he was something of a late bloomer and much of his success still lay ahead, not to be realized until the second half of his life. He went on to invent the Model T (1908), improve the assembly line at the Highland Park plant (1913), introduce the five-dollar day (1914), and break ground at the River Rouge plant (1918).[47] Around this time, in the 1920s, he was credited with the creation of "Fordism"—the use of vertical integration to enable mass production and mass consumption. Yet, no matter how large and prosperous Ford Motor Company became, it remained an oversized mom-and-pop shop, with Henry Ford setting the tone in top-down manner, with little input from board members or company executives. Even the closest family members were set limits in their roles. From behind the scenes, Ford as an individual remained dominant—from 1918 to 1943, he made his son Edsel the nominal head of the company, but this was entirely a sham, with Henry still running the show.[48] This situation led to a well-documented poor relationship between father and heir. Nonetheless, the ability to survive as a one-man business was remarkable for its day, especially since rival automobile manufacturers were increasingly embracing the corporate model, which featured a more horizontal hierarchy. Perhaps this singularity explains the ongoing proliferation of books about Ford Motor Company's history.

Given the complexity of Henry Ford, his company, and the literature written already, no single approach to understanding this topic can be enough. This is why this study takes a broad view, zooming in on Dearborn as a model community and then pulling back to look at Detroit and its metropolitan area, as well as considering national trends in suburbanization. It also comments on the profound cultural impact of Henry Ford, a businessman with profit-driven ambitions who nonetheless was running a company that he envisioned as an instrument of social change. Unlike the Carnegies and Rockefellers who had come a generation before, Ford wished to be more than a philanthropist handing out charity; instead, he wanted to change our society and economy in some fundamental way, and he did so successfully. So, although this is primarily a work of history, it is not exactly a narrowly defined monograph; instead, it draws upon other fields such as sociology and geography. At times, it uses an American studies approach, in order to address the underlying values and beliefs motivating Ford, which deserve particular attention since they were shared by so many compatriots and provide insight into the national character. Only this interdisciplinary method can best wrap around Henry Ford's plan for the American suburb, as played out in Dearborn, the Detroit area, and the nation.

1

The Urban Plans of Henry Ford

Ford and Suburbanization

Henry Ford possessed a unique ability to connect culture and technology; after all, it is difficult to imagine another individual who was able to influence such a great number of people with the invention of a single mass-produced consumer product.[1] Up to the point when the Model T was conceived, the automobile was merely a form of recreation for the affluent, a luxury that provided convenience and entertainment. Only after Ford reinterpreted the automobile as something within the reach of average people did it become an everyday necessity and bring about a transportation revolution. Although competitor automakers soon copied Ford Motor Company's dissemination of an affordable and easy-to-maintain car for daily use, no other maker retained a dominant market share in such a steady streak throughout the 1910s and early 1920s. An immediate impact of the mass-produced automobile was a dramatic transformation of the national landscape, with radiating urban growth following newly accessible corridors that led out of central cities.[2] Yet, little has been written on how Henry Ford himself viewed this upending turn of events. As it happens, he was a strong supporter of the rise of suburbanization brought in on the tide of spreading automobile use. To some extent, he actually seems to have intended this new kind of urban development.[3]

The unstoppable quality of Henry Ford continues to generate interest in his defining impact on American society.[4] Some of Ford's influence can be attributed to his unusual personality and lively imagination, which made him someone who could identify and predict trends and then drive the bandwagon to make them widespread. Also to be considered, however, was the degree to which Henry Ford, the man, was conflated with Ford Motor

Company, the firm he founded.[5] Ford Motor Company was essentially a family business, a model more typical of the nineteenth century than of the twentieth. In this personality-driven environment, the values and beliefs of Henry Ford mattered as much as any business acumen, and to some extent, he wanted his company to be an instrument of social change, which was somewhat odd compared to other automakers. Really, there was no one within the firm to oppose him on this—he was a majority stockholder, and besides, the company was wildly profitable, making him one of the richest and most influential men in the country, if not the world. Despite his high status, he remained something of an Everyman, and the fact that we are still quoting him today proves what a hold he had on the nation's psyche (as did Mark Twain or Benjamin Franklin). Given this folksy vein of his, it seems only natural that he concerned himself not only with the best mode of transportation for everyone but also with what kind of homes they inhabited—looking far beyond his own workers to see how every American should live.[6]

Just as Henry Ford wanted to make a "car for the multitude," he also intended to create a *suburb for the multitude*. Indirectly, he was already accomplishing this through the transportation revolution he himself had set into motion, which brought about swift urban change throughout the United States. In a much more literal way, he created suburbanization firsthand by relocating his industrial headquarters from Detroit to the outskirts of the city, in a location that would become Dearborn, Michigan. Additionally, Ford promoted this new site by commissioning a model subdivision called the Ford Homes. Also, he had at his disposal the deployment of company policies to motivate employees who needed aid in buying houses and cars. Within a single decade (the 1920s), Dearborn grew from a population of 5,000 to ten times that number, with automobile workers soon constituting half of all employed residents.[7] Dearborn embodied a rising trend of the times—suburbs that sheltered upwardly mobile, working-class people who could newly afford to own houses and cars. In the end, Henry Ford was singularly responsible for promoting suburban development in the Detroit area, ultimately setting an example for a nation of people adopting the automobile who wished to relocate outside of central cities. One reason Ford could do this was his ability to spread ideas through the many channels of communication under his control, some of which attained circulation throughout the country, like the *Dearborn Independent*.[8] For example, this newspaper featured an ongoing series about the Ford Homes, presumably inspiring its audience to create a like-minded community.

Of course, Henry Ford—however powerful—was not alone in transforming Dearborn into a model suburb. As a major landowner and the single largest taxpayer, he likely had the elected officials in his vest pocket, who must have been complicit in his plan. He also had the help, wittingly or not, of private developers and anyone else in the real estate business as well as bureaucrats with oversight for zoning and other regulation whose interests coincided with his. After all, most of Dearborn grew in a conventional way, with dozens of developers building out entire subdivisions on a speculative basis, selling hundreds of individual houses to prospective homeowners. Government regulation of this development was provided by ordinances typical of the time, intended to preserve property values. In this sense, Dearborn was a rather ordinary community—the product of market forces—that orchestrated the supply and demand for residential development. Here, the Ford Homes subdivision developed by Ford Motor Company on a speculative basis for sale to employees was part of the larger pattern and subject to the same process of development as the rest of Dearborn.[9]

This is where Henry Ford diverged from the industrial titans of the past, taking on a much more modest role than the monopolists who founded self-contained company towns owned entirely by a single corporation. Dearborn was the exception rather than the rule because so little of its residential area was directly under the influence of the automaker. Ford's responsibility in creating a suburb for the masses was primarily conceptual; although taking the step to build the Ford Homes was crucial to the realization of Dearborn as a community, he left it mostly to others to implement his idea.

In the end, Henry Ford's influence on urban development, after widening for so many years, was constrained by changing times. At his peak, Ford was able to offer high wages, on an unprecedented scale, to his workers, which made it possible for them to afford the suburbs. With the onset of the Great Depression, however, the role of a single individual in assuring a basic standard of living for an enormous number of people was curtailed by economic uncertainty, which brought chaos to every level of society. Ford's ability to promote suburbs for the masses, in Dearborn and throughout the nation, simply could not ride out a downturn this precipitous, and his efforts were halted for a time. Ultimately, recovery was brought about through the rise of unionization and a greater role for big government. Of course, Fordism—the linking of mass production and mass consumption—was slowed down only temporarily, and it was far from disappearing as the century reached its midpoint and the country entered into postwar expansion. This system remained the foundation for the economy, but now it was buttressed by union demands for high wages and government provision of entitlements.

The success of this new system was evident in the elevated standard of living for the average worker, who continued to achieve a suburban lifestyle. Henry Ford himself did not live to witness these lasting changes, as he died in 1947. Yet it is clear in retrospect that he was committed to promoting a rising suburban trend for all classes, and this study will argue that those effects were still evident long after his death.

The Move to Metropolitanism

When Dearborn mushroomed in growth during the 1920s, it necessarily impacted the destiny of Detroit. For many inevitable reasons, cities and their suburbs exist in a state of dynamic tension; one would not exist without the other. Suburbs get their start as the offspring of the urban center—as the result of increased congestion that pushes the population to the outskirts where land is more available and often cheaper. By their very nature, suburbs rarely attain self-sufficiency: they are usually lacking in a strong tax base, high assessed valuation, major employers, or qualified labor pool, and sometimes they are missing key infrastructure components and valuable natural resources. Cities, although more independent because of their concentration of population and geographic advantages, are nonetheless reliant upon their suburbs. For instance, suburbs that function as bedroom communities supply the city with a labor pool commuting to work. The popularity of annexation—in which bordering suburbs are incorporated into the central city—illustrates how attractive the additional tax base and voter population of a desirable suburb might be.

Here, the relationship of Dearborn and Detroit is a case in point. When Dearborn leaped to a population of 50,000 from only 5,000 within a single decade, its *pace of growth* needs to be compared to that of the central city. Detroit, after all, had become one of the biggest cities in the nation. By 1920, it had a population of close to one million residents, and from then until 1940, it was ranked as the country's fourth-largest city.[10] In other words, Detroit was still expanding during the same period that Dearborn was doing the same. However, an important difference to be noted is that the rate of growth for Detroit was being outpaced by that of Dearborn—its multiplier was far less than the factor of ten experienced by its suburb. In fact, this was becoming a nationwide trend within major metropolitan areas: suburban population in these places surged by a third while the population of central cities expanded by only a quarter.[11]

This trend is the reason this study takes on a wide lens, pulling within its view both Dearborn and Detroit, to look fully at the impact of Henry Ford's urban policies. It is difficult to study Dearborn in isolation during the 1920s, since many Ford Motor Company workers at its factory commuted there from Detroit and from other suburbs. Some of these wage earners were displaced from employment at the Ford Motor Company facility in Highland Park, which was gradually decommissioned. Many automobile workers still lived near their first plant, even if they no longer worked there, and then commuted to Dearborn. Almost all African American workers commuted in from segregated communities elsewhere, as discrimination barred them from living in Dearborn. The dispersion of workers who lived throughout the Detroit metropolis eventually spurred Henry Ford to consider an addition to the region's mass transit system, proposing a new streetcar line in order to facilitate the commute into Dearborn. With the Great Depression, many workers who lost jobs at the Ford Motor Company but still lived in Detroit became a disproportionate burden on the social services of the central city. After all, Detroit could not levy taxes upon the auto company because it lay outside the city's tax base. So the central city was in competition with its biggest suburb, as they struggled over how to provide a safety net to citizens without a united tax base to provide adequate revenues. These are just a few examples of the need to address urban history with an approach based on "metropolitanism."[12]

Fordist and Post-Fordist Cities

In many ways, Henry Ford perfected the concept of vertical integration. This was a centralization, under one roof, of numerous manufacturing steps that had previously been outsourced to suppliers. His gigantic River Rouge plant in Dearborn was a manifestation of this philosophy, the physical perfection of an idea to maximize efficiency through economies of scale. The massive size of the River Rouge site—fifteen times the amount of land for the Highland Park plant—was complemented by access to transportation at an advantageous intersection of land, water, and rail routes. Nearby was a highway connecting Detroit and Chicago, and there were two major rail lines for freight, the Michigan Central and the Pere Marquette. Bordering the site was the River Rouge, which led to two Great Lakes linked via the Detroit River. The complex developed there became the world's largest manufacturing facility under a single operator. Designed by architect Albert Kahn, it spilled across a vast area, 9.5 million square feet of floor space spread out among two dozen glass-and-steel, single-story loft buildings. Vertical integration ensured that at every stage the same owner was involved: from gathering raw materials at company-owned timber tracts and iron mines, to transporting them by company-owned ship and rail, to the creation of semi-finished products like steel at company-owned foundries, and the assembly of a final item: in this case, the automobile. The closed loop of vertical integration was essentially a type of monopoly, with all the middlemen cut out.[13]

Some geographers have referred to postwar urban development as "Fordist," asserting that Fordism and its "fixed"—or vertically integrated—production were responsible for generating centralized cities surrounded by concentric rings of bedroom communities.[14] This period, they say, was the height of American suburbanization; while suburbs had existed a century earlier or more, they were never before spread on such a broad scale. Then, in the late twentieth century, these geographers claim, the economy entered a "post-Fordist" stage that relied on "flexible" production, and urban growth in turn became more fungible—industry spun off smaller units, which leapfrogged across municipal boundaries, state lines, and even national borders; cities first emptied and then gentrified in boomerang fashion; and meanwhile suburbs became "edge cities" interspersed with office parks, malls, and factories.[15] Suburbs still existed, but they were no longer exclusively residential, and more inhabitants began to do reverse commutes. Thus, these geographers argue, "post-Fordist" development is tied to both deindustrialization and white flight as well as the devastating urban crisis these brought on.[16]

One of the purposes of this study is to re-periodize our understanding of "Fordist" urban development by showing that the mass production of suburbia dated to the 1920s rather than the 1950s or 1960s. At the same time, this work will question the usefulness of "Fordism" in understanding urban development, especially the way it attempts to connect "fixed" production with centralized urban form. After all, as industry became more vertically integrated, this produced the exact opposite in urban formation. As a result, sprawling residential development throughout the metropolitan area became the norm at the precise moment that manufacturing was at its most compact state. For example, when Henry Ford moved his industry from Detroit to Dearborn, it spurred intensive unplanned growth surrounding the urban core. Suburban residents no longer commuted in a predictable way, entering and exiting the central city for their jobs; they commuted across suburbs, and bedroom communities were also their workplace destinations. Furthermore, this appears to have been intentional on the part of Ford: he seems to be a proponent of decentralization as well as centralization, even when his production method was in its most "fixed" period. The immediate effect of this diversion of industry was to decimate the central city's tax base, which became a major factor in the urban crisis there. Therefore, the urban crisis dates from a "Fordist" rather than a "post-Fordist" period, or so this study will illustrate.

Henry Ford as De Facto Urban Planner

This work will also argue for a sharper picture of Henry Ford by looking at him through the telescope of urban planning. It seems unlikely that Ford took up urban planning in any kind of formal way—he was a farm boy at heart, not college educated, and for relaxation he much preferred tinkering with his hands to reading. To imagine that he sought out information on the Anglo-American "Garden City" or the early twentieth-century Regional Planning Association of America (RPAA) would be a stretch. Yet, many captains of industry before him had taken an interest in developing company towns, and he was likely familiar with this tradition, since he socialized with his fellow capitalists.[17] Certainly, when it came time to commission the Ford Homes district, he knew enough to hire Leonard Willeke, an accomplished architect and urban planner, who further broadened Ford's knowledge of community development.[18]

So although Henry Ford did not personally research the leading theories of urban planning, he was part of a circle of people who did. Just as important, those notable thinkers were learning about Ford and studying his attempts to implement urban plans. For instance, it is documented that Lewis Mumford and Frank Lloyd Wright took an interest in Henry Ford, and they were probably as much influenced by him as he was by them.[19] The company-town communities of Ford were flung far and wide throughout his commercial empire—in suburban Dearborn, in the countryside surrounding Detroit, in the backwoods of the Upper Peninsula, at the future site of the Tennessee Valley Authority, and as far away as Brazil.[20] Even replica Greenfield Village, part of the museum complex Ford established, can be seen as an "urban plan" of the automaker, although it was intended as a historical demonstration, rather than a place for actual people to live.

To put Henry Ford in the role of urban planner is to comprehend his lasting impact on Dearborn and the Detroit metropolis, places that exemplify the dynamic relationship of a suburb with its central city. He intended Dearborn to become the prototype of a uniquely American community that would feature a middle-class lifestyle attainable for many. This icon of a new place to live was reproduced throughout the nation, through Ford's ideological sway as much as through his economic policies of high wages and cheap goods, all of which were adopted on a widespread basis.

Early Twentieth-Century Suburbs

During the early twentieth century, suburbs for the masses seemed to pose a solution to many urban problems, especially traffic congestion and crowded, unhealthy housing. In contrast to the city, these suburbs were developed on site, with residences located efficiently near outlying industrial employment and other kinds of jobs, thereby eliminating long commutes. Land was cheap and plentiful in these areas, and inexpensive single-family detached houses could be developed, creating a stock that was modern, sanitary, and roomy. The new suburbs were often portrayed as healthy alternatives to the polluted city, even when factories were present. These communities allowed a standard of living that was high, yet affordable, and offered a low tax rate, reliable employment, a fair level of municipal services, pleasant outdoor recreation, convenient shopping, and access to the amenities of the city. All the same, some flaws in mass suburbanization also became apparent, primarily due to discrepancies in the housing choices offered. Often, less skilled workers were not able to live in such suburbs due to economic, social, or racial barriers, and they were forced to make a reverse commute out to the suburb from the central city in order to work there. Other problems were environmental pollution, runaway growth, fiscal unsoundness, and inadequate infrastructure.[21]

Of all the Detroit suburbs to which Henry Ford could relocate, Dearborn was the most advantageous geographically (see figure 1). It featured a quantity of inexpensive, undeveloped land that would enable Ford to build a much larger plant than the one in Highland Park and even give him some leeway for future expansion. Dearborn also had the skeleton of a transportation system that could easily be developed on an industrial scale. In addition to the highway that ran through the center of the city and lines for rail freight, Dearborn featured the River Rouge, which was linked to two Great Lakes via the Detroit River and once dredged could be used for shipping. Somehow these important resources had been overlooked by other industrialists in Detroit, and the land nearby remained undervalued. Between 1915 and 1918, Ford acquired twenty-five hundred acres in Dearborn, close to fifteen times the amount of land occupied by the Highland Park plant. The vast size of the River Rouge site as well as its accessibility to transportation by land, water, and rail permitted a degree of vertical integration that never before existed in industry. The plant would be fed with raw materials from the company's own timber tracts, iron mines, and rubber plantation. Then, it would process the raw materials into semi-finished products, since not just foundries but entire steel mills were to be placed

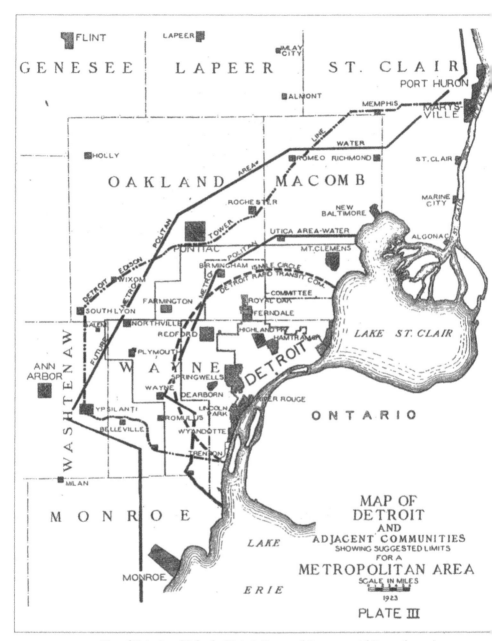

FIGURE 1. Map of Detroit and Suburbs (Detroit Bureau of Governmental Research, 1923)

at the location of automobile assembly. Indeed, by attaining this scale of vertical integration, the Ford Motor Company eventually outdistanced all its peer corporations.[22]

Of all the urban plans Henry Ford toyed with throughout his empire, Dearborn was the only one that could be considered suburban: the rest were far in the Detroit outskirts (village industries), on the Upper Peninsula (Kingsford and Pequaming), in the undeveloped South (Muscle Shoals, AL), or within a Latin American rubber plantation (Fordlandia and Belterra). In luring workers out of the city, Dearborn as much as any suburb for the masses was characterized by both advantages and disadvantages. After all, when a captain of industry such as Ford moved to a greenfield site to develop a new facility, and by default a new community, there were few checks and balances to assure that adequate political representation, physical infra-structure, pollution management, commuting options, and other necessities would be in place. Thus, for much of the 1920s, the communities imme-diately surrounding the River Rouge plant found themselves in a state of crisis, with Dearborn lacking an adequate tax base and neighboring Fordson experiencing a housing shortage. Ford's leading role in the consolidation of a community adjacent to Dearborn failed to address inequities in the tax structure for the two groups of residents. While his company-built housing helped some wage earners live where they worked, the drastic reduction of his original plan meant that many workers went unaided. All in all, the unregulated quality of these suburbs for the masses simultaneously raised and dashed the hopes of many reformers.

Consolidation Issues

In 1920, before Henry Ford targeted the region for the location of the River Rouge plant, the Dearborn area was primarily rural, relatively undeveloped, with few social services, little infrastructure for roads and transit, and min-imal utilities such as sewer, electricity, gas, and telephone lines. Dearborn's future boundaries were not yet set (see figure 2). Originally, the River Rouge plant was developed on the area's outskirts, in the township of Springwells. Over the next ten years, Springwells would first incorporate as a village, then as a city, and later change its name to Fordson. Dearborn would incorpo-rate as a city in 1927 and consolidate with Fordson in 1929.[23] Throughout the 1920s, consolidated Dearborn gained inhabitants, buildings, businesses, and much more, because of the growth spurred by the relocation of Ford Motor Company.[24] The area, whose economy had been based on farming, brickyards, salt mines, breweries, and a Ford Motor Company tractor plant,

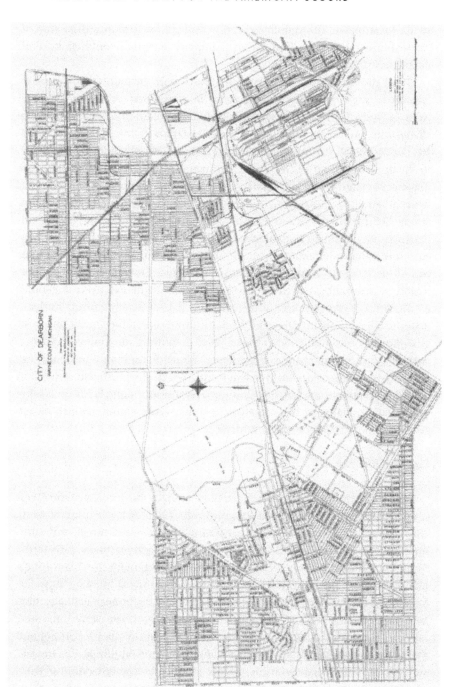

FIGURE 2. Map of Dearborn, 1941 (University of Chicago, Regenstein Library, Map Collection)

now attracted numerous heavy manufacturers, many of which supported the automobile trade. Houses were constructed in the thousands, and a high school, library, and country club were founded. Dozens of streets were paved, and as the roads improved, the number of automobiles increased. More streetcar lines were created, buses were added to the transit system, and an airport was established. As the population grew, the racial composition changed, and although native whites remained in the majority, the number of foreign-born whites increased, ultimately representing thirty-five different nationalities. Many African Americans commuted into Dearborn to work at the River Rouge plant. As the Great Migration increased and Ford Motor Company continued to hire black workers, they eventually numbered ten thousand. However, African Americans were excluded from living in Dearborn due to racial intolerance enforced by de facto and de jure means.[25]

As Dearborn and its neighbor Fordson experienced this rapid and sometimes awkward growth spurt, Henry Ford observed inefficiencies in municipal management that increased the burden for his company and its workers in their efforts to support themselves and their communities. The most obvious problem was that although each of the cities needed to develop public improvements and services at the same time, they had no program for sharing resources. If such a program were implemented, it could mean a lower tax rate for both cities and, as a result, significant savings for all taxpayers, individuals and businesses alike. Ford, as the largest taxpayer of either community, would benefit the most from such a program, but his workers would benefit, too. "One central government," Ford believed, "would be better able to direct the future development of this area, instead of each local community endeavoring to build a city within its own boundaries." To him, this was a matter of rationalizing municipal management following efficient business models. In regard to the merger, he declared, "The tendency in business today is to lower costs through more efficient methods to eliminate expenditures that are unnecessary—all for the purpose of reducing prices to the public. . . . Public funds should be spent in a manner that will serve public need for a greater and longer purpose, which can only be done through centralized administration."[26]

Henry Ford, though, had a few other reasons to push for consolidation. After all, he needed a place for his workers to live, and a consolidated Dearborn and Fordson better accomplished this task. Second, Ford needed efficiency in managing his greater Dearborn holdings, previously situated in three different governmental units: his engineering laboratory in the city of Dearborn, his estate in Dearborn Township, and his River Rouge plant in the city of Fordson. Dealing with a single government would make his financial and legal matters easier. Finally, Ford wanted to assure himself the unilateral decision making needed to run an international corporation, with locally elected officials answering to him and not the other way around. The logistical challenges of doing business in an urban setting had become apparent to him while running the Highland Park plant—although Highland Park remained separate from Detroit, it was surrounded by the city in the 1920s, making industrial expansion there impossible. Dearborn and Fordson now faced their own jurisdictional problems: unless joined together, they were in danger of consolidation with Detroit; or if not consolidated, they, too, could be fenced in by the central city as it grew outward and annexed areas bordering them. In fact, Detroit had annexed part of Springwells Township as early as 1916. Thus, it was in Ford's interest to reinforce the independence of a greater Dearborn, assuring himself an ample greenfield site for the growth of his industrial operations and an arena for his own political power.

Meanwhile, as early as 1920, the dual natures of Dearborn and Fordson were emerging. The village of Dearborn, incorporated in 1893, consisted of two and one-third square miles lying within the Dearborn Township.[27] The River Rouge plant was isolated from Dearborn Village, as it lay well outside the village in neighboring Springwells Township (later incorporated as the city of Fordson). Dearborn had a small population, only twenty-five hundred people, and few industries, functioning mainly as a site of truck farming with about four hundred acres for the cultivation of orchards and vineyards.[28] By 1923, however, the research and development center of the Ford Motor Company was built there, and despite the addition of the Stout Metal Aeroplane Company and Frink Concrete Products in the mid-1920s, Dearborn stabilized as the white-collar twin of industrial Springwells. It was described in a 1926 magazine as a place where "stagnant swamps have become beautiful gardens or willow-bordered pools, magnificent paved highways stretch here and there; cow pastures now hold large apartment buildings; potato fields have become the social center for golf, bridge, and dancing."[29] Dearborn's main street, Michigan Avenue, held banks, stores, a movie theater, a post office, and the town hall. Throughout the community there were churches, a large library, a high school, a country club, and an athletic field.[30] In the next year (1927), Dearborn became incorporated as a city of nine thousand.

Despite this promising picture, Dearborn soon found itself in debt, unable to keep up with the cost of public improvements because of a patchwork tax base. The ratio of industry to commerce was relatively low, and since industry was the more lucrative for generating tax dollars, the revenue of the city never reached a high level. Plus, its tax base received a blow in the early 1920s when Ford relocated his tractor plant from Dearborn to the River Rouge complex in Springwells. Without a voluminous tax base producing a thick flow of revenues, it was only a matter of time before Dearborn became financially overextended.[31]

During this time, Springwells, home of Ford Motor Company's River Rouge plant since 1917, was going through its own changes. By 1920, the community contained the largest brick and tile factories in the state, serving as the primary supplier of bricks to Detroit. In the same year, two metal companies were founded in Springwells: Harwick Stamping and Detroit Seamless Steel Tubes. The River Rouge plant was not the only car manufacturer in Springwells; Paige Motor Company, albeit much smaller than Ford Motor Company, had relocated there in 1919.[32] In 1924, as the River Rouge plant operations expanded, the citizens of Springwells responded by incorporating the entire township into a city in order to absorb the plant into their tax base and raise revenue, putting themselves in position to guide the growth spurred by increased industrial activity.[33] They began a public improvements program of several million dollars, creating a disposal plant and a complete sewer and water system. Between 1923 and 1926, new construction starts totaled 3,134 houses and apartments, sixty-five stores, eighty-one combined stores and apartments, and fifty-nine industrial buildings, as well as thirteen hotels and two theaters. Also, ten schools were built, along with one bus garage, one fire station, one town hall, and seventy-five miles of paved streets. By 1927, Springwells had changed its name to Fordson and grown to a population of twenty-five thousand, covering an area of eight and a half square miles with an assessed valuation of $131,250,000. Fordson became a center of industry—served by four major railroads, highways, and a port— and host to thirty industries, employing fifty-five thousand workers and creating an annual output of $2 million of manufactured products.[34]

Although thriving (especially relative to Dearborn), Fordson was not without its problems. For instance, it featured similarities to the port-of-entry neighborhoods typically found in urban settings. It was ethnically diverse—home to many immigrants, including Romanians, Italians, Poles, Germans, Russians, Yugoslavians, Syrians, and Turks, to name a few. Many of these immigrants were less-skilled wage earners who preferred to live within walking distance of the Rouge plant. As a result, Fordson was denser than Dearborn, containing two-flats, four-flats, rooming houses, and apartment buildings in addition to single-family houses. It was also more likely to have housing of poor quality, which remained in demand due to an ongoing shortage of places for new arrivals to live.

Eventually, the community became congested and derelict.[35] According to the 1940 master's thesis "Sociological Survey of Dearborn" by Albert Ammerman, slightly over a thousand families lived in substandard conditions. Ammerman refers to the housing as reaching "near slum conditions in many places" with "much doubling up of families." He reported that, along a stretch of only four blocks, sixty-three houses were found where two families were living in a house originally intended for only one. Within the same district, as many as four families were living in dwelling units made for one family only.[36] Iris Becker, a community organizer, attributed the uneven housing quality to the rapid growth of the South End. "Those fields just sprouted houses," exclaimed Becker. "Oh yes. They moved right in around on the fields around the Ford Motor Company and walked to work." She noted that many foreign-born workers built their own housing, with the result that the housing quality was quite uneven; some came over with Old World construction skills, and others just built something quickly and shoddily to tide themselves over.[37]

When consolidation was proposed between Fordson and Dearborn in 1927, Henry Ford was one of its instigators, and he was responsible for much of the public relations that caused it to succeed. According to Joseph Karmann, mayor of Fordson at the time, Ford approached him and said, "Let's put the two towns together and eliminate the name Fordson. . . . You got a job to sponsor the movement of consolidating these two towns." In return, Ford offered to build a new police headquarters, fire department, hospital, and office space. To win people over, Ford held a dinner at his estate to which he invited local civic and business leaders. Yet even in this backroom setting, Ford evaded being identified as the initiator of the consolidation movement, saying, "I don't know too much about what's going to happen in the future but whoever suggested this idea, that's a bright and brilliant one."[38] A week before the election, he then unabashedly published a front-page letter supporting consolidation.[39] Joseph Cardinal, resident of Fordson, also recalled Ford initiating a consolidation petition on which his signature headed the list.[40]

Between Henry Ford's support, Dearborn's debt, and Fordson's housing shortage, there were many reasons to go ahead with consolidation. It still did not come about easily, however, as several opposing factions emerged from the population. At stake, after all, was the future of two communities that together had held no more than five thousand residents ten years before. Opponents to consolidation were found mostly in Fordson, which had a lower tax rate than Dearborn and already enjoyed many completed paving, sewage, and water main construction projects that its neighbor lacked. For example, in 1927, Dearborn's valuation was $28 million, with a tax rate of $27 to $28 per thousand, and a budget of $785,000; in comparison, Fordson's valuation was $135 million, its tax rate was between $19 and $20 per thousand, and its budget was $2,700,000. This discrepancy had existed since 1920, when the assessed valuation of the village of Dearborn was $10,501,125 with a tax levy of $89,000 and a general bonded indebtedness of $327,000, and the village of Springwells had a valuation of $17,380,200, a tax levy of $145,000, and a general bonded indebtedness of $31,000.[41] Fordsonites worried that joining forces with Dearborn meant they would have to subsidize the smaller city's public improvements, thereby increasing their own tax rate.[42] Meanwhile, a faction in Dearborn resisted consolidation because they favored smaller government.[43]

In the end, a couple of compromises sweetened the deal for both sides. First, the name Dearborn, which referred to the Revolutionary War general, would be used for the consolidated city, and Fordson would be dropped. People were pleased that the Dearborn name was historical, and it happened to be favored by Henry Ford, who was born on its border and considered it his hometown. Second, special assessments on property owners in Dearborn were promised in order to keep the cost of public improvements from adding to the tax burden of former Fordsonites.[44] Probably the most compelling reason for Fordsonites to consolidate, though, was their fear of a merger with Detroit, which would bring about a higher tax rate.

The proposal passed with a three-to-two majority, and support came overwhelmingly from Dearborn, whose leaders had argued that consolidation would boost their city, creating lower tax rates, more efficient transportation, better city planning, improved business conditions, development of the Rouge River as a commercial waterway, and establishment of a municipal hospital.[45] Clyde Ford, the mayor of Dearborn before consolidation and a cousin of Henry Ford, was elected as the first mayor of the consolidated city. Results for the Fordsonites were mixed, however. Although they succeeded in not being merged with Detroit, consolidation with Dearborn meant a higher tax rate—apparently, the special assessments on Dearborn never materialized, and Fordson ended up shouldering some of the cost of developing the neighboring community. Henry Ford, though, had many reasons to be pleased, and if the interests of Fordson had not been entirely served by consolidation, at least his own had been protected.

Ultimately, this chain of events raises the question as to how the consolidation of Dearborn-Fordson prevented an even larger consolidation with Detroit. Individually, each community was lacking in tax base and the revenues to provide adequate services during a period of spiraling growth when needs were increasing, so they were both vulnerable to merging with the central city. By coming together, however, they could provide services in a self-supporting way without being dependent on the larger city nearby. Otherwise, the only choice would have been to join up with Detroit, a more mature city with an established system of services (such as streets and sewers) that it could easily extend outward—which could have happened, but only with a referendum from voters. Once Dearborn and Fordson consolidated, the voters no longer had an incentive to merge with Detroit, as either they were satisfied with their level of social services and infrastructure or they were able to create this environment with the revenues flowing from a newly reinforced tax base. They also nipped in the bud any chance for Detroit to annex those parts of Dearborn Township that lay between the two communities, since relevant areas of the township became incorporated as part of the consolidation. Given that Detroit had more than doubled its footprint through annexations between 1900 and 1920, this scenario was a realistic threat that was now neutralized. Through the process of consolidation, Dearborn capped off a decade-long trend to establish itself as a premier suburb for workers, with a demographic base, housing options, and amenities such as schools and shopping that far exceeded any other community in the Detroit area.

Why a Suburb?

Dearborn's transformation from a small farm-market community that had barely evolved in the previous two centuries could not have been more dramatic, traveling suddenly from preindustrial times to a time of mass-produced industry. Henry Ford's ultimate goal was to turn it into a suburb for the masses, one fitting for American wage earners and capable of turning workers from any background into good citizens. Articles published by Ford portrayed Dearborn as an "ideal suburban" development, full of "cozy homes," where workers could "enjoy the advantages of suburban life and the accommodations and privileges that go with the city." Evidently, a suburb like Dearborn offered not just amenities but also safety and affordability. A *Ford News* article emphasized the soundness of the community, declaring:

> Constantly increasing numbers are seeking to purchase homes in the little village on the Rouge where taxes, schools, and water are such that parents may feel safe in bringing their families, confident that the facilities afforded will not cost too much for a purse only comfortably filled.[46]

Journalists commented on the democratic possibilities of Dearborn, noting its intimate size and sociable residents, in contrast with nearby Detroit.
"The builders of this Dearborn community hope to see the purchasers settle
down as permanent residents and take an active part in the growth of Dearborn village," stated the *Dearborn Independent*. "The builders have in mind
(though this is for the future to decide) schools, community meeting-places,
classes of various sorts and other assemblages which will foster health, comfort and solid Americanism."[47]

Henry Ford's interest in the social possibilities of suburbs derived from a
fear that cities and their cosmopolitan culture were threatening the nation's
values. He was particularly concerned about the concentration of unassim-
ilated immigrant labor in urban centers. A company newsletter noted that,
after working a ten-hour day, the typical laborer "goes home to a smelly and
sordid room in a tenement house or to a house which is merely one in a row
of slouchy and poorly planned, poorly built houses." Since the "city with
its high buildings" would not appeal to immigrants of "peasant stock, farm
bred and raised," factories in the fields posed a potential solution:

> The plan of decentralization of population and the giving away of urban con-
> gestion by the development of many smaller rural plants that workers may
> have more natural living conditions that are fast becoming possible only for
> the man of more substantial means is one plan to aid this situation.[48]

For Ford, place of residence was important to citizenship as it was only
outside the city that true community could be found. Thus, suburbanization could be used to acculturate workers. "Cities have no soul," he claimed.
"[I]n small communities the better qualities of our nature have a chance;
but in large communities it is the looser standards and the more heartless
qualities that set our fashions and our customs."[49]

In fact, Henry Ford's anti-Semitism may have contributed to his bias against
cities. According to the diatribe published by Ford entitled *The International
Jew*, the city was where Jews congregated, and there they exerted a monopoly
on real estate, imposing exploitatively high rents on Gentiles and becoming
the "Landlord of America."[50] In the pages of the *Dearborn Independent*, Ford
went so far as to entitle one editorial, "The Modern City—A Pestiferous
Growth." In it, he asserted that the "problem of the city"—which he placed
in quotes the same way as the "Jewish question"—was a "bundle of the most
baffling [social] problems."[51] In another essay, in which "immigrant" is used
somewhat interchangeably with "Jew," he complained that "not all modern
immigrants are of pioneer quality." Ford worried that such immigrants were

importers of "dangerous and false ideas," that is, they were political revolutionaries. He demanded that "the custom of immigrants settling in the cities should . . . be stopped."[52] In sum, cities were centers for immigrants, labor organizers, and bankers, who all made Ford shudder. He identified instead with agriculturists and artisans, people who were rugged individualists, rooted in the soil, working with their hands, and dealing solely in cash—ironically, he continued to align himself this way long after becoming one of the richest and most powerful men on the planet.

On the other hand, Ford, as an industrialist, recognized that it was "nonsense" to expect everyone to go back to the farm.[53] Suburbs appeared to be the perfect mediation between city and country, and a *Ford News* article referred to Dearborn as realizing the plans of Ford "to get a large part of [his] manufacturing away from the large cities."[54] "Perhaps we may at first conclude that there are so many conveniences in city life that a suburban existence would not be so desirable," stated another article:

> However, it is hardly proposed to return to the life of an isolated country community devoid of conveniences. There is nothing more profitable to the health, the pocketbook and life in general than by living in such a way [as] to benefit not only from the advantages of country life, but also from the added conveniences of the city.[55]

To Ford, suburbs were "quieter, cleaner, sunnier, airier and in every way more healthful for children and adults the whole year round." He emphasized their bounty, noting "you can work farther from home where living conditions are better and expenses are not so high."[56] Overall, he considered moving workers out of the city to the suburbs a return to the "early American idea."[57]

Henry Ford took credit for the role played by his own product, the automobile, in bringing about suburbanization. A company publication boasted, "The automobile is distributing mankind over the landscape" and claimed it will "level down the seething masses of weltering humanity" and bring people "back to nature." Already the "man of moderate means" had relocated to the suburbs, and following him next would be the "wage earner."[58]

That Ford believed workers should use the automobile to escape to the suburb is evident in another article, which stated:

> The car owner can reach his work from a distance twice or three times as great in less time, can reside in the suburbs, with ground for garden and flowers, room for chickens, if he cares to keep them, and opportunity for pleasant and inexpensive recreation at any time.[59]

This article then set up a contrast, describing a worker without a car. The author explained that a "high cost of living" is incurred by the wage earner who lives far from the place of employment. This situation resulted in limited "recreation and amusement," habitation in "cramped quarters," and ultimately a life of "mere existence."[60] Last, the congratulatory note struck in an advertisement from 1925 suggests again the automobile's wider implications intended by Ford. "[The Model T] is hastening the development of such new districts—out beyond the car lines," the advertisement declared. "It has enabled thousands of families to escape high rents, the confines of crowded cities, and to satisfy their longings for fresh air, open country and a healthier, happier environment."[61]

Other Urban Proposals

Between leading the cause for consolidation and setting aside the Ford Homes District, where he built houses for workers, Henry Ford left a singular imprint on the community. Yet Dearborn was not the first or the last urban plan for him. Ever the utopian, Ford had an enduring interest in the kinds of communities in which workers lived. Moreover, this sort of idealism was not limited to him personally as this was the era of company towns, envisioned by industrialists as an extension of social services already offered to workers, such as programs for health, education, and recreation.[62] Company towns were created to subsidize the most basic needs, such as housing and consumer goods, making them more affordable. In remote areas—like mining or forestry locations—the company town was sometimes a necessity as no urban infrastructure yet existed.

Perhaps best epitomized by Pullman, Illinois, company towns became more frequent as industrialization increased. George Pullman, the inventor and manufacturer of the sleeper car, founded his eponymous company town in 1880. It was originally located outside Chicago and later annexed to it in 1889. By 1884, the population of Pullman reached a total of eight thousand residents living in fourteen hundred dwellings—mostly sturdy, multi-family brick row houses, set on wide tree-lined streets and connected to utilities. There were also parks, a library, a theater, a hotel, a store, and a church, all built at company expense. An important aspect of the housing in Pullman was that it was completely rental, with no opportunity for homeownership. This later led to a well-known labor struggle, as an 1894 strike ensued when Pullman maintained rental rates while pushing down wages. Later, an Illinois Supreme Court decision forced him to break up his holdings, declaring them a monopoly.[63]

Still, employers continued taking the risk of developing company towns well into the early twentieth century, although some shifted to providing housing for purchase rather than for rental in order to avoid future conflicts.[64] The "new" company town was distinguished by its use of speculative development—the entire community was gradually sold off parcel by parcel to the workers themselves, a process that eventually eliminated the company as owner. Such towns were comprehensively planned and picturesquely designed with low-density development emphasizing single-family detached houses. Sometimes housing types varied—ranging from single-family detached houses to multiple-family attached or semi-detached houses and fairly large boardinghouses. Some public buildings such as churches, schools, clubhouses, or community halls were provided as well. A town square or park acted as a focal point, upstaging the factory. Regulation was implemented in the form of zoning and building codes, since the original patron would otherwise lose complete control of development once the speculatively developed property was sold. Often ordinances outlawing liquor and discouraging loitering were also implemented.

Henry Ford remains a case in point, in the way he held sway over the communities of his workers, whether directly or not. In some situations he was in a position to start such a community from scratch, funding upfront the cost of housing, infrastructure, and utilities and other resources such as stores and schools. At other times, he subsidized the expansion of an existing community. Although Ford commissioned a number of company towns, Dearborn cannot be counted as such because he was not the sole developer. Among the company towns that were indeed controlled by him are those located on the Upper Peninsula of Michigan, such as Kingsford. Within the region of southeastern Michigan, Ford spurred the growth of Ypsilanti, Flat Rock, and others that were part of the "village industries," which turned existing communities into company towns. Far away in South America, he organized a pair of towns associated with a Brazilian rubber plantation, Fordlandia and Belterra. His proposal for a "75-mile city" in Muscle Shoals, Alabama, was not a typical company town in the sense that he intended to own the entire community. However, it reveals the scale of his ambition that he had plans for it drawn up, after placing a bid to purchase a major hydroelectric dam owned by the federal government. This bid failed when it was met with political opposition, so it will never be known if Muscle Shoals would have evolved into a company town. Of all his urban plans, Dearborn was the most significant in size and success.

Village Industries

Henry Ford implemented his ideas for company towns in his program for "village industries," in which nineteen facilities were developed throughout the Michigan countryside to house small-scale manufacturing of lightweight automobile parts (see figure 3). Often these sites already contained old hydro-powered mills that were renovated or replaced for modern industrial purposes. Integrated with production at the River Rouge and Highland Park plants, the village industries were located within easy distance in order to promote cost-efficient transportation between the hub-and-spoke facilities. Built on the Rouge, Raisin, Saline, and Huron Rivers, these subassembly sites were limited to within a sixty-mile radius of Dearborn and Detroit, and they remained functional from 1918 to the 1940s. An implicit goal of

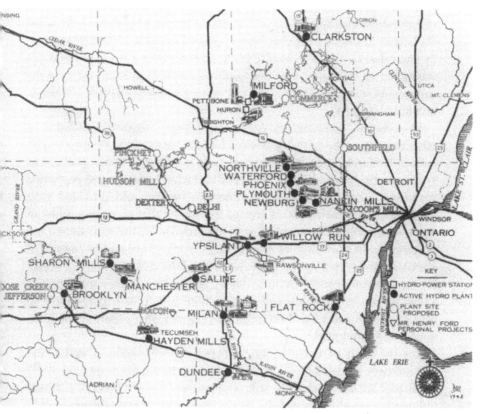

FIGURE 3. Map of Village Industries (Collections of The Henry Ford)

village industries was to reduce the company's dependence upon numerous outside suppliers, whose numbers rose to fifty-three hundred firms in Detroit and nearby areas by the early 1930s. In addition, they would draw upon a labor pool of rural workers who could return to farming at times when manufacturing was slack. Emphasis was placed on hiring locally rather than attracting workers from outside the community; a six-month residency requirement was initially established, but this was then relaxed later.[65]

Located in areas that were rural (neither urban nor suburban), the village industries sought a balance between nature and technology, striving for a pastoral aesthetic even when juxtaposed with industry.[66] For example, after renovation of an old water mill, newly installed state-of-the-art machinery was shielded by a rustic exterior. When modern facilities were required, they were designed to be unobtrusive in the landscape. Since most of the village industries began as a renovation or a replacement of an old mill, their size and purpose could be somewhat idiosyncratic. Quite a few village industries employed a workforce of fewer than a hundred workers, but the largest, Ypsilanti, peaked at fifteen hundred workers. Of limited versatility and capacity, each site usually made no more than a few kinds of parts: valves, horns, regulators, switches, taps, or gauges. Their footprint upon the community was likely rather light, not causing a drastic increase in population or boundaries.

Nonetheless, communities containing village industries expanded in other ways upon the arrival of Henry Ford. His intervention in these locales is clear. He funded new infrastructure such as electrical, water, and sewage systems or bridges and roads. He subsidized school districts and supported vocational curriculums, built or restored churches, and provided plots for growing vegetables. Lakes created by the installation or upgrading of dams were carefully landscaped at Ford's expense for the recreational use of residents. In the village of Nankin Mills, Ford furnished free municipal electricity and water. At Flat Rock, he covered the cost of a railroad bridge for the company-owned Detroit, Toledo, and Irontown Railroad as well as a road for use by the public and a one-million-gallon capacity reservoir. In Milford, he sponsored a "beautification program" that removed rundown houses and a junkyard.[67]

For the most part, Ford foresaw that the combination of agriculture and industry modeled by the village industries would occur on a relatively small, perhaps artisanal, scale. Still, conversion of a site to become a "village industry" markedly changed the employment base of the existing municipalities: in the case of the Milan factory, its workforce totaled "10 percent of the community's two thousand residents."[68] There were obvious economic impacts upon the community as a result of Fordism: workers were turned into consumers, through their receiving higher wages, which resulted in increased automobile sales.[69] In return, Ford Motor Company also acted as a consumer and stimulated the local economy through its own purchases. For example, in 1935, within the communities hosting the village industries, fifteen rural suppliers with three hundred employees sold an estimated $1 million in goods to the company.[70]

Although romantically publicized by Henry Ford, the village industries nonetheless incurred a high overhead because of the pricey renovations of outmoded buildings, the costliness of training rural workers, and the limited scale of production permitted by the sites. Based on the surmises of Ford Motor Company managers and outside experts, these industries could not have been profitable. Clearly, though, the village industries were important to Ford, if for no other reason than as a kind of social engineering—and the integration of living and working achieved in them was something he attempted in Dearborn and elsewhere.

Upper Peninsula

More similar to conventional company towns were the communities influenced by Henry Ford on Michigan's Upper Peninsula, the site of company-owned lumber tracts and iron mines that supplied the vertically integrated River Rouge plant with raw materials. Ford's presence was so extensive there that he was one of the region's largest private employers from the 1920s through the 1950s. An estimated ten thousand workers labored in his iron mines, logging camps, and factories for woodworking, automobiles, and chemicals. Wood was especially important across the automobile industry as all-steel car bodies were not yet prevalent, and wooden floorboards and body framework were common. Wood was also used throughout Ford Motor Company for shipping containers, pallets, and pattern work, as well as for railroad ties and boxcars. In 1920, Henry Ford made an initial purchase of 350,000 acres of timber forest for a price of $2.9 million. In addition to land for logging, he needed to create centralized facilities that would funnel the lumber from the widespread forests and turn the wood into semi-finished products.[71]

This happened first in Kingsford, Michigan, a small community on the Wisconsin border that was drastically changed upon his arrival. In 1920, Ford purchased a three-thousand-acre tract, which mostly overlapped with Kingsford, although the rest was in adjacent Iron Mountain, a declining city of eight thousand. The ambitious complex intended there would process logs imported from timberlands as far as one hundred miles away. Eventually containing a sawmill, dozens of drying kilns, and some wood-manufacturing plants, the size of the complex caused it to be dubbed the "River Rouge of the North."[72] Powering these industrial facilities was an eleven-thousand-horsepower hydroelectric station built by Ford on the Menominee River. By 1923, Ford's Kingsford factories employed up to three thousand workers, which gave the entire community an economic boost. In the same year, Kingsford incorporated as a village. Around this time, Ford built about one hundred rental houses in the so-called Ford Addition in order to accommodate employees who had families.[73] For single workers, Ford built bunkhouses and a mess hall. A commissary was also constructed, which supplied the town with food and clothing at little above cost. Eventually, employment for Kingsford and nearby Iron Mountain peaked at seventy-six hundred in 1925. By this time, the company was paying more than 60 percent of Kingsford's taxes. One wood by-product created in Kingsford was the charcoal briquette, which is still popular with today's grillers.[74]

Also notable among Henry Ford's Upper Peninsula ventures was the town of Pequaming. Founded in 1870–1880, Pequaming had originally been built by another industrialist, Charles Hebard, a timber speculator from the East. A picturesque lumber town located on the edge of a forty-thousand-acre hardwood forest, it overlooked the Keweenaw Bay on the shores of Lake Superior. Almost entirely funded by Hebard, the community was a classic company town, consisting of about one hundred rental houses, three churches, schools, a town hall, a post office, a commissary, a clubhouse, and a hotel, as well as a powerhouse, a sawmill, and docks and railroad for transporting the wood. In 1923, Henry Ford bought the entire town and its adjacent timberlands for $2,850,000 and thus became virtually the only employer and taxpayer for the community of six hundred residents. After the purchase Ford installed a modern waterworks and improved the fire protection services. In the ensuing years, he created a regional school system that emphasized a vocational curriculum and attracted students from Pequaming and nearby communities.[75]

Muscle Shoals

In the early 1920s, Henry Ford was attracted to the government-owned project in Muscle Shoals, Alabama, which consisted of a major hydroelectric dam and the adjoining defense industry factories it powered (see figure 4). This undertaking had been started through the 1916 National Defense Act, a wartime initiative. Construction of the dam, named the Wilson, followed in 1918, with the purpose of powering chemical plants for the production

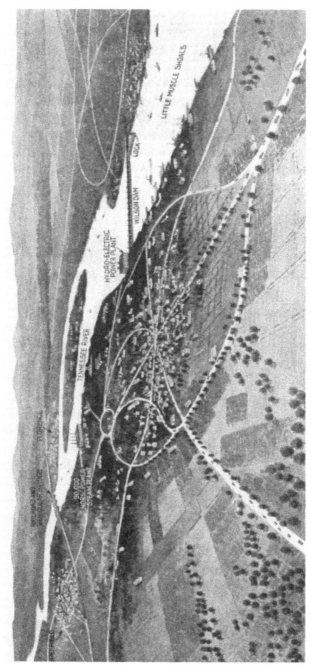

FIGURE 4. Map of Muscle Shoals, AL (Littell McClung, "The Seventy-Five Mile City," *Scientific American* 127, no. 3, 1922)

of explosives. Designed to reach 140 feet in height and span a mile across the river, the Wilson Dam when finished would be capable of generating 260,000 horsepower. In 1921, however, the dam was only one-third complete, and the factories it supported were designated for peacetime conversion to the production of nitrates for fertilizers. However, with World War I at an end and increased scrutiny upon spending, the government now wished to sell this major piece of infrastructure for private use, and altogether the properties were valued at $150 million.[76]

In 1921, Henry Ford submitted two bids to the federal government: one bid for the completion and long-term leasing of the dam and the other bid for purchasing the two nitrate plants and the quarry. Ford's intention was to receive a good return on his investment as he foresaw a profit-making side to this business. At the same time, he wished to create products and services that were affordable to consumers through achieving economies of scale. He envisioned the ability to produce cheap agricultural fertilizers that would help farmers, and he hoped to use the massive hydroelectric power of the dam to furnish electricity at reasonable rates throughout the region. The dam would also mitigate flooding of the Tennessee River and make it navigable for commercial transportation purposes. Ford even had plans drawn up of a linear "75-mile city" that would grow along the Tennessee River as a result of the development generated by the Muscle Shoals project.[77] He believed the location of this sprawling city—half-urban, half-rural—would be advantageous for the locals, who could easily switch between factory and farmwork, depending upon the season. Ford even hoped his company could serve as a lender, supplying low-interest mortgages to promote house building and homeownership. In this scenario, the seventy-five-mile city would be owned neither by Ford nor the federal government but would develop conventionally, in response to the supply and demand of market forces, and growth would be spurred by the availability of financing from the powerful industrialist. By emphasizing the need for regional leadership within this economically lagging area, Ford's proposal was something of a precursor to the Tennessee Valley Authority (TVA) later developed under the New Deal.[78]

Some of Henry Ford's political opponents objected to the idea of selling a government asset—they noted the moneymaking incentive of such a venture and estimated that the gain would line an individual's pockets at the expense of the public. Ford was careful to line up many allies on his side to disperse this criticism. He gathered the backing of farm organizations nationwide as well as most members from the House of Representatives. However, a few senators, particularly George Norris, fought the Ford offer. Norris was a champion of the dam's potential to bring affordable electricity rates to the area, which featured substandard living conditions and was in great need of economic development. He believed a public ownership plan was the only guarantee to further the interests of the region. Also lining up opposite Ford were industrial interests such as the National Fertilizer Association and Andrew Mellon's Alcoa, who feared monopolization. By 1924, Ford had withdrawn his bid. Almost ten years later, in 1933, the Tennessee Valley Authority—modeled precisely upon the vision of George Norris—was created under Franklin Roosevelt through the legislative efforts of a New Deal Congress.[79]

Fordlandia/Belterra

From 1927 to 1945, Henry Ford undertook the establishment of a Brazilian rubber plantation colony to supply material for automobile tires (see figure 5). This was an attempt to break an existing monopoly on this crucial automotive material held by the Anglo-Dutch owners of plantations in Southeast Asia. These colonists illegally imported Brazilian rubber seeds to Europe for cultivation and study and then successfully grew the trees in the Far East for international trade. At the same time, the Firestone Company developed a rubber plantation in Liberia, West Africa, and Goodyear did the same in Costa Rica and Panama. The Brazilian government invited Henry Ford to consider investing in rubber production there; Brazil was losing ground in the competition for rubber production because of cultivation of the trees outside their native country. After visiting the site, Ford's agents acquired the land by concession from the Brazilian government, who would share in a small percentage of the profits from rubber production. The plantation, named Fordlandia, consisted of 2.5 million acres—the size of a small American state—located upon the Tapajos River, a tributary of the Amazon, six hundred miles from the Atlantic. It took eighteen hours to reach the plantation by riverboat from the nearest town.[80]

Given Henry Ford's resources, the isolation of the site did not deter him from creating a replica Michigan-style town, featuring landscaped bungalows equipped with indoor plumbing, paved streets lined with fire hydrants, tree-shaded central squares and sidewalks, an electric plant, a lumber mill, an up-to-date hospital, three schools, a golf course, a swimming pool, and a tennis court. By 1933, Fordlandia employed about 340 workers, who were accommodated in 230 homes for families and a single-men's bunkhouse that could shelter up to 900 residents.[81] The living conditions of Fordlandia stood in stark contrast to the nomadic existence of native South American workers who had previously tapped rubber trees scattered in the vast jungle. Labor

FIGURE 5. Photo of Fordlandia, Brazil, 1930–31 (Collections of The Henry Ford)

conflicts were the unsurprising result of acclimating these workers—and migrants from all over the continent—to industrial time discipline when they started working for Ford Motor Company. A particular bone of contention was the expectation that single male workers live together in bunkhouses, eat Midwestern food from the employer-run cafeteria, undergo required health inspections, and be banned from drinking. Indigenous families now living in the thick-walled and underventilated bungalows found them oppressively hot, and they missed the smoky fires they once kept perpetually burning under their huts to fend off insects. Workers also objected to employment during midday when the heat became intense, as they were used to the traditional routine of laboring during predawn and postdusk hours.[82]

In addition to labor problems, the plantation's rubber trees failed to flourish because of the lack of horticultural expertise among the people Henry Ford had placed in charge.[83] More specifically, the dense placement of rubber trees in a monocultural setting made them susceptible to insects and disease, which were avoided in the natural environment by their growing at a distance from each other. The rolling land had been stripped of vegetation before planting the rubber trees and now required extensive terracing to prevent the rich soil from washing away. The trees were being grown from seeds, but more success had been reached elsewhere through a process of grafting, especially onto established trees that were already disease-resistant.

Around this time, when the setbacks of Fordlandia were becoming evident, Henry Ford was offered a better piece of land in nearby Belterra, which he then obtained. This time, trees would be grown through grafting rather than from seeds, and Belterra was planted with an illicit shipment of two thousand buddings of rubber trees from the Far East. With this improvement, the focus on rubber production shifted to Belterra. Fordlandia continued to be productive in a reduced fashion, and its sizable sawmill was kept running for hardwood harvesting and the export of lumber products. Belterra contained an experimental laboratory built by Ford to explore the commercial potential of rain forest resources such as exotic woods, spices, tea, coffee, nut and vegetable oils, and fibers such as jute, sisal, and hemp. Belterra quickly expanded upon the arrival of the rubber enterprise, and by 1940, there were seven thousand residents, of which two thousand were Ford Motor Company workers. From afar, Henry Ford commissioned the construction of 850 houses. His local agents subversively assured that half of these were of the thatched style preferred by the Native Americans. As in Fordlandia, there was a 950-man bunkhouse. Ford also built a powerhouse, a sawmill, a hospital, churches, stores, a recreation building, a library, a golf course, and some schools. Belterra, which exceeded Fordlandia in its smooth operations, soon became a showcase for Ford Motor Company, which considered it a model community. Years later, both Fordlandia and Belterra were abandoned when synthetic rubber became widespread after World War II, displacing rubber from natural sources.[84]

Conclusion

Among Henry Ford's many urban plans, Dearborn was unique in its suburban location within an expanding metropolitan region. With a population totaling fifty thousand by 1930, it was certainly the largest of the communities he influenced. In keeping with the example provided by the Ford Homes, Dearborn became a place where many wage earners lived, able to own their own homes in a relatively bucolic setting with access to amenities such as good transportation, shopping, and parks. Much of this growth, of course, was due to the presence of Henry Ford and his industry. Nonetheless, when commenting on Dearborn, Ford remarked disingenuously that its transformation was "a product of the Pioneers and the Builders," with the implication that a multitude of actors had contributed to its development rather than one prominent patron. Its foundations, he continued, "were laid by farmers laboring on the land" and by "industrial enterprise." He concluded that "as long as citizens co-operate to maintain high standards of health and security, as long as they see to it that good wages may always be translated into true values of living and education, the progress of Dearborn will be protected."[85] By this reference he invoked the image of a democratic community built from the ground up by a time-honored American icon, the yeoman farmer—as well as by a new symbol of republicanism, the factory wage earner.[86] More than just skirting his own role in developing Dearborn, Ford tried to position it as a typical American community, connected to a boot-strapping tradition and worthy of reproduction elsewhere.

As it turned out, one of Henry Ford's blind spots was the naive belief that mass suburbanization could be backward-looking instead of revolutionary. Throughout, he had remained nostalgic of the old agrarian society he experienced as a youth—witness his development of the Greenfield Village museum (see figure 6). Yet, the suburb for the masses that Ford envisioned functioned less as the bridge between city and country than as a harbinger of a rising social order displacing what came before. Ford's attachment to the past meant that he consistently underestimated the modernizing force he

FIGURE 6. Map of Greenfield Village, 1934 (Collections of The Henry Ford)

himself had unleashed with the development of a novel form of production as well as the transformation of workers into consumers. Eventually, these suburbs for the masses were transformed from places where wage earners were empowered as consumers to sites of increasing political contestation, where civil rights advocates focused on the integration of housing and enlightened women questioned their role as homemakers. No one would have been more surprised at this turn of events than Henry Ford, who did not live to see these long-term consequences. After all, he had been careful to exclude African American workers from living in the Ford Homes, and he did not permit women to have jobs on his factory floor. Altogether, Dearborn and other suburbs from that time reflect Henry Ford's genius— wittingly or not—in remaking American culture.

2

Suburbs and the Working Class

THE NEWFOUND PRESENCE OF Henry Ford and his company spurred increased suburban development in Dearborn and contributed to its mushrooming growth. Ford himself had a twofold effect upon the rise of this community: the relocation of his industrial facility to the outskirts of Detroit together with his efforts to turn workers into car owners reinforced each other in prompting wage earners to move out of the city. The high wages he paid enabled workers to buy suburban homes. All in all, Dearborn is best understood as Ford's attempt to create a suburb for the masses. Ever the populist, Ford had once claimed the Model T would become a "car for the multitude," and now he wanted to create a suburb for the multitude. Ford's own references to Dearborn show he saw it as an expression of existing American values as well as a tool of Americanization—and as such he intended it as a model to be copied elsewhere. It was also a community to be mass-produced. Eventually, Dearborn came to embody many of Ford's values: it was a place where workers became homeowners, where industry was reconciled with the countryside, where residents grew their own vegetable gardens, where the environment was healthier than in the city, where uncongested roads meant the automobile could be used freely, and where quality of life would improve because money stretched farther.

At the same time, the question arises as to who was included in Henry Ford's concept of the "multitude." Although Dearborn was successful in attracting a high percentage of working-class people among its population (more than half of its employed residents were Ford Motor Company workers), not all wage earners could live there. Less-skilled workers were likely deterred from living there for economic reasons, and African Americans were excluded almost completely. On this topic, Ford himself made rather contradictory statements, particularly in connection with his attempt to create a subdivision of affordable housing called the Ford Homes. On one hand, he declared himself an advocate of wage earners seeking suburban relocation:

> One of the most hopeful facts is that, whereas only the well-to-do once found it possible to get away from the city, now the workingman finds it not only possible but advantageous to live in the country, and thousands of them of doing it even while they work in the City.[1]

Yet, he resisted appearing to give workers a handout, stating, "We are not catering to the thriftless people in building these houses."[2] Apparently, Ford was at least somewhat ambivalent about how far to go in his empowerment of workers, perhaps drawing the line at supporting skilled wage earners who best fit his ideal of American labor and could help him situate Dearborn as a prototypical community.

Opportunities for Wage Earners

Of the people who moved to Dearborn during its rampant expansion in the 1920s, many became homeowners. By 1930, Dearborn's homeownership rate was already reaching a relatively high rate—55 percent locally versus 46 percent across the country.[3] This figure (55 percent) is quite remarkable as it was not until the post–World War II period that homeownership rates of more than 50 percent become common in the United States. The figure is also significant because this community was primarily working class, with automobile manufacturing the major source of employment. Dearborn's homeownership rate was also high within the Detroit metropolis, despite the central city's long association with working-class homeownership.[4] In comparison, Detroit's homeownership rate was 41 percent, and Highland Park, the site of Ford Motor Company's previous plant, had an even lower rate (37 percent). The median value of houses in Dearborn was higher than the national median ($7,914 compared to $4,778).[5]

An examination of how Ford Motor Company workers fared in Dearborn compared to other residents there is even more revealing. Based on a randomized sample from the 1930 manuscript census, about half of all employed Dearbornites worked for Ford Motor Company—and they could be found across almost every occupational category, with the exception of executives, who tended to live in more fashionable places, such as choice

Ford Motor Company Workers in Dearborn Who Are Household Heads
Tables 1 through 4

TABLE 1

WORKERS OF ALL LEVELS - *Managerial, Skilled, Semi-Skilled, Unskilled*

Home-ownership rate	57%
Median house value	$7200
Wife works remuneratively	22%
Other relative in household works	19%

TABLE 2

WORKERS - *Skilled*

Home-ownership rate	75%
Median house value	$7000
Wife works remuneratively	9%
Other relative in household works	13%

TABLE 3

WORKERS - *Semi-Skilled*

Home-ownership rate	34%
Median house value	$6750
Wife works remuneratively	27%
Other relative in household works	23%

TABLE 4

WORKERS - *Unskilled*

Home-ownership rate	62%
Median house value	$6600
Wife works remuneratively	41%
Other relative in household works	24%

Source: US Bureau of the Census, *1930 Manuscript Census.*

Detroit neighborhoods or suburbs to the north and east of the central city.[6] Of the Ford Motor Company workers living in Dearborn, low-level managerial workers such as clerks or foremen made up 15 percent; skilled industrial workers were 20 percent; semi-skilled workers were the majority at 38 percent; and unskilled workers were 27 percent.[7] In households headed by Ford Motor Company workers, the homeownership rate was 57 percent (slightly higher than elsewhere in Dearborn), and the median house value was $7,200 (a little lower).

Overall, the housing opportunities in Dearborn were unusually good for workers, and descriptions by its boosters verged on the rhapsodic. An article described the satisfaction in homeownership experienced by Dearborn resident and family man Stanley Case, a tool inspector for a nearby automobile manufacturer, presumably the Ford Motor Company. "Some of the happiest American homes of today," asserted the article, "are to be found, not necessarily where the ultra-ultra in comfort and luxury can be provided, but in the modest homes of the American workmen." On $1,600 a year, Case supported a wife and two children, and although they believed themselves unable to afford going to movies, they did manage to own a refrigerator, a washing machine, a vacuum cleaner, a sewing machine, a radio, and an automobile—or, to be precise, they were close to paying off these items. Their house was described as teeming with the activity of the children. "All their life is interwoven in their home," declared the article, and the Cases agreed, describing their feelings about owning a house and starting a family as "perfectly swell."[8]

Other homeowners expressed pride in and gratitude for their houses in Dearborn in firsthand accounts. Resident John Baja attested that, although he had lived in many apartments in his life, only after owning a house did he know "what it's like to be with a home," adding, "No where in the world can a person live and enjoy a home like the American. And no where in this country is a better place to have a home located than the City of Dearborn."[9] Of his childhood home, which was a modest three-bedroom Colonial, Bob Biermann recalled, "It was 1939, during the Depression, when my parents took their life savings and invested in a home at 6030 Kendal in East Dearborn. It was their dream home, but they could never have imagined all the joyous, angry, humorous and sad moments they and their five children were to experience over the next 60 years."[10] Michael Adray, recounting how his father enjoyed being a suburban homeowner, remembered, "Dad worked and put in his day at Ford and he loved to keep a garden. Boy, he had a big garden and that was his pride and joy. He loved having a garden of his own."[11] Another recalled living in Dearborn during this period as "a golden age of opportunity."[12]

Housing Inequities

Less skilled workers in Dearborn did not always fare as well. Typically, they were found in the South End, in the former Fordson community, which contained the River Rouge plant (see figure 7). The South End was

FIGURE 7. River Rouge Plant, Aerial Photo, 1948 (Collections of The Henry Ford)

geographically isolated, separated from most of Dearborn by the large real estate holdings of Henry Ford. It was also Dearborn's most ethnically diverse neighborhood, home to many immigrants. This heterogeneity was notable since, across Dearborn, native whites represented close to three-quarters of the population. Meanwhile, of the foreign-born Dearborn residents, easily assimilated English-speaking Canadians were the biggest group.[13] "The kind of people and the separation of the Ford plant between us and the rest of the town made it a separate kind of community and later on became the 'South End,'" stated resident and activist Iris Becker. "People outside of Dearborn often didn't know it was a part of Dearborn [as] it was closer to Delray and Detroit."[14] Becker portrayed the South End as a "little town" within Dearborn, notable for its churches and clubs representing different ethnicities such as the Romanians, Serbs, and Hungarians. Along Salina, which functioned as the "main street" for the South End, there was a row of coffeehouses for Arabic residents.[15]

As a result of the housing shortage, some residents in the South End resorted to the "garage home" as a solution.[16] In this situation, a worker would construct a five-hundred-dollar building consisting of a single story and a footprint no larger than twenty square feet in size, on the rear of a lot where the garage would normally be located. Such a structure would be much less costly than the type of house required by deed restrictions on the front of the lot, which needed to have a minimum property value of around five or six thousand dollars. Developers attached these restrictions because, in the absence of zoning, there was no other way to control land use and keep up the marketability of housing. Local officials, meanwhile, looked the other way, even when it was obvious that residents were building the garages for housing rather than for cars. After all, with the housing shortage going on, they had no reason to crack down. A local newspaper congratulated the workers on their entrepreneurship in becoming homeowners, calling the garage homes thrifty, cozy, and comfortable, noting that they could be equipped with heat, electricity, water, and sewer connections.[17] By 1924, the garage homes numbered in the many hundreds, and although modestly sized, consisting of only one or two rooms, they served as a stopgap measure during this period (see figure 8).

When Ford Motor Company workers occupied garage homes, the semiskilled led with 44 percent, unskilled were 36 percent, and skilled were 22 percent (8 percent were low-level managers such as clerks or foremen). Close to 60 percent were foreign born. Most were married, and household size averaged 4.2 people. In about a quarter of the households, the income of the head was supplemented by the presence of boarders or secondary

FIGURE 8. Photo of "Garage Home" (City of Dearborn)

breadwinners.[18] In other words, even in small houses consisting of only one or two rooms, often more than four people could be found under the same roof. Despite this frugal standard of living, multiple breadwinners or boarders were still needed to make ends meet. On the other hand, the Sanborn maps and building permits show that many garage homes also had actual garages on site, implying that the residents could afford automobiles.[19] The ownership rate of the garage homes was notably high at 84 percent, which compares to 55 percent across Dearborn, although the median value ($3,000) was less than half the median for all of Dearborn ($7,914).[20] In fact, the ownership rate and the median value made the garage home population more comparable to that of nearby Inkster Gardens than to other Ford Motor Company workers in Dearborn. This probably reflects the common plight of less skilled workers, who were overrepresented among residents of both Dearborn's garage homes and Inkster Gardens, which was predominantly African American.

For the typical worker, the process of becoming a homeowner in Dearborn—even of a garage home—required a degree of sacrifice. A glimpse into this struggle is offered in the oral history of Harold Vartanian, whose autoworker-headed immigrant family moved to the outskirts of Dearborn in the mid-1920s. Although their roughed-in house was not technically a "garage home," their experience offers some parallels with the hardships encountered by garage homeowners. Vartanian recounted that the house was made out of "beaverboard paper" and consisted of only three rooms. It lacked a kitchen, as well as the most fundamental utilities: a well, electricity, and indoor plumbing. There was an outdoor toilet "made out of old doors" and a "black-top roof." A potbelly stove provided them with heat, and kerosene lamps gave them light. At times, he refers to the house as a "shanty" or a "cabin." It was, he recalls, "not even straight with the road. It was about parallel with the creek, which went on an angle." Vartanian thinks the house was originally "a real estate office," although he also wonders if "the home was actually built for my stepdad or what because I think it could have been."[21]

The family gradually improved the property by digging wells, setting up rain catchers for bathwater, and replacing the original ramshackle toilet with a "two-room outhouse."[22] Sometimes the wells would dry up in the summertime, and the family had to buy water in bottles, or the pumps would freeze in the winter, compelling them to melt snow as their source for water. To supplement the income of the father, who worked for Ford Motor Company, the family raised cows on their property and delivered the milk in a Model T. Over the course of the next decade or so, the family's conditions improved: their house was connected to municipal electricity, running water, and sewers, and they replaced the potbelly stove with a "laundry stove," which also acted as a water heater. Eventually, in 1932, they "put the new house in."[23]

The garage homes were often portrayed as temporary residences, like the one owned by the Vartanian family, to be replaced by a more permanent structure on the front of the lot when resources permitted. However, despite this romanticization as "starter houses," there is little evidence that this happened with any frequency. In many cases, the original families either continued to live in the garage homes or they sold the garages to new owners who also used them for residential purposes, and when they did so the original families, rather than moving to the front of the lot, moved away entirely. That the garage homes were equipped from the beginning with utilities and even automobile garages also points to their use as permanent residences. Over six hundred garage homes were still occupied in the 1960s, so it appears it was too burdensome a process for occupants to develop and relocate to more permanent housing on the front of their lots.[24]

Ford Homes

Within Dearborn, the Ford Homes ranked at the high end of the housing spectrum (see figure 9). This subdivision consisted of three hundred houses near the site of the original tractor plant in the West End of Dearborn, which were intended for occupancy by high-end wage earners. The subdivision was relatively modest in scale, with the housing types limited to single-family detached houses only and no commercial development. As small as the project was, it was still to offer some amenities, including a park to buffer the houses from a bordering railroad line, a community center, and a school, of which only the latter was built. The infrastructure for the subdivision was fairly extensive, with paved streets and sidewalks, boulevard lighting with buried electrical wires, telephone poles hidden from view in alleys. Six different types of houses were built, varying in size and appearance, but all of them were two stories with a kitchen, a living room, a dining room, sometimes a vestibule, and most had three bedrooms. Upon request, automobile garages were provided for prospective buyers.

Aesthetically, the Ford Homes subdivision exhibited the aesthetic influence of its designer Leonard Willeke, and this characteristic became a selling point used in press releases drafted by the Ford Motor Company.[25] Willeke achieved this pleasing effect by creating a picturesque plan throughout the subdivision, varying the housing models and slightly staggering the spacing of each house from another. The architectural style of the housing was quaint in a somewhat contrived way, consisting of a cross between English cottage and Colonial revival, with square bases, sharply pitched roofs, slightly projecting eaves, regular and hipped gables, rectangular and crescent windows, and hooded arches over the doors. The quality of the materials and construction was quite high. The houses boasted full basements, with steel girders across the foundation walls to support the structure above; interiors with walls double-boarded and covered with plasterboard and floors made of oak or fir; and exteriors of frame, cedar shingles, brick veneer, or combinations thereof. In addition, the houses came with coal bins, furnaces, humidifiers, fireplaces, and laundry tubs, as well as bathrooms fully accessorized with enameled iron bathtubs, vitreous iron toilet fixtures, and tiled floors.[26]

The overall goal, according to a company statement, was to help the workers—but not by cutting corners, since the plan was instead "to furnish to the employees a modern type of house, well equipped and tastefully designed."[27] Garages would be included since "the Ford employees . . . are nearly all motor car owners." The *Dearborn Independent* explained that they were "artistically beautiful, . . . well laid out, . . . prettily surrounded, . . .

FIGURE 9. Photo of Ford Homes District, 1919 (Collections of The Henry Ford)

the best-looking, best-constructed, longest-lasting homes possible within the financial limitations of well-paid working men."[28] "Monotony" and "cheapness" were avoided in the overall design,[29] with the result that the subdivision could not be mistaken for a "factory village" full of "row houses" that looked "machine-made."[30] Instead, the Ford Homes would contribute to Dearborn's reputation as the "most desirable Detroit suburb," a "home city," free of a "factory spirit," despite the presence of a major industry. This article continued:

> There has never been the incentive to make of it a hustling factory town with belching smoke, hurrying workmen, and unpleasant dirt and noises. Rather, the beauty of the little place has grown greater as, away a few blocks from the business district, modern little houses and bungalows have risen to shelter those with the foresight to seek a home away from the distractions of Detroit the Dynamic.[31]

The houses were built quickly, using Fordist methods that took advantage of standardized materials and Taylorized division of labor: for example, one crew did all the foundations, another did the framing, and another did roofing. Most of the houses were completed by 1921, although all of them were not sold and occupied until 1925. The tractor plant was relocated to the Rouge plant in 1921 for consolidation reasons, although this had been the raison d'être of the housing in Dearborn. Ford Motor Company employees were not deterred, though, from living in the new subdivision: blue-collar workers simply commuted to the River Rouge plant by interurban and by bus, and later white-collar workers walked to the nearby administration and laboratory building built in 1923. The company marketed the Ford Homes in a newsletter to employees and made the houses affordable by offering easy financing. In mid-1921, the houses were selling for between $6,900 to $8,500, with down payments as low as 10 percent and monthly installments varying from $38 to $85 according to the type of house, amount of down payment, and the term of years required for payment.

Close to half of all the households were headed by Ford Motor Company workers by 1930—the first year for which comprehensive data is available after the Ford Homes subdivision houses were built, sold, and occupied.[32] Of that group of household heads, more than half were managerial (54 percent). The rest of the household heads were split between skilled and semi-skilled at a fifth each, while unskilled workers trailed at 6 percent. The relatively high percentage of managerial Ford Motor Company workers found here was something of a reversal, as elsewhere in Dearborn they made up only one-third that amount. Within the subdivision, the household size was only 4.4 people, much lower than most households with a Ford Motor Company worker present (5.6), but exactly typical for throughout Dearborn. In 39 percent of the homes, some member other than the household head worked remuneratively, which was about the same for Ford Motor Company families across Dearborn. About three-quarters (74 percent) of the Ford Motor Company household heads were native whites, which was close to the typical composition of Dearborn. In comparison, only about half of Ford Motor Company workers in the rest of Dearborn were native whites.

Most significant, the subdivision's homeownership rate by Ford Motor Company household heads was 87 percent, compared to 55 percent across all Dearborn household heads, and the median value was $8,000, slightly higher than the median for Dearborn ($7,914) and higher yet than the median for Ford Motor Company household heads across Dearborn ($7,200).[33] Of course, not all levels of workers could afford to live in the Ford Homes, nor was the standard of living there generally found elsewhere in Dearborn. It is also ironic that, while the housing was intended for skilled workers, they ended up being outnumbered by employees in managerial jobs. Still, the subdivision is representative of Henry Ford's intention to make access to high-quality housing available to workers.

Proximity of Industry and Residences

One of the most obvious issues faced by Dearbornites was simply the existence of a mammoth industry amid the residences. Eventually the River Rouge plant became the world's largest manufacturing facility under a single operator.[34] Henry Ford himself did not see industry in a suburban setting as posing much of a problem, interestingly enough. He predicted, for the future, holistic communities that combined agriculture and industry to create self-sufficiency, claiming that it was no longer "logical to divide the country into agricultural and industrial groups" and noting that manufacturing had shifted from its historical concentration in the Northeast and was more commonplace than ever in the South and the West.[35] "The shift is everywhere from wholly manufacturing or wholly agricultural to a balance between the two," he stated. "This is not a revolutionary idea. In a sense, it is a reactionary one. . . . It suggests something that is very old."[36] Ford implemented these ideas in his program for "village industries," whereby nineteen facilities were developed throughout the Michigan countryside during the interwar period to house subassembly manufacturing of lightweight automobile parts.[37] For the most part, Ford foresaw the combination of agriculture and industry as occurring on a relatively small scale. Here Dearborn was a significant exception because of the vast scale of its industry.

Newspaper accounts noticed the utopian quality of Henry Ford's intentions toward Dearborn. A local newspaper described the area around the River Rouge plant as a "modern new city" and even went so far as to compare it to Port Sunlight, the English industrial community designed by world-renowned landscape architects "with the definite purpose of giving the entire population the working stimulus of beautiful park-like surroundings and the peace and contentment that comes from nature's best setting."[38] *Detroit Saturday Night* proclaimed Dearborn a "veritable workers' paradise" and credited Henry Ford with a dream of providing "employment for many" within a place of residence where "every prospect pleased" and a "lovely, quiet, helpful, neighborly existence was the rule."[39] A *Chicago Daily Tribune* article declared of Ford that "he has gathered around him not only . . . blocks of factories with black chimneys pointing like cannon toward the sky, but fields and gardens where people are happily at work, workshops where they are turning out things to sell, laboratories where they are experimenting for the future."[40] According to a Ford Motor Company publicist, the suburbanization of industry was evidence that "industrialism does not necessarily mean hideous factories of dirty brick, belching smoke stacks and grimy workmen crowded in ramshackle hovels." Instead, "the spots you would select for a picnic Henry Ford has picked for factory sites."[41]

Dearborn's boosters also emphasized the benefits of having industry and residences in close proximity to each other. One developer, Edith Mae Cummings, asserted that workers would have the best of all worlds, where "paved highways, the automobile and the auto bus give them transportation" and "homes of the better type are being built." In fact, her subdivision could "be reached in fifteen minutes from the Ford plant, making it possible for the men who work in the River Rouge District to live in Dearborn." Because "great industrial institutions located on the west side give them employment at the highest wage being paid to factory employees in the United States," she added, they could enjoy modern conveniences available to "only the very rich man" a few years earlier.[42] Supporters argued that Dearborn was a healthy, even curative, place to live, despite the presence of manufacturing. Most of Dearborn's residential development, in fact, was located west of the River Rouge plant, and with prevailing winds blowing toward the east, many residents were in fact spared the ill effects of pollution.[43] Local newspapers were unabashed in calling for citizens to "move out in ozone district," claiming that "Dearborn throbs, but without smoke, noise" and noting that the "city's growth was in suburbs,"[44] "where fresh air, sunshine, and beautiful grounds make life more worth the living."[45] An article with the saccharine title "Dearborn Is Called Smiling, Happy City" asserted that "throughout the city is an air of health and well-being which gives visitors a distinctly pleasant impression."[46] Finally, a locally published poem described both the suburban and the industrial aspects of the community in sentimental terms, referring to Dearborn as "a home-land near the work-land."[47]

A more diverse range of reactions appeared in descriptions written for wider audiences. *Munsey's Magazine* writer Judson Welliver generally saw the Detroit metropolis as an "object-lesson" in "the new art of making a distinctively industrial center beautiful, livable, attractive; of making a factory town good to look at; of making show-places of vast, clanging, whirring machine-shops." He found this striking, especially as Detroit's industries were of the kind that "commonly imply a smoky, grimy, unkempt, drab, sunless town—industries that one surveys with the thought that they have produced palaces at one end of the town and slums at the other," as found in England and older manufacturing centers of the United States. Although "industry grew and furnaces and chimneys reared up with threats to smoke it out," he argued that Detroit's efficient production overcame the old paradigm and described its plants as "ornaments rather than eyesores." He attributed the improved designs to the architect Albert Kahn, known for using steel, glass, and concrete to create modern buildings that were open, ventilated, and filled with light, and he noted their settings in "grass-plots, gardens, and fountains rather than cinders and slag-heaps."[48] This could easily be a description of the Ford Motor Company plants in either Highland Park or Dearborn, since they both featured buildings designed by Kahn that were revolutionary in their sanitary working conditions and streamlined aesthetic.

Edmund Wilson's description of the River Rouge plant is more bitingly critical, however, and he commented on its junkyard appearance:

> One approaches the plant itself through the used materials and the dead equipment of old projects not yet salvaged—a line of croquet-wickets tracing the disused electrified freight-line of the D.T. & I, a rusty junk-heap of still-tough steel vertebra from old merchant marine hulls bought by Ford from the government after the War.

Wilson acknowledged, however, "The buildings of the plant have a certain beauty . . . black-tipped silver cigarette chimneys above long factories of a pale dull green the color of very thin pea-soup, with large darker rows on rows of little rectangular windows." Yet he also noticed, "[Beyond] appear the black silo-shaped ovens, white smoke pouring low in front of them, and the angular black cranes and the round silver cylinders of the blast furnace."[49] Local historian Arthur Pound found fault not so much in the factories but in the contrast with their settings. He commented, "Disconcerting is the contrast between the spic-and-span industrial structures in which Detroit's workingmen toil and the shabby districts in which many of them reside. One sees here our penchant for doing small things badly and big things well."[50]

There are few surviving accounts of complaints by Dearborn citizens about the polluting impact of Ford Motor Company industry. One of these is Becker's oral history, in which she recounts the South End as "stinky, dirty and dusty." She recalled "clean-up parades" since "they had to do a lot of cleaning in the South End because it was dirty and smoky from the Ford Motor Company as well as other industries around there." Becker continued, "A lot of the people were very neat and they would get discouraged because the streets were dirty." She described environmentalism as not gaining momentum in Dearborn until the 1940s, when Mayor Orville Hubbard appointed committees for smoke abatement and the "city beautiful" movement. Before then, Becker stated, it was not uncommon to be "considered kind of a kook" if one insisted that "air ought to be cleaner."[51]

Runaway Growth

As a side effect of prosperity, Dearborn experienced phenomenal change in its built environment, ranking it among some of the nation's fastest-growing communities.[52] "That's the period of such huge growth," observed Becker. "The Dearborn area—what is now Dearborn—grew 1000 percent between 1920 and 1930," she said, adding that much of the growth was in the South End.[53] The author of an article about Springwells (later annexed to Dearborn) remarked, "Whatever conditions may have brought it about, it is a fact that more detached homes have been constructed in Springwells and other Detroit suburban villages in the past two years than experienced in [almost] any other city. . . . Square mile upon square mile of new territory is being developed, and as quickly occupied with splendid new homes of every description, around Detroit generally and Springwells particularly."[54] Another article in the same newspaper confirmed this: "Detroit is rapidly expanding in every direction. What was formerly green fields on Detroit's north, east and west is now a part of the city. It is only a matter of years until Springwells, including its own outlying green fields, will become thickly populated."[55]

This mushrooming growth was particularly disorienting to those who had been part of Dearborn's rural culture before the arrival of Ford Motor Company.[56] Henry Haigh, a longtime resident, was astonished that his "quiet little sylvan hamlet" was transformed into a "superlatively prosperous industrial suburb."[57] As subdividers acquired farmland for development, the original occupants were displaced. "When the Ford people came out," reminisced Joseph Karmann who became mayor of Fordson in the late 1920s, "and bought our old farm, our old homestead, and all the others in the area, why, we were like pigeons in the barn when the barn was torn down. . . . We just had to get out and look, seek for places elsewhere."[58] According to Clyde Ford, cousin to Henry Ford and mayor of Dearborn in the 1930s, the new development caused "farm land values to rise slowly at first and finally to prices undreamed of a few years previous with the wildest speculation bringing about changes constantly." He added that real estate activity eventually erased the landscape of almost all its previous features, including the well-fenced fields and farm buildings that had once served as landmarks. "People who had lived from the early times," he ruminated, "moved and scattered to all points."[59]

The growth of Dearborn drew attention from a range of critics as the development of infrastructure fell behind the rate at which housing was built. According to resident Joseph Cardinal, "It was almost impossible to put in sewers and sidewalks and water and . . . streets to keep up with this terrific growth that we had as a result of the Ford plant coming out here."[60] Road development especially lagged, even in the Ford Homes model subdivision. "Just mud. Just mud," lamented Theodore Graham who lived in the subdivision, when asked about the unpaved streets. He and his neighbor "pulled so many Model T's out of that mud. . . . It got so Pete and I left our spade outside the front porch. [We] used to dig them out there every day, well, pretty near every day after a rain. My own got caught in there once."[61] Municipal engineer Robert Erley complained that, "In the smaller activities, Dearborn began 'to put on the trimmings,' but in the larger activities it began to stand still." He added, "'Garage houses' on the rear end of lots were built in large numbers wherever restrictions would permit, the owners hoping that some day, someone would provide the proper improvements."[62] Karmann recalled, "The subdividers would buy farms . . . and develop them. They had just temporary homes on the bigger share of these lots. Today they [would] call them slum areas, shacks and shanties, no sewage, no water, and the problems . . . with sanitation."[63] The poor quality of some of the housing prompted editorials with titles such as "City of Shacks or Fine Homes?" "Housing Facilities Are Lacking," and "Realtors Pledge Aid for Better Homes."[64]

Unattractive housing was just one of many building types springing up in suburban areas now accessible by the automobile, causing the Detroit metropolis to be characterized by what local historian Arthur Pound referred to as "slovenly spaciousness." He explained that there were "shacks next to churches" and "rookeries in the very shadow of skyscrapers," as well as "household decay almost under the eaves of industrial neatness." There was no pressure, he reasoned, "to use land thriftily [as] fussy citizens can always move farther out on several hundred square miles of nearly level plain."[65] Author Jonathan Norton Leonard was more harsh, remarking that, "beyond the Ford plant lies Detroit, separated by five miles of the most complete ugliness in America. Open country of a few years ago is half built-up with flimsy houses, gas stations, hot dog stands. Lesser factories drool rusty among the weeds."[66] The loss of open space was mourned by many locals. "The city is still spreading out in all directions and occupying more and more territory which just a few years ago were farm communities," lamented Clyde Ford. "Old landmarks are gone so much so that at times the sentiment of it grips us in a strange way."[67] Another Dearborn resident complained of this turn of events as well, stating, "All the rural areas within 20 miles of Detroit and more are gobbled up in one great mass of people, homes, factories, shopping centers almost every mile."[68]

In 1930, automobile-dependent growth was also criticized by *Harper's* writer Robert Duffus, who went so far as to compare Detroit to Los Angeles and to argue that both suffered from the "American disease of growth," an affliction that resulted when a city "has been able to spread itself over an almost limitless area, with few natural obstacles" because of "the almost universal adoption of the automobile and the frantic use thereof." The unpredictability of this growth made it difficult to plan within the urban limits of Detroit, much less its entire metropolis. Duffus continued, "The city went forward, as all boom towns do, by jerks. It grew by a series of convulsions. . . . A city growing by jerks, too rapidly for planning, presents a curious pattern. Perhaps one should say absence of patterns." He placed the blame for this on the automobile and the corresponding rise in suburban population. Of the Detroit metropolis, he stated, "The automobile with a million and more new inhabitants riding on the running board shattered it completely. It scrambled it. It made an omelet of it." He mused, "Two or three years from now there may be another furious spurt." Making the connection between suburbanization and consumerism, he then quipped, "Perhaps this will come when the slogan of a car for every member of the family, with an airplane or two thrown in, is successfully impressed upon the American consciousness."[69]

However, metropolitanization in Detroit had its boosters as well as its detractors. Descriptions of the region's suburbs emphasizing their affluence and beauty stood in contrast to those of the central city. "On all sides are reflected the many activities that reach far out into the suburbs," stated a writer for *Outlook*, who commented on the "great stretches of residential sections and streets and boulevards" and noted that two of the most "fashionable thoroughfares" were Chicago and Boston Boulevards, "flanked by imposing residences [that were] little more than a year old." This writer also noted that property along Lake Saint Clair "that a few years ago sold for sixty-six dollars a foot now brings in one thousand dollars."[70] *Munsey's* writer Judson Welliver even compared some of the grand houses in Detroit's suburbs to those in Newport, stating that "palatial 'cottages' in wonderful grounds look out over the blue waters of the lake, miles of them lining the shore."[71] "Every Detroit suburb is now enjoying . . . [a] building campaign," declared *Springwells Independent*. "Square mile upon square mile of new territory is being developed and as quickly occupied with splendid new homes of every description."[72] *New Republic* writer Cyril Player observed, "[Detroit] finds its own energy pushing ever to the rim of the hills, and the gay radiance of the Michigan countryside becomes precious enough to incorporate and preserve in the new home-growing districts."[73] Even Dearborn, a modest working-class suburb, was depicted glossily in comparison to Detroit, featuring modern little houses in demand by those seeking a quality of beauty found away from the central city."[74]

Mass Suburbanization Debated

Dearborn as a suburb for the masses was part of a rising trend well documented by contemporaries in the early twentieth century, a geographic trend that appeared during the interwar period in a region now known as the "Rustbelt." Industry was growing in the Sunbelt, but it was often located within the city limits or in unincorporated areas rather than in suburbs— Los Angeles is a case in point. Within the Rustbelt, twelve cities including Detroit produced more than thirty industrial or diversified suburbs, which experienced rapid growth in the 1920s and featured large populations, ranging from about 25,000 to 75,000 by 1930. Suburbs most comparable to Dearborn are found in the following metropolitan areas: Akron (Barberton), Boston (Brockton, Quincy), Chicago (Cicero, Waukegan, Illinois; Hammond, Indiana), Cincinnati (Norwood), Detroit (Highland Park,

Hamtramck, Pontiac, Wyandotte), Milwaukee (West Allis), New York (Port Chester, New York; Norwalk, Stamford, Connecticut; Clifton, Hackensack, Hoboken, Irvington, Kearny, New Brunswick, Passaic, Perth Amboy, Plainfield, Union City, New Jersey), Philadelphia (Chester), Pittsburgh (Washington, McKeesport), Providence (Pawtucket), St. Louis (East St. Louis), and South Bend (Mishawaka).[75]

The high hopes held out for such suburbs are best summarized by Carol Aronovici who wrote in 1914, "The suburbanizing of the wage earner is a great social and economic opportunity." He wondered "whether garden communities will look upon the bleak horrors of our urbanized existence and give men, women, and children a new lease on life and industry [a] chance to serve men rather than to enslave them."[76] Ten years later, *American City* writer William Bailey concurred, claiming, "Outstanding industrial experiments are represented in the suburbs of satellite character. . . . [These] are being realized to be a frontier of opportunity by the newcome foreigner, and by the negro."[77] Federal policy makers studying the issue in 1932 agreed, declaring, "[There are] many advantages of industrial decentralization over industry located in an overpopulated city." These policy makers envisioned "trimmed lawns with shrubs and flowers, wooded areas and parks, conveniently located schools and churches, with good highway and transit facilities. . . . All within walking distance of the factory." Such an arrangement would dispense with "cold lunches and expensive transportation often with wasteful unremunerative and fatiguing trips strap-hanging in street cars, local trains and buses." Moreover, "blocks of tenements" would be eliminated and be replaced by "healthful houses with ample sunlight, air circulation, comparative freedom from smoke, dust and noise, and affording much desired privacy." Cost of living would be reduced "because of the development of adjacent truck gardening, dairies, poultry yards, and farming."[78]

Critics, however, worried about the creation of local economies dependent upon a single industry. The policy makers who authored *Our Cities: Their Role in the National Economy* noted that "localities, by means of subsidies, tax exemption, and free sites, have indiscriminately attracted enterprises which did not mesh with the rest of the community's industries and which sooner or later helped to throw the entire industrial pattern out of gear." They concluded that "under such unbalanced conditions, it is impossible to achieve a maximum employment for the available labor supply and a minimum of seasonal and cyclical fluctuations in the total payroll of the community."[79] According to urban planner M. L. Wilson, this was a situation that both employers and employees might resist. "This type of employer objects to a personal relationship which sets up a sense of obligation in time of unemployment," he observed. "They object to decentralized locations because it might tend to place them 'at the mercy' of a limited number of wage-earning people." Moreover, "the workers desire to be so located that they have a reservoir of industries where they can find jobs."[80] George Ford, urban planner, also noted this disadvantage, remarking, "If the worker loses his job he has to pull up stakes and move to some other part of the metropolitan area where he can get work."[81]

Inadequate housing in these new suburbs was another complaint of reformers. "When industry moves out from the city center it is seeking economic advantage," noted Graham Taylor, an expert on manufacturing. "It may provide also a made-to-order 'model' town, or merely build rows of 'company houses,' or leave housing to haphazard real-estate enterprise, or depend on traction to bring workers to the suburban shops." Often, industry simply shifted to the edge of the city, he commented, and workers continued to live in crowded urban neighborhoods, causing workers to make a reverse commute to their jobs.[82] "It is a well-known fact," declared George Ford,

> that the majority of workers, in many if not most, of the larger industrial plants that have moved out into the suburbs are still living in the heart of the city and daily spending much time and energy in commuting back and forth. . . . In Cincinnati and Providence today, at the evening rush hour, as many people are using the transit lines into the center of the city as away from it. . . . While it may be a good thing for the transit lines[,] the decentralization of factories in America has not served as yet in any marked degree to decentralize population.[83]

The reverse commute of wage earners turned upside down the expectations of the white-collar world, causing Taylor to suggest:

> The suburbanite who leaves business behind at nightfall for the cool green rim of the city would think the world had gone topsy-turvy if at five-thirty he rushed out of a factory set in a landscape of open fields and wooded hillsides, scrambled for a seat in a street car or grimy train and clattered back to the region of brick and pavement, of soot and noise and jostle. Yet this is daily routine for many thousands of factory workers.[84]

Finally, the new suburbs drew criticism for the speculative development they spurred. On this point, Taylor remarked, "Compared with [the] thought-out, well-joined, craftsman-like organization of equipment to meet the common needs of these various manufactories," any effort to meet the needs of the workers presented a marked contrast, especially regarding the development of their communities. He added, "Subdivisions have been laid out without any reference to each other, and the whole arrangement of the town had the appearance of a crazy quilt."[85] George Ford, commenting on the lack of infrastructure for community life, stated, "School facilities are apt to be poor, churches and sect groups, theatres, billiard parlors and other leisure time employments are lacking or inadequate; it is difficult for their friends or compatriots to get in and out to see them."[86] "The removal of the factory to the rim of the big city is not an adequate solution of our civic-industrial problem," asserted Taylor. "If it leaves the workers' home behind in a congested area, or even if it transplants it to a region where the whole system of community life is left to remain undeveloped."[87]

In fact, the rise of mass suburbs was an increasing worry among the nation's urban policy makers, who wondered how central cities would be impacted. "The motor age has brought 'boom' suburban towns planted with as little planning as the 'boom' towns which burst into existence in the railway age," wrote the authors of the Hoover-commissioned *Recent Social Trends in the United States*. "This unanticipated type of aggregation has not only meant a reorganization of city planning, but has precipitated many adjustments of social habits." They continued, "Large cities throughout the United States have been confronted with the task either of extending municipal services to surrounding suburban communities or of developing some new form of political association." They warned that the cost involved in maintaining obsolete central cities was becoming a subject of concern and the problem should not be neglected much longer.[88]

Reformer Aronovici agreed, emphasizing not just the dislocation created by new suburban growth but also its devastating social and economic costs for central cities. He noted that, as the automobile made suburbs possible, the city in comparison was becoming outmoded, "largely devoid of the conveniences of modern efficient living." He added that the "drift of population from congested areas to the periphery" left a "vacuum not only in the physical structure of the city but in its economic and social values. . . . The blighted areas are being drained slowly of their economic values by their inability to produce revenue and the additional burden imposed by taxation which is based upon the value of hopes long ago lost by the property-owners."[89]

Conclusion

The case of Dearborn offers insights into the rise of the suburb for the masses, an increasingly common American community during this period.

Dearborn, like many suburbs of its kind, featured inadequate housing, runaway growth, a reverse commute for many workers, and an economy dependent on a single industry. While skilled workers living in Dearborn benefited exceptionally, housing opportunities could vary wildly along lines of class and race, with less skilled white workers limited because they lacked the financial means, and African Americans barred for racial reasons. As for the less skilled workers who did live in Dearborn, they often put up with substandard housing, such as the garage homes. Still, communities such as Dearborn can be seen as a watershed, anticipating a time in the postwar period when suburbs would become more open than ever before, containing more of the national population than either the cities or the countryside. The desirability of the suburbs from the perspective of Ford Motor Company workers is evident in the sacrifices they made to live there. At the same time, these suburbs were the subject of new lines of segregation, some of which have persisted even until now.

3

The Automobile and Urban Growth

THE RISE OF AUTOMOBILE use during this period impacted the Detroit metropolis in a number of ways: it introduced a means of transportation that was affordable, provided freedom to move about individually, and conveyed a sensation of speed, efficiency, and power. At the same time, however, automobiles were life-threatening hazards to urban centers and created inconvenient and annoying traffic jams. The use of automobiles promoted the decentralization of urban growth—both within the city proper, which witnessed an increase in subdivisions near its limits, and outside the city, in newly developed suburbs. Inevitably, the flow of traffic away from the center of the city brought about a decline in its downtown district. Finally, the growing reliance on the automobile—as it shifted from a recreational object to a utilitarian one—at times created a financial burden for working-class people who increasingly needed a car for commuting purposes. The barrier for them to afford an automobile is evident in the statistic that only half of all Ford workers owned one, and of those who owned a car only one in ten used it to commute.

Criticism of the automobile-dependent urban development that now surrounded Detroit was particularly biting. Speculative subdivisions like Dearborn were now typical. One policy maker, commenting on such subdivisions that extended for miles outside the city, complained that "lots were in many instances only staked out on the land . . . ," adding, "As far as the eye could see, the white painted posts bearing street names stretched out in all directions, a band sometimes a mile or more in width along the traffic artery."[1] Cyril Arthur Player commented about these eyesores in the *New Republic*:

Less than ten years ago, Detroit was so surrounded by farm lands traversed by thin, sometimes anemic, roads. . . . Today Suburbia stretches easily for a score of miles around the city from water's edge to water's edge, and he who wishes to find a quiet spot for courtship must travel a weary way for a rural road. . . . The "filling-in" of these suburban districts has been surprisingly rapid and consistent. One unfortunate development has been the so-called working-man's home; . . . it is represented by a shoddy, regimented type, often without suitable foundation, and these barrack-like colonies begin to encircle the community proper.[2]

Detroit, however, had not gone through this period of rapid expansion without at least a few attempts to plan its development. As early as 1919, *Detroit Saturday Night* writer Harvey Whipple complained that Detroit

is sprawly and awkward and heterogeneous. . . . Detroit's growth has been like Topsy's; it has been without plan; it has *happened;* it has *occurred* as the immediate occasion dictated and individual development has always been paramount to the general public good. . . . There has been no scheme by which future growth could be directed and controlled; no plan by which investors could be reasonably sure of the values of their property. A valuable piece of real estate today might be utterly worthless tomorrow [original italics].[3]

In calling for the creation of a zoning ordinance, Whipple noted, "Other cities have been through this struggle of heterogeneous and undirected growth and development." He concluded, "It is not so long since that the problem was solved in New York city only after great damage had been done and many personal losses experienced."[4]

In addition to zoning, there were demands for planning on a metropolitan level. One advocate for this was Frank Burton, Detroit commissioner of building and safety engineering. Upon noting that a survey of construction throughout Detroit and its surrounding area "shows single home building forging far ahead," he asserted that "this building expansion will continue until the city runs into all the adjacent counties." He then declared that "new civic problems" must "be provided for in a really big way, and some form of incorporation [on a city-county scale] must be adopted if policing and sanitary features are to be controlled."[5] Although a number of similar plans were proposed throughout the 1920s, there is no evidence they were implemented in more than a piecemeal fashion.[6]

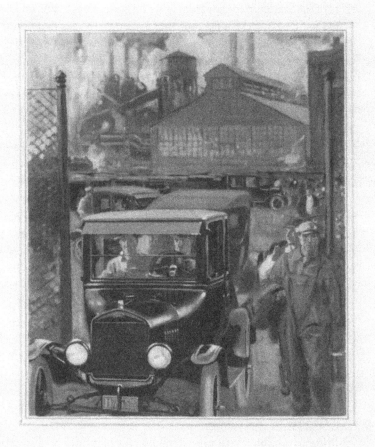

Within the means of millions

Automobile parking grounds adjacent to factories may be seen today in every American industrial center. They offer a striking proof of the better standard of living that workers in this country enjoy.

Here Ford cars usually outnumber all others. Their low cost and operating economy bring them within the means of millions; and in families where the cost of living is high even in proportion to income, the purchase of a car is possible with little sacrifice through the Ford Weekly Purchase Plan.

Runabout $260 Tudor . $580
Touring . $290 Fordor . $660
Coupe . $520   All Prices F. O. B.
                         Detroit
On Open-Car equipment and Demountable Rims $85 Extra
Full-Size Balloon Tires Optional
at an extra cost of $25

FORD MOTOR COMPANY   .·.   DETROIT, MICHIGAN

THE UNIVERSAL CAR

M A K E   S A F E T Y   Y O U R   R E S P O N S I B I L I T Y

FIGURE 10. Advertisement for Ford Motor Company, 1925 (Collections of The Henry Ford)

Methods of Commuting

Detroit, home of the automobile industry, was one of the leading cities in the country when it came to the rate of car ownership among its citizens. By 1930, it featured a ratio of one car for every 3.6 people, exceeding that in any other major city save Los Angeles.[7] The automobile had at last become an item of mass consumption, and this was true in varying degrees all over the country. The shift can be attributed to a combination of factors: manufacturers pushed down the price of the automobile, an improved infrastructure of paved roads and highways made its use more feasible, and finally, the decentralization of jobs and residences caused it to become a daily necessity. By the end of the 1920s, there was a national average of one car for every 4.5 people—in other words, enough for each American household to have its own. This compares to one car for every eleven people at the beginning of the decade.[8]

Henry Ford was particularly influential in bringing about this phenomenal change since he focused on making the automobile affordable; it was indeed a bit of a populist crusade of his. At the founding of his company he declared, "I will build a motor car for the multitude. . . . It shall be so low in price that the man of moderate means may own one—and enjoy with his family the blessings of happy hours spent in God's great open spaces."[9]

However, the use of cars did not immediately displace transit in Detroit during the 1920s. This was because automobile use, though rising, simply could not meet the challenge of conveying 1.5 million people across a scattered metropolis. As a result, the city still featured a variety of transportation modes, with citizens able to choose among streetcars, buses, and jitneys, as well as walking. In fact, the major carmakers recognized this situation and worked with Detroit to increase its transit service and infrastructure. No one was more involved in this than Henry Ford, and with good reason. His River Rouge plant was the largest single factory in the metropolis, drawing tens of thousands of workers daily, yet requiring employees to make a rather formidable reverse commute to its suburban location. With only one in ten wage earners commuting to the River Rouge plant by automobile, transit improvements were the only solution. Thus, Ford found himself in a paradoxical situation where he acted at the potential expense of his own product. The best illustrations of Ford's role in promoting transit are offered by his partial subsidization of the Northwest Belt line extending from Highland Park to Dearborn, his support of the municipalization of streetcars, and his endorsement of a proposal for subways.

An insurmountable obstacle arose because the demand for a metropolitan transit system was occurring at a time when the only tax structure to support it was contained within the boundaries of the central city. In other words, the relocation of industry created a need for transit lines to be extended into the suburbs, yet there was no mechanism for municipalities other than Detroit to be taxed for this. A plan for Detroit to subsidize suburban transit was highly unpopular with city residents, who voted it down. Ultimately, not even Ford himself, who had a hand in creating this situation, could reverse it. Thus, the gradual erosion of Detroit's transit system, which began in the 1930s, continued until the years after World War II, when the last streetcars were removed. In the end, both the lack of a metropolitan tax structure and the competition offered by the automobile must be taken into consideration when explaining the demise of transit in Detroit and other major cities in similar circumstances.[10]

Ford Workers Commute

Back in the late 1910s when Henry Ford was scouting a location for his new industrial colossus, Dearborn was not entirely without transit. At the time it featured a system of both passenger and freight rail and an interurban train, and these advantages became a deciding factor in Ford's choice to move there. Still, the passenger rail and the interurban would be far from adequate for moving tens of thousands of workers using transit at three daily rush hours coinciding with the factory's shifts. Not one but many streetcar lines needed to be added to the existing layer of transportation; buses would also be used to complement the streetcar system. Designing transit for Ford Motor Company wage earners, however, was complicated by the location of their homes, which were clustered near the Highland Park plant or scattered throughout the city of Detroit and in some of its suburbs. For many workers, traveling to Dearborn via transit necessitated a trip into the center of the city and back out, waiting for a transfer in the process. This posed a problem not only for the workers who were inconvenienced while commuting but also for the entire downtown, which suffered from intense congestion.[11]

Meanwhile, the number of Ford Motor Company wage earners was already far from trivial; as early as 1920, when both the Highland Park and River Rouge plants were operating, the count at the two facilities combined was about fifty-seven thousand, about a third of the entire workforce in Detroit's automobile industry.[12] Over the next decade Ford Motor Company shifted operations from Highland Park to the exponentially larger River Rouge plant, which would employ as many as one hundred thousand at its peacetime peak. Unless resolved effectively, inadequate transit to Dearborn could cause tardiness, fatigue, and turnover among employees, prompting a measurable loss of valuable industrial productivity. For the workers themselves, a difficult commute meant a setback in the quality of life they had achieved while employed at the Highland Park plant preceding the rise of the River Rouge. Beginning in 1915, when Henry Ford first envisioned the development of the River Rouge plant, he recognized the need for improved transportation to convey workers there. According to a *Detroit News* article written that year, a "tremendous investment of money and time" would be involved with "the establishment of blast furnaces and plants in which to manufacture his new farm tractor" staffed by a "throng of workers." The article speculated that "between Michigan Avenue and Fort Boulevard, on the wide stretch of suburban country that lies between these two arteries, will be a means of transportation" and concluded that Ford had given "considerable thought" to a streetcar line connecting the two thoroughfares.[13]

The shortcoming of turning Dearborn into an ideal community of workers was revealed once huge numbers of people were compelled to commute into it. For some workers this was because they could not afford to live there; for the ten thousand African Americans who worked for Ford Motor Company, it was because they were prohibited from living there. At times when the River Rouge plant labor force reached its peak, up to thirty thousand workers arrived daily with each shift, which meant a total of ninety thousand a day. Commuting was one subject of a 1930 study commissioned by Ford Motor Company and conducted by the Bureau of Labor Statistics, which sampled one hundred Detroit families headed by Ford Motor Company workers. On average, the workers lived 8.2 miles from the River Rouge plant, and close to half of them commuted by streetcar. In addition, about one-fifth (19 percent) commuted by bus and a little over one-tenth (12 percent) by automobile, while 5 percent took a combination of streetcar and bus, and 3 percent walked. Another 12 percent used varying modes of transportation throughout the year. Although the largest percentage (31 percent) had a commute of between thirty and sixty minutes in length, another one-fifth (21 percent) had a commute of over ninety minutes, and 15 percent had a commute of between sixty and ninety minutes. Only one-fifth (21 percent) had a commute of under thirty minutes, and 12 percent fell into the category of "other," since they used varying modes of transportation that resulted in different lengths of commute.[14]

The shift toward centering operations in Dearborn rather than in Highland Park intensified the problem of commuting, at least initially, as many workers made the long commute by streetcar until they could relocate their residences. A booster from Springwells (later part of Dearborn) appeared to brace himself when he said that, now "the gigantic steel plant will soon be running at full speed, the city must prepare for the greatest influx of workers from Highland Park and the surrounding country that it has ever seen in any city in the country."[15] The labor statisticians remarked, "The large area covered by the city of Detroit and its suburbs made it necessary for most of the employees to ride to and from work," and due to operations moving to Dearborn, "the distance to and from work was materially increased for many of the workingman."[16] Confirming the findings of the statisticians, who had noted that one-fifth of the workers commuted for over ninety minutes, a *World's Work* article commented, "Detroit is spread out. Even in normal times workmen sometimes travel two hours to get to work and two hours back."[17] These observations probably did not fully reflect the experience of African American workers who tended to have the longest commutes because of the restrictions about where they could live. According to Detroit Urban League head John Dancy, "Because of inability to find homes outside the ghetto, Negroes working in large factories sometimes had to spend as much as four hours a day traveling to and from their work."[18]

Chester Kuta, a Ford worker who lived in Detroit until he could move to Dearborn, portrays vividly his streetcar commute on the Baker line. "Going to work and coming home was a real experience in itself," he recalls, noting that when he got on a streetcar at Livernois and Vernor Highway, "it was already pretty well crowded because the thing came from the east side. So I stood all the way to work, and I stood all the way home, too." Ford Motor Company workers were not allowed to sit at work, so this was a lot of standing. He added, "Those things were so crowded. Just to prove something to myself, I actually lifted my feet off the floor. Do you know that I didn't even sink?"[19] Commuting was just one part of an exhausting day for these workers. "Every worker could identify Ford workers on the streetcars going home at night," asserted autoworker Charles Denby. "You'd see twenty asleep on the cars and everyone would say, 'Ford workers.' Many times the conductors looked over the car and shook a man to tell him it was his stop."[20] According to a muckraking article in *Forbes*: "The men and women on the way home from work [at Ford] slump down in the buses and street cars so near dead that they often go half-a-mile beyond their destination."[21] Such a situation was described somewhat more tenderly by a *Pipp's Weekly* article, which stated, "Coming down in a Woodward car this morning, a toiler was on one of the side seats. His legs were spread out, his arms hung out loosely, his head hung on his chest. He was sound asleep. . . . It is a familiar sight, these tired-out Ford workmen. . . . But men and women both stood and let him sleep rather than disturb him."[22]

As early as 1918, a prescient newspaper editor lamented Dearborn's lack of balance between job opportunities and affordable housing, calling it "woefully lax." He warned, "Out of an army of 2400 or more employes [*sic*] of the Wonderland on our outskirts, fully 80 per cent are compelled to make a journey of 20 miles per day," adding that this was "a trip that almost all would forego were conditions such in Dearborn to allow them to reside here."[23] Years later, Depression-era federal policy makers criticized Dearborn for not resolving the reverse commute for many Ford Motor Company workers. Frustrated with this trend they stated that, regarding the movement of population out of the larger cities:

> there are enough conspicuous examples of factory decentralization to suggest that in some instances, at least, the workers have not followed factories. . . . Detroit is a case in point. It seems quite certain that most of the men working in the new Ford plant at Dearborn live in Detroit since, when on full time, this plant employs more than twice as many men as there are persons in the entire city of Dearborn. . . . In so far as the lack of housing in the neighborhood of the plants which have moved out into the suburbs is the reason for the workers still living in the large cities, there is need for a program that will provide homes and thus assist in the decentralization of population.[24]

On the other hand, wage earners who could afford to move to Dearborn and other suburbs may have remained in Detroit in order to remain centrally located near multiple employment opportunities, and thus commuting was their own choice. The journalist Myron Watkins, writing on labor issues in Detroit, commented on this mobility between jobs:

> Except for a very few "old-timers" there is absolutely no loyalty to the establishment or organization in which these men daily labor for their living. . . .They are continually on the alert for "better pay," and a difference of five cents per hour in favor of a new job will lead them to "throw up" an old job without delay. . . . Constancy in employment relations is no longer a virtue, at least not a common one.[25]

Century writer Webb Waldron concurred: "Workmen move restlessly from shop to shop as the mood strikes them or as this or that concern bids slightly higher." He added, "Where multiple manufacture has been pushed to the last degree, so that men's jobs consist in performing one very small operation over and over in endless monotony, the sense of attachment to the concern is naturally at a minimum."[26]

Northwest Belt Line

The start of manufacturing at the River Rouge made the problem of transporting workers suddenly acute. Production was initiated with a war contract in early 1918 for the manufacturing of submarine-chasing boats, and it
did not switch to the making of automobiles until the onset of peace. At this
time, no streetcar line terminated near the River Rouge plant, so Ford Motor
Company workers lacked any easy way to get there via transit. As a stopgap
measure, the company used Model T trucks with trailers to bring in as many
as six thousand workers daily from Highland Park.[27] Negotiations to build
a streetcar line were taking place with the Detroit Urban Railways (DUR),
which was a private franchise monopoly that ran Detroit's transit system. In
June 1918, an article announced plans for the extension of streetcar lines that
would terminate at the Eagle Loop, claiming, "In deciding on the new line
the D.U.R. will relieve many workers at the Ford shipbuilding and blast furnace plants of a mile walk."[28] According to the minutes of a meeting by Ford
Motor Company directors, it was proposed that either the carmaker or the
Navy (or a combination of the two) loan the DUR up to $500,000 for con-
struction.[29] As this matched the cost estimate listed in the newspaper article,
it can be assumed some sort of deal was worked out between the parties.

The completion of this line solved only part of Ford Motor Company's
problems, though. Workers, it was true, could now arrive at the plant by
streetcar, but for the thousands who still lived in Highland Park, the route
into downtown and out again was circuitous. What was required was a belt
line skirting the city that would connect the two plants, and indeed, as early
as 1923 discussion began as to Henry Ford's prospective role in building
this.[30] The pressing need for the Northwest Belt Line was made clear in a
petition circulated by workers, who complained, "We are compelled to ride
several miles out of our way in going to and from our place of employment,
thus consuming much time that we should have for our own use and for
our families." They concluded, "The present condition is intolerable and
works a great hardship upon us, threatening the continuity of our employment."[31] On the topic of the new line, Ross Schram, general manager of the
Department of Street Railways (DSR), predicted it would shave between
twenty and forty-five minutes every day off the commute for up to three
thousand riders.[32]

Fortunately for Henry Ford, there was an entrepreneurial developer with
close ties to the transit industry named Robert Oakman who was already
planning such a line and had indeed started building it (see figure 11).[33] Oakman hoped to profit in two ways: first, by renting or eventually selling his

tracks to a transit operator and, second, by the speculative development of land he owned nearby that would increase in value once a line was running. Negotiations between Oakman and the Department of Street Railways (who had taken over the DUR) dragged on, and it was not until two years later in 1925 that an agreement was reached.[34] By that time, Ford had long contemplated building two spurs on Oakman's Northwest Belt Line, one that would connect it to a Detroit crosstown line on Warren Avenue and another that would extend its terminus down Schaefer Avenue to the grounds of the Rouge plant.[35] By June 1925, the Northwest Line was opened, and shortly thereafter it included extensions financed by Ford on Warren and Schaefer.[36]

Transit improvements for the River Rouge plant were hardly over, though, and before the end of the 1920s, another major project was undertaken, again involving the cooperation of Ford Motor Company and the DSR. The problem was the Eagle Loop, in use since the late 1910s when Henry Ford

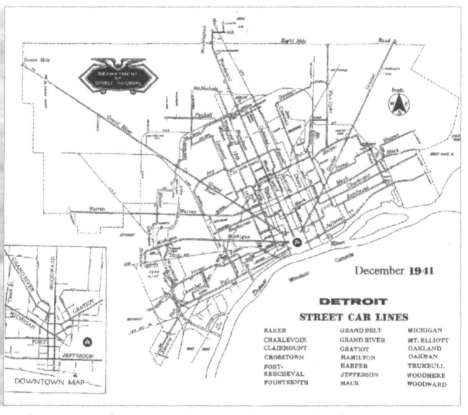

FIGURE 11. Map of Detroit Street Railways, 1941 (Jack Schramm collection)

had negotiated an extension from the DUR to get workers to his plant for wartime production. From this loop, workers had to walk a quarter mile in order to reach the plant, crossing at the Pere Marquette Railroad, then going on a bridge that went over Miller Road.[37] To expedite the workers' commute, assure safety, and increase capacity, Ford in 1927 arranged for a streetcar line tunnel to be built under the railroad tracks to serve two new terminals, referred to as Miller Road South (completed in 1927) and Miller Road North (1929). From the existing overpass on Miller Road, two bridge-ways were extended to lead to the terminals, and on each bridge were three pre-payment booths at the top of the steps leading to the loading tracks. In addition to the extension of tracks westward from the former Eagle Loop, the DSR also extended a spur from Michigan Avenue southward on Wyoming so that the new terminals were connected to more than one streetcar line. For this project, Ford Motor Company loaned $263,882 to the DSR for the costs of the extension and invested an additional $273,498 for the facilities on their property leased to DSR.[38] Eventually, the final cost totaled about $1 million.

By the end of the 1920s, approximately thirty thousand workers arrived at the River Rouge plant for each of the three daily shifts, most of them coming by streetcar. In other words, the transit facilities had to process a population equivalent to that of a small city, not once or twice but three times a day. To do so, seven streetcar lines served the plant, terminating at three yards. An example of the schedule from 1930 gives an idea of the logistics involved. As street railway historian Jack Schramm put it:

> Between 3:35 P.M. and 4:35 P.M. this one plant was served by seven car lines operating 165 runs, many of which were two-car motor-trailer trains. The three yards had a simultaneous capacity to load 54 cars, unload 35 cars and store 90 cars. . . . Electric power came from three substations with a capacity of six million watts.

According to Schramm, the culmination of transit improvements at the Rouge made it "unique in the western hemisphere and perhaps the world."[39]

Municipal Ownership

Extensions to the Northwest Belt Line and development of terminals at his plant were not Henry Ford's only foray into transit issues. In the early 1920s, he became involved with policy making on a metropolitan scale through his support of municipal ownership. Municipal ownership was

Detroit's answer to the private franchises running its street railway system, which put the citizenship at the mercy of monopolists who controlled fare hikes and the routing of lines. This had been a political topic since the 1890s, when Hazen Pingree was mayor, but it got a whole new burst of support with the 1918 election of Mayor James Couzens, a former Ford Motor Company executive, who made it a plank in his campaign platform. The DUR had earned the distaste of the public and city leaders alike for the poor management of its operations, although, it must be said, the private transit company was not entirely at fault. Conditions for the renewal of its franchise had been a political tussle for years, and without any certainty of being able to continue in business, the DUR stopped making any capital improvements. As a result, between 1899 and 1913, the city's track mileage per capita fell by almost half, which of course reduced service.[40] Meanwhile, the formation of the DUR in 1900, which involved buying up other transit companies, caused it to become overextended financially, and it struggled with debt for many years to come, which further hindered it from investing in its system.[41]

Still, even with Couzens in office, toppling the DUR was no simple matter. In the end, Couzens used a series of compromises to undermine the franchise of the DUR, eventually lowering the price needed to buy them out. Shortly after taking office, Couzens appointed a new street railway commission, which provided an appraisal of $31.5 million to be offered to the DUR, but in April 1919, this was voted down by the public in a fairly split referendum, with seventy thousand votes against versus sixty-four thousand in favor.[42] Opponents to the plan complained the price was too high. In response to this setback, Couzens decided to develop a competing system of municipally owned streetcar lines. With the support of the electorate, an amount of $15 million was allocated to build 100 miles of new track, with service by 400 new streetcars and 150 trailers. Construction began in 1920, and within a year the new system, although not completed, went into operation.[43] Another step was made toward municipal takeover of the DUR when some of its franchises expired and the electorate agreed to purchase 31 of its 300 or so miles of tracks, 105 of its streetcars, and 23 of its trailers, all for a cost of $2.3 million.[44] By now, the DUR was backed into a corner. Unable to expand because of the municipally operated lines, a profitable operation was no longer feasible, and for a price only two-thirds of that originally offered by Couzens in 1919 the DUR agreed to sell out. After a referendum supported this plan with 89 percent of the vote, municipal ownership of the entire system, now operated by the Department of Street Railways (DSR), went into effect in May 1922.

From the 1910s onward, Henry Ford had given municipal ownership his verbal support. In 1915, he proclaimed it "one of the safest business propositions I have ever heard of."[45] In 1922, he stated, "In Detroit . . . we have . . . able business men who have made a success of municipal operation. . . . I believe the time has come for [it]. Give them a chance to make good."[46] He developed a personal connection to transit policy in 1920 when his chief engineer, William Mayo, was appointed by Couzens to the Street Railway Commission. In 1922, Ford's tie to political power was further increased when Mayo was asked to take over operation of the DSR when manager John Goodwin took a leave of absence. Mayo would remain on Ford Motor Company's payroll, but he would devote half of each day or more to running the DSR.[47] The new relationship between Henry Ford and the DSR through the role of Mayo as manager created much speculation in the newspapers. One article asserted, "The unseen hand of Henry Ford is expected to pilot Detroit's municipal street railway." Another predicted that Mayo would "introduce some of the well-known Ford efficiency methods into the street railway system."[48]

Henry Ford now had unprecedented access to a transportation system that carried a significant portion of the metropolitan population into the River Rouge plant each day. With Mayo in charge, Ford took the opportunity in January 1923 to send an auditor in to inspect the books of the DSR. Less than a year later, he lent $2 million to the DSR for streetcar extensions. He also offered electric power from his plant at a cheap rate to run the streetcar system, although it is not clear if this was ever pursued. In July 1924, Mayo resigned and returned full-time to his job at Ford Motor Company, although he was retained by the DSR as a consulting engineer for the remainder of the 1920s. Even after Mayo officially stepped down, the relationship between Henry Ford and the DSR remained strong. This is evident in the successful undertaking of two major transit projects affecting the River Rouge plant: the extension of the Northwest Belt Line and the development of two new terminals, Miller Road North and South.

When Detroit completed the municipal ownership of its transit, it became one of only three major cities (the others were San Francisco and Seattle) to municipalize its transit, and its system was said to be the largest of its kind.[49] Although this was an accomplishment in itself, municipal ownership in many ways only created a new set of issues for Detroit and its surrounding area. For starters, Detroit's new transit system inherited many problems from the old system. According to Schramm, of the 363 miles of trackage the DSR came to own, fully two-thirds were in poor condition. In addition, the streetcars themselves were deteriorated, and as a result entire fleets had to be scrapped. A set of 250 Birney streetcars bought in 1921 by the municipally owned lines during the time they were competing with the DUR turned out to be a mistake, because they were not equipped for the loads that could be reached in urban settings during rush hours, and of these cars only 56 could be sold. The DSR initially had problems obtaining affordable electric power at a time when it was trying to expand its service. For a while the department was locked into an expensive contract with Detroit Edison, which had been negotiated by the DUR.[50]

All the same, between 1922 and 1930, the expansion of DSR service represented a considerable improvement over what was provided by the DUR: miles of trackage increased by almost 100, reaching a total of 450; there were now 1,835 streetcars in operation, compared to 1,260 previously; and an entire bus system had been added with a fleet totaling close to 600. During this same time, the DSR acquired an equity of $16 million in assets, paid the city $7 million in taxes and fees, and caused property valuation to rise from $36,659,913 to $58,675,739. All this was accomplished despite a six cents fare that was among the lowest in the nation.[51] Detroit's municipal ownership overall earned praise from the *American City* journal, which asserted, "New trails have been blazed both in engineering and in transportation."[52]

1929 Subway Proposal

Even with all the improvements under municipal ownership, though, the street railways by the end of the 1920s still managed to bump up against some limits. Detroit had, after all, increased its population from about 1.0 million in 1920 to 1.5 million by 1930, and during this time a significant number of jobs had shifted to the fringes, which created new burdens for transit. For instance, at Ford Motor Company alone, the ratio of jobs in Highland Park versus Dearborn was about six to one in 1920 but switched to almost the reverse in 1929, when it was one to seven. Not only did the location of Ford Motor Company jobs flip but the sheer number of jobs changed; while Highland Park's workforce peaked at sixty-two thousand in the mid-1920s, the number at the Rouge topped off at double that by the end of the decade, at least according to some accounts.[53] Besides having reached their maximum capacity, the efficiency of streetcars was hampered by automobiles, which used their tracks, creating congestion.

Rather than setting an exclusive right-of-way for the streetcars, however, the mayor-appointed Rapid Transit Commission (RTC) recommended taking transit off the surface of the streets altogether and putting it underground in the form of a subway. When this was suggested in 1929, it was the revival of a proposal that had been repeatedly discussed as early as 1909 by various commissions and that had been defeated at referendums a few times in the 1920s because of disagreement over its financing. Also, it should be noted that, since 1924, the Detroit subway proposal had been part of a package of transportation improvements referred to as "super-highways," which were automotive thoroughfares developed in tandem with transit (see figure 12).[54] The coexistence of such modes was possible because of a unique belief among the city's political leaders that

FIGURE 12. Illustration of Super-Highway. "Proposed Super-Highway Plan for Greater Detroit" (Rapid Transit Commission, 1924)

automobiles and transit could be complementary rather than competitors. The super-highway received the backing of the city's carmakers who, after all, needed to get tens of thousands of workers to their scattered plants every day. The biggest champion of the Detroit super-highway was Sidney Waldon, a transportation planner and tireless advocate of mass transit. In 1927, he stated:

> History has proven over and over again that we pay for adequate facilities whether we have them or not. We pay through delays and reduced efficiency. We pay through nervous wear and tear, through loss of property in blighted areas, and lessened values. And as a last resort we pay enormously for a few defensive measures that too often fail because [they are] inadequate.[55]

By 1929, when the subway proposal was again put on the table, some aspects of the super-highway plan were already underway, with money allocated for buying up property necessary for road widening. The subway component, though, and more specifically the money to construct it, had never been approved by the electorate, and it would need to go through another referendum in order to be built.[56] Meanwhile, getting voter approval of financing for the subway would be difficult for two reasons: one was the ambitious scale of the plan and the other was the way the cost would be distributed across the population. In the original super-highway plan from 1924, transportation corridors accommodating both automobiles and transit would extend in a pattern of radiating spokes throughout the Detroit metropolis, knitting together the central city and its suburbs. This network was to stretch for 240 miles and into three counties, with roads a little over 200 feet wide. Within the city limits transit would be placed underground, and in the suburbs it would be put on surface-level median strips. Because the super-highways were to be developed in more than one political jurisdiction, finding sources of funding was complex. For instance, beyond the city boundaries, super-highways would be constructed with revenue from a state gasoline tax. Within Detroit, however, this was not an option, and rather than relying on the state for money, funding would come mostly from assessments placed on local citizens whose property lay in a zone containing the proposed improvements; the rest of the money would come from a special citywide tax and from revenue generated by a relatively expensive ten-cent fare (the streetcars charged only six cents).[57]

The cost structure immediately posed a problem, since the city of Detroit was receiving the least financial assistance of all the jurisdictions involved, and yet it was responsible for the most expensive element of the entire plan, which was the subway. Homeowners subject to the assessment because their property abutted the planned subway lines were particularly vocal in their objections; they were, after all, to be assessed at the same rate charged for the ground floors of downtown merchants whose business would increase exponentially from a subway that brought consumers to their doors. On the other hand, the carmakers would shoulder a portion of the costs, as their property would be subject to the same assessments and citywide tax as the homeowners and downtown merchants. It took special legislation even to make this possible as by now many major automotive plants were located outside the city limits: Ford had centers in Dearborn and Highland Park, and Dodge had facilities in Hamtramck. Still, the cost borne by property owners (including the leading carmakers) in the three communities of Dearborn, Highland Park, and Hamtramck would amount to only about 10 percent of the cost for the whole system, despite the fact that the subway was engineered to deliver gigantic workforces to their doorstep every day.[58]

Meanwhile, the RTC, which had first proposed the super-highway plan in 1924, did not have a complete proposal for the subway component until two years later. When ready, they released a plan for a $280 million four-line system, forty-seven miles in length with routes designed, in the words of its engineers, so that "420,000 out of 445,000 workers [would] have their jobs within a half mile of a rapid transit line."[59] This version of the plan, however, met with intense political pressure due to its scale and cost, drawing opposition from the city administration, the city council, and small property holders as well as the Manufacturers' Association, which represented the interests of the automotive industries.

Thus began the whittling down of the subway proposal. At the end of three years, in 1929, the RTC came up with an alternate plan that its members believed to be adequately reduced to be submitted to the public. This plan was only about one-third the size of the original, featuring in place of four subway lines a single one known as the Vernor-Mack, which would traverse the city on an east–west axis, terminating at one end at Ford's Rouge plant in Dearborn. Its cost was also much smaller, estimated at $91 million.[60] The proposed Vernor-Mack subway line was situated to serve a section of the city in which residences, jobs, and amenities were highly concentrated, and its location would permit it to connect to twenty-seven of the twenty-nine existing streetcar lines and to twelve bus routes. According to the RTC, about 30 percent of all Detroit's industrial and business workers were employed within half a mile of the line, as this zone contained not only Ford Motor Company's River Rouge plant but also the many factories clustered on the West Side.[61] Also within this service area were destinations such as ball parks, downtown stores, city hall and municipal offices, the Eastern Market and the West Side Market, railroad stations for the Grand Trunk and Michigan Central, Baby Creek Park, and Woodmere Cemetery.[62] The running time on the Vernor-Mack line from its beginning at Connors Avenue to the Rouge plant was estimated to be forty-five minutes, which was twenty-eight minutes shorter than the amount of time to go the same route via streetcar.[63]

The revised subway plan was intended, no doubt, to serve as much of the Detroit population as possible. Still, it can be argued that no single person or organization would benefit as much as Henry Ford. By 1929, Ford was unique among all Detroit manufacturers in needing to transport close to ninety thousand workers a day to a suburban location; meanwhile, the Vernor-Mack line, which terminated at the River Rouge plant, was projected to have a daily capacity of eighty-eight thousand passengers—hardly a coincidence. Yet Ford's share of the subway cost was disproportionately small. Despite the many changes made in the subway plan between 1926 and 1929, the financing structure remained essentially the same, with outlying communities served by the subway paying for about 10 percent of the cost. While at one time these communities included Hamtramck and Highland Park as well as Dearborn, they now consisted of only the latter due to the re-routing of the subway line. Thus, Ford, as the major taxpayer in Dearborn, could expect to pay just a small portion of a $91 million subway proposal designed to funnel tens of thousands of workers directly to what was now his flagship plant.[64] Naturally, Henry Ford approved of the subway proposal, as is evident in the newspaper coverage devoted to the topic in the weeks leading up to the referendum on April 1, 1929. By now Mayo was serving as a spokesperson for Ford on the topic of the subway, and in one article he stated, "[In] Dearborn . . . the general feeling with regard to this plan . . . is favorable to it. I have talked it over with Mr. Ford at length and I can say that in his judgment he is very much for it."[65] Another sign of Henry Ford's support was the action of Edsel Ford to join the Citizens' Better Transportation Committee, formed to promote the subway.

Moreover, the RTC openly acknowledged that their goal was to transport industrial workers to recently decentralized plants, including that of Ford Motor Company. "As cities increase in population and in area," observed the commissioners, "new industrial plants are located farther out from the residential districts." They noted, "People employed [in] Highland Park, Hamtramck and Dearborn live largely in Detroit," causing both the distance to be traveled and the number of people handled to increase during peak hours.⁶⁶ They had previously stated that "if the City is to maintain its position as the third industrial city in the United States," leaders must see that wage earners can get to work within a reasonable travel time. "The workers of the city," the commissioners concluded, "should not be compelled to spend more than 45 minutes in travel morning and evening," and they added, "A great many now have to ride more than an hour and a half each way, or a total of three hours spent in travel or in awaiting a chance to ride."⁶⁷ More specifically, policy makers mentioned Ford Motor Company's River Rouge plant as a consideration in their decision to route the subway. One commissioner admitted frankly that "we were not altogether prepared [for] the shifting of the industrial workers from Highland Park to the Ford Rouge plant" in the space of only a few years, which "placed a heavy burden on the street railway."⁶⁸ In an article titled "Subway Seen as Necessity," another commissioner stated, "I know of workers in the Ford plant at the Rouge who spend 3 1/2 hours every day going to and from work."⁶⁹ Del Smith, general manager of DSR estimated that 50 percent of Ford workers would use the subway lines.⁷⁰

In the meantime, there were some indications that the general public was open to improving transit by way of a subway. This is attested in the dissatisfaction with the streetcars expressed by wage earners in letters to the editor written as the subway referendum approached. Coming from the River Rouge plant on the Northwestern Belt line, wrote one worker, "a deplorable scene occurred. . . . There were more than 100 men waiting at that point so imagine what happened. We were anxious to board the car but could not do so on account of the pushing, etc. . . . Much precious time was lost in this way." In conclusion, he asked, "And what will happen when all those now working in Highland Park are transferred to the Rouge plant? This condition should be remedied at once."⁷¹ Another wage earner complained, "In the northwest locality a working man or woman hasn't the ghost of a chance to getting to work on time in the mornings. . . . I live close to what seems to be a super highway and no city service has been installed yet. But, for a few buses . . . running down Coolidge highway in the morning, I don't know what most of the workmen in this section would do to get to work."⁷² At a hearing before the city council, a Ford Motor Company worker named Charles Le Brown declared himself a member of the "Straphangers Union" and asserted that although the "D.S.R is giving splendid surface transportation . . . its service is limited during peak hours so it can not provide more service . . . despite the growth of employment and the growth of population." He then discussed how lacking Detroit's transit system was compared to other cities.

After concluding that "the demand for rapid transit is acute in Detroit," he was "applauded vigorously."[73]

However, opposition to the subway plan also materialized over the crucial months before the vote was taken, and most of the objections were oriented toward the cost structuring. One citizen argued for a private franchise to develop the subway "so that the property owner of the City of Detroit does not have to gamble away his property on a rapid transit proposition."[74] Another asserted:

> The rich should bear the heavy burden of taxation. . . . If the subway increases the value of John Smith's home from $4000 to $6000 and one-half the increase is taken as a special tax, he will pay $1,002.40 taxes, while William Jones with a home worth $100,000, out of the special tax district, will pay 44 cents per thousand, or $440. I believe that such a division of the subway tax is unjust.[75]

Other factions protested the discrepancy between those benefiting from the subway, such as industrialists, downtown merchants, and residential subdividers, and those who would pay the most for the proposal, namely, homeowners. "If downtown merchants and outside-the-city-limits manufacturers desire special rapid transit advantages," stated one letter to the editor, "it is high time for them to club together, become philanthropic, and make a present to the city of a model unit of a rapid transit system."[76] Another echoed his sentiment, remarking that industrialists, business proprietors, realtors, and property owners who desired a subway could "form a company, put up the money, build and operate it," and the role of the city should be limited to granting a "right-of-way and not one cent toward the cost of construction" as the tax roll was "already too high."[77] One citizen spoke out against the long-range consequences of such an unfair cost structuring: taxes would rise and cause residents to relocate to the suburbs. Those supporting the subways, he commented conspiratorially, were subdividers and speculators "who will at once advertise to go out and live outside of the city limits and avoid the big town, [and thus] shoot the pay envelopes outside of the city at the expense of the city taxpayers."[78]

Ultimately, opponents to the subway organized against the lack of responsibility taken by Henry Ford for a transit system that would disproportionately benefit him. "We would spend $91,000,000 and probably twice that amount," wrote one citizen, "for only the beginning of a subway system that will carry us nowhere but to Ford's, and during the long period of construction and even after it is completed, what are we going to do about our traffic problem?"[79] An attorney for a coalition of neighborhood improvement associations that united against the subway was even more to the point in commenting that the subway "will be a great benefit" to Ford Motor Company. Then he asked "how much money they would be willing to give the city to relieve the burden of construction costs, how much relief they would give the taxpayers for the undoubted and unquestioned benefit that they would receive."[80] It is not obvious from this statement if the attorney knew that Ford would indeed be contributing in the form of taxes and assessments to at least a portion of the subway cost. Even so, it was a common perception that Ford and other manufacturers were not contributing as much as they might. In the end, the subway plan was defeated by a wide margin, with the cost structuring cited as the number one reason for its failure.[81]

The defeat of this bill, however, should not be interpreted to mean the citizens of Detroit were in any way philosophically opposed to transit—after all, in the late 1930s, they supported a New Deal proposal for a subway that would be subsidized with federal money, and the only reason this did not go through was that the state of Michigan, which administered the grant, dropped the ball.[82] Thus, to assume Detroiters preferred driving automobiles to riding public transportation is simplistic. What the citizens demanded instead—and rightly so—was a fair and just cost structuring to support such an expensive public amenity.[83]

Henry Ford and Rail Transit

Ultimately, not only was the subway plan lost in 1929 but all types of rail transit in Detroit declined in the following years. Although a multitude of factors contributed to the demise of rail, it is worthwhile to examine the role Henry Ford alone may have had in its fall. To begin with, from the late 1910s and throughout the 1920s, Ford periodically expressed ambivalence about the future of urban mass transit, and this makes a contrast to his overall endorsement, and at times subsidization, of rail transit projects ranging from the Northwest Belt Line, municipal ownership, and the subway proposal. For instance, in 1919, Ford announced a plan to develop gasoline-powered streetcars in the belief they would be cheaper to run than electric streetcars. This statement, and its implication that electric streetcars would soon be outmoded, was considered an attack on Couzens's first attempt at municipal ownership taking place in the same year. In another situation, when Mayo was about to take over the DSR operations, Ford criticized the price of the streetcar fare, at the time only six cents, one of the lowest in the country.

On more than one occasion, Ford predicted the end of streetcars altogether. In 1919, even while putting together his own modification for a gasoline-powered streetcar, Ford suggested, "I think all street car tracks will be out of American cities within ten years. All the trolley companies want to unload. They know better than anyone else that their day is done."[84] A 1922 company publication stated, "Passenger auto buses are running on roads paralleling electric lines and are competing successfully."[85] In 1923, a number of years before the 1929 subway proposal that he so favored, Ford claimed subways would someday be used for parking automobiles.[86]

Given Henry Ford's ambivalence, even contradictions, on the topic of rail transit, it should not be too surprising that he became involved with the development of one of its competitors, the bus, and it was only a matter of time before he obtained a contract to supply the DSR with buses. Detroit, like other major US cities, became drawn to the idea of replacing rail with buses, which were attractive for a number of reasons: they required less capital investment since they did not need any special infrastructure; they could be operated by one person rather than the two people common on streetcars, so their cost of labor was lower; and because their motorization made them compatible with the automobile, they were easy to incorporate into the growing highway system. Finally, their flexibility in routing made them adaptable to crisscrossing the metropolis in a grid, which was increasingly important in a decentralized built environment that could no longer be adequately served by the hub-and-spoke pattern typical of rail transit. In 1932, the DSR bought out the Detroit Motorbus Company, which enabled it for the first time to operate extensive bus service in the central business district. At the time, the DSR still operated more miles of streetcar lines (520) than miles of bus lines (430). However, this ratio would start to shift, and as extensions of streetcar lines ended in the 1930s, the replacement of rail with buses began to pick up. Starting in 1934, Ford Motor Company became one of the main suppliers to the DSR.

Of course, it was the automobile that posed the largest threat to transit in Detroit, and it is interesting to note that Henry Ford himself admitted as much. After all, he had a greater impact on the viability of transit than other automobile manufacturers since it was he who designed and marketed a car for the masses. In 1923 Ford provided a provocative interview to William Stidger on the topic of the competition between the automobile and transit in the form of both rail and bus. Ford first scoffed at the idea of a subway, getting Stidger to admit that whether streetcars or a subway were available, he would still find it "handier and quicker" to take his automobile down-town. At the possibility of manufacturing buses, which he later decided to do, Ford at the time expressed little interest, claiming, "We shall keep on manufacturing the car that the people want and will need and in the end we will haul the people with the little unit car." By the end of the interview Stidger, convinced by Ford, stated that in the future "we will all get cars," and someday streetcars will be used as infrequently as by the "average man" as the current "business man who is in a hurry," adding, "The poorest of us will have them to drive to work every day just as the employes [sic] of the Ford motor works are doing already to a large extent."[87]

Throughout the 1920s and 1930s, Henry Ford's attitude toward transit, particularly rail transit, was never easy to summarize or predict. Certainly when it served his interest, he was all for it. As the single largest manufac-turer in Detroit, his impact in promoting transit cannot be underestimated; he undoubtedly contributed to the rich mix of transit options available in the Detroit metropolis during this period. Yet Ford's role in undermining rail transit cannot be discounted either, as his choices led to the diminish-ment of the types and amount of transit offered. His marketing of a car for mass consumption was perhaps the largest single factor in the decline of Detroit's rail transit, but it was not the only one. Ford, in deciding to posi-tion a factory that was record-breaking in size on the periphery of the city, practically doomed any attempts on the part of the DSR to create a via-ble transit system. Logistically, it was difficult to route transit to flow into the factory since it was a reverse commute from the city center; second, it placed a crushing demand on the system at three daily rush hours; and last, it diverted a good part of the industrial tax base away from the city that was supplying the transit system and paying for it. Ultimately, rail transit failed in Detroit for more or less the same complex set of reasons as in any comparable city, reasons that went well beyond any actions taken by Henry Ford. Still, because of the unique relationship between Ford and the Detroit metropolis, his role must be addressed.

Conclusion

Overall the metropolitanization of Detroit was undertaken without much foresight, spurred as it was by industrialists spreading their factories around the city's periphery and by residents who pioneered the "crabgrass frontier" in their automobiles. Ultimately, Detroit could do little to bridle the booming growth of its metropolitan area without the cooperation of the Big Three. The automakers, however, had their own agenda, as Dearborn and suburbs like it offered ever cheaper land and labor the farther away from the city they were situated. At the same time, the eventual promotion by local and federal officials of automobile use (through road building) and homeownership (through mortgage standardization) meant the automakers could count on wage earners coming to them to live and work. Finally, sponsoring suburbanization, both industrial and residential, was in the interest of the automakers as it increased dependency upon their own product. To Henry Ford at least, suburbia appeared to offer a better life for his workers, something in which he as a welfare capitalist took a genuine interest.

The result of all this was the metropolitanization of Detroit during the interwar years, a process by which suburbs became prosperous while the city was drained of resources and became burdened with new problems. Unplanned urban development was now a feature throughout the landscape of metropolitan Detroit, much of it spurred by automobile-dependent growth.

The rise of Dearborn and suburbs like it ravaged Detroit, weakening the commercial center, increasing slums, enforcing boundaries of race and class, shrinking the number of jobs, and decimating the tax base.[88] Although this situation culminated in the Great Depression when the city found it no longer had the ability to support its citizens, the full ramifications were not to be detectable until after World War II when the urban population began an actual decrease.

4

Rising Standards in the Suburbs

A TRADEMARK OF HENRY Ford's welfare capitalism was his desire to raise the standard of living of workers to a level that was indistinguishable from that of the middle class. Although other welfare capitalists sought to improve the conditions of wage earners, none dared to empower them to the point attempted by Ford, whose vision of welfare capitalism directly implied that workers should live in suburbs. "His plan," recalled personnel manager John Lee, "is for every family working for him [to have] a comfortable home; a bath tub in it, and a yard with a little garden, and ultimately, he wanted to see every employee of his owning an automobile."[1] A key to developing this new lifestyle for workers was to present them with a combination of increased time and money. Toward this end Ford designed a high minimum wage with the intention that a family could be supported by a sole, male breadwinner. He also provided workers with more leisure time by shortening the workday and standardizing time off on the weekend. In describing his goals to raise the standard of living, Ford stated that workers should be able to provide their families with some of the "luxuries of life" such as education or a good neighborhood as well as the "necessities" such as decent housing.[2]

In discussing his motives, Ford revealed a dramatic change in his thinking on these matters. When he first established the five-dollar day in 1914, the high wage was available only to those workers who met strict criteria for eligibility. They had to prove themselves worthy through inspection of their character and conduct, and such investigations extended even to their homes. Only those who were thrifty, kept orderly houses, refrained from drinking and gambling, and supported dependents in a responsible way met the requirements. Additionally, even after they were granted the high wage, workers were supposed to continue meeting standards for conduct and character, both on and off the job. In Ford's own words: "the man and his home [should meet] certain standards of cleanliness and citizenship. . . . The idea was that there should be a very definite incentive to better living and that the very best incentive was a money premium on proper living."[3] According to company literature, workers must "learn to spend more money for living and efficiently enjoy freedom and citizenship."[4] One newspaper article remarked, "[Ford] insists that the men who receive the wages must live after a decent American fashion."[5] In other words, it was up to the workers to prove themselves worthy of these benefits.

However, starting with 1920, when the six-dollar day was established, Henry Ford now expressed a belief that all workers were equally worthy and that it was not useful to divide them into categories of deserving and undeserving. Simply put, wage earners across the board were entitled to a high standard of living by virtue of their hard work and their status as Americans. On this point, a company newsletter declared:

> [This standard of living] the American workman takes as a right, won by honest and strenuous labor, and gladly given by those with and for whom he works. . . . That is to say, their labor not only meets their needs, but much more. Their savings are surprisingly large. Many of them come to work in their own motor cars and they converse with everyone as their equals. In the United States, the workman . . . has reached the highest rank, that of being a CITIZEN. . . . Here, in America, the workers do not only exist, they LIVE.[6]

In this regard, Ford's vision for workers fit into an exceptionalist model: he busied himself with turning wage earners not only into good citizens but, more specifically, into good Americans. Unlike the wage earners of other industrial societies, American workers deserved affordable consumer goods and plentiful leisure time, and ultimately, they would become members of a society that was not as divided by class as those of the Old World. This shift toward higher standards of living was never more evident than in Dearborn and similar suburbs for the masses.

Welfare Capitalism

Henry Ford was an innovator of welfare capitalism, an early twentieth-century management practice that sought to improve the standard of living of workers through a professionalized department of personnel, which took a proactive, even interventionist, approach to dealing with employees.[7]

Practitioners of welfare capitalism varied in their techniques: they standardized wages and hours, or they subsidized essentials not covered by workers' paychecks such as health care, education, recreation, and housing. In doing so, industrialists attempted to redefine their relationships with employees, transforming an impersonal business transaction—in which workers traded labor for pay—into a relationship like that of an extended family, with concern articulated for the well-being of all members. Manufacturers had good reason to implement such programs. Mass production had begun to reach its engineering limits, and since machines could not be further redesigned, workers had to change. Welfare capitalism dovetailed with Taylorization to sharpen wage earners into more efficient manufacturing tools by creating stronger, more motivated employees who worked faster and stayed with the company longer. Freeing the income of wage earners from necessities translated into increased spending power, which meant that workers were turned into consumers, often of the company's own products. Satisfied workers were less likely to unionize, and improving conditions both on and off the job was a way to pacify and satisfy the labor force. Finally, by providing programs on a voluntary, privatized basis, industrialists could avoid the formation of a welfare state and increased powers of the government to regulate and tax their companies.

In 1914, Henry Ford made his first foray into welfare capitalism by establishing the five-dollar-day wage, which was made available only to workers who demonstrated they were industrious at work as well as thrifty, sober, and family-oriented when at home. To keep track of this, welfare workers employed by the company's sociological department checked up on the wage earners both on and off the job. However, as of 1920, this policy was abruptly overhauled, and a universal wage of six dollars a day took its place—no longer would conduct and character be considered as an eligibility requirement to be assured a high minimum wage. In explaining the sudden rejection of his first program, Ford declared, "Paternalism has no place in industry," and thus the five-dollar day was dismissed as a passing social experiment.[8]

Ford reorganized the sociological department so that workers would come to it when they needed help, not the other way around, and investigators would not be sent uninvited to the homes of employees. Instead, promotional literature and marketing incentives would be used to guide the choices of workers. Ford created a system of bonuses based on length of service and productivity and an investment plan with a guaranteed return of at least 6 percent. Four years later, he shortened the workweek from six days to five. Thanks to these new policies—which provided both increased income and more leisure—workers enjoyed a quality of life possibly unprecedented in the history of industrial wage earners. Their empowerment as consumers was further heightened through mass production techniques that made goods such as automobiles more affordable than ever.

Under this laissez-faire approach that dominated the company throughout the 1920s, Ford Motor Company wage earners were more assured than ever of enjoying a high standard of living. For workers to attain this status, Henry Ford needed to do more than relocate his factory, pay high wages, and provide more leisure time—he also had to instill a desire for commercial consumption at levels usually associated with the middle class. As Ford put it, "We want our people to desire more and better things, and demand a higher standard of living."[9] In this regard, he attempted nothing less than the bourgeoisification of native white workers, the assimilation of immigrant workers, and the industrialization of Great Migration black workers. Ford accomplished this through the relentless propaganda of company publications as well as through specific marketing programs to aid employees interested in buying houses and cars. Ford's goal to acculturate workers was likely an extension of the Americanization programs undertaken by him and other welfare capitalists of the period. Meanwhile, his innovations in management complemented the efforts of labor advocates who fought throughout the early twentieth century for higher pay, shorter hours, better housing, and the ability of single, male breadwinners to support entire households. Such activism probably made wage earners more receptive to Ford's program of acculturation. Fordism, in other words, was a cultural and social project as well as an economic one. Only when this was undertaken could the connection between mass production and mass consumption be linked as well to mass suburbanization.

Altogether, the changes Henry Ford made in his management practices were fairly radical, and yet his programs of the 1920s are best understood as a new kind of welfare capitalism rather than a dismantling of it. After all, Ford was still motivated by the same issues that prompted welfare capitalists everywhere to provide workers with subsidies and benefits: he wanted to reduce turnover, promote longevity, and increase loyalty among wage earners as well as discourage governmental interference that would make workplace improvements mandatory rather than voluntary. Ford also wished to benefit from the public goodwill created by welfare capitalism, which served to offset his record on labor issues. Additionally, Ford's attempt to systemize and streamline personnel practices in his company was in keeping with the longtime goals of welfare capitalism, whose latest focus was on so-called scientific management. Finally, Ford wished to improve the life circumstances of his workers by assuring them a standard of living fitting for Americans. This preoccupation with quality-of-life issues was another distinguishing feature of welfare capitalism, which emphasized the responsibility of employers in taking care of the overall well-being of their employees.

Ford's Ideas of Welfare

Although Ford was undeniably a pioneer in the area of welfare capitalism, his policies were not atypical for the period. After all, many other industrialists were embarking on their own experiments in new management techniques. Throughout the 1910s, the practice of welfare capitalism spread, especially at large companies, and by 1914, over fifteen hundred firms practiced some form of it.[10] These policies focused on standardizing wages and hours, regulating job advancement, and increasing employee representation, as well as providing services such as health care, education, and recreation or goods such as housing. Welfare capitalism was most likely to be found at companies that had reason to be concerned about attracting and retaining workers, like any companies that relied on skilled laborers or those located in geographically isolated areas such as mill, mining, or timber towns. It was also typical in industries employing large numbers of women, where their presence attracted governmental scrutiny and the legislation of protective measures. Welfare capitalism was a common resort when there was a need to counter image problems created by labor unrest, anti-trust investigations, the exposés of muckrakers, or defects in consumer goods. Finally, welfare capitalism became popular as industrialists professed a growing concern with making workers into better citizens, improving both their morale and their morals at the same time.

What set Henry Ford apart from the others was the scope and timing of his innovations—he made changes on a bigger scale than his peers and he implemented them before others did. For instance, when the five-dollar day was introduced in 1914, his new wage was about double the nationwide average for industrial workers. This made headlines across the country, stirring responses that ranged from outrage to skepticism to amazement. The high minimum wage was only one of many reforms Ford implemented around this time. He reduced the workday from nine hours to eight with three shifts a day, and he standardized the workweek to six days and many years later shortened it further to five days. He mandated that hiring and firing take place in the personnel office, a reform in the arbitrary powers that foremen once had over workers, and he assured that shop conditions be improved through the organization of a department of safety and health. Ford developed commissaries to make consumer items available to workers at or below market rate, and he established a savings-and-loan association. He created two educational programs: the Ford Trade School, which provided vocational training to boys, and the Ford English School, which taught language and citizenship to immigrant employees. Finally, alcohol and tobacco were banned from the factory floor.

Ford's philosophy changed over time because he perceived a connection between a high standard of living and the demands of citizenship in a democracy. Giving workers a sense of independence by empowering them with time and money was important to cultivating free-thinking citizens. Although his laborers might function in a slavish manner on the job, mindlessly repeating a single task, Ford preferred that outside the factory they be anything but robot-like. He saw equal danger in workers degraded by a capitalist system that paid low wages and in workers transfixed by a communist ideology, and he believed that only high wages could create worker-citizens not beholden to anyone, able to exercise their rights freely. After all, a man who could not support himself or his family was susceptible to being manipulated by political elements. In fact, Ford recognized that democracy depends as much on economic as on political equality and that there could be no true freedom without living wages. He observed, "Civilization in terms of material well-being indicates a degree of intellectual well-being, for without economic independence there can certainly be no intellectual independence. If a man spends twelve hours a day hunting his daily bread, he is not going to have much time [left over] for clear thinking."[11] Time spent thinking was a chance for a man to "consider his children and their education; morals and their sanction; literature, science, politics. . . . it is when all the people think, normally and wholesomely, that the world will become what it might be."[12]

Henry Ford also believed the physical and mental strength a man gained from working made him a better citizen. He declared, "Work is sanitative, it is educative, it is preservative. It produces results in the man himself as well as in the material that passes under his hand."[13] Ford used the concept of civic duty to offset the potential emasculation of the artisan by automation, prioritizing the contribution of the workers as citizens over pleasure taken in exercising skill. "Even when the extreme specialization of the work obliges the man to make the same motion over and over again," stated a company publication, "the monotony of the action has not smothered the consciousness or the importance of the task. . . . He is building something that is a benefit to humanity and should not his work be a pleasure."[14] Manliness was as much a qualification for working for Ford as a product from it, and one commentator remarked, "The conviction that character and manhood are requisites for employment has spread throughout the entire shop; in fact throughout the whole city of Detroit."[15] Thus, according to Ford, the type of manhood necessary for citizenship depended on both hard work and high wages, and it could be achieved as much by an unskilled factory hand as by an artisan.[16]

Ford believed the social order of the factory floor could embody the lessons of democracy and citizenship, prompting him to advocate for the idea of the "American shop," which would "reflect the Republic in its highest ideals."[17] Of course, the American shop also meant one that was open, without the presence of unions, and it was common for industrialists of the period to promote it. According to Ford, this system would protect the idea of equality, since all workers would be treated alike and given the same opportunity for advancement: "It is the transcription of the Declaration and the Constitution into industrial terms. It is the act of making our political liberty complete by adding thereto economic liberty also."[18] To Ford, workers were the true Americans, and he believed there was an inherent dignity in laboring that was being eroded by larger societal changes. He protested against this, adding, "What we want in this country is that the workingman shall have the best of it all around."[19] In making these points, Ford put a twist on Jeffersonian philosophy: by placing industry on the same level as agriculture as the highest occupation for a citizen in a democracy, he held up a model of republicanism in which factory wage earners as well as yeoman farmers were the foundation of a community. The desire to develop workers into good citizens likely originated in Ford's programs during the 1910s to assimilate immigrant workers. Calling his plant a "melting pot," Ford enrolled workers in citizenship and English language classes. An article in the company newsletter, *Ford News,* offered a nation-building rationale for Americanizing immigrant workers, announcing, "If America still continues to be the refuge and dumping ground of all the world, we must, that is, industry and government, take some steps toward making real citizens of our aliens."[20]

Welfare Capitalism and Suburbs

Ultimately, Ford wanted his workers—native-born and immigrant alike—to become good Americans through participation in a high standard of living, and persuading wage earners to become homeowners was a first step toward this. Ford's belief that workers should feel entitled to own their homes was fairly radical for the time, given that in this pre–Federal Housing Administration period, the American homeownership rate was below 50 percent. In any case, Ford embarked on a unique marketing campaign using company publications that preached the virtues of homeownership. A *Ford*

News article asserted, "America is getting back into the home these days, for in it lies every requisite for infinite happiness." Americans, so it claimed, have an "inherent love . . . for their homes" that makes communities "keen rivals for first position in home ownership." Owning a home was "one of the achievements of life, for which we willingly struggle for years through trials and difficulties that might be compared with those of the pioneer who pressed into the wilderness."[21]

Ford himself, as a former farmer, may have seen homeownership as a way of connecting people to the land, in both a literal and a patriotic sense. Ford called the United States "a nation of pioneer blood" and remarked, "Every man needs elbow room."[22] In reaction to the tendency of immigrants to locate in cities, he complained, "It is not the number of the newcomers that constitutes the problem, but their unwillingness to begin as pioneers, with the land," suggesting that "settled on the land, the immigrant would more readily imbibe American ideas."[23] One benefit of suburbs was connection to the land in the form of vegetable gardens and outdoor recreation. Ford declared, "If anyone would figure up the production of the small truck gardens, which so many factory workers may now have because of the automobile, the total would undoubtedly be astounding."[24] Ford indeed pushed his home owning workers to maintain a relationship to the soil by growing their own vegetables. A company newsletter suggested, "We are better workmen and better men for spending a part of our time in our gardens."[25]

One company publication acknowledged that turning immigrant wage earners into homeowners would not come about immediately yet called for them to consider doing so. Although "some of those of foreign birth . . . were living and sleeping in over-crowded rooms and tenements," stated the guide, they were expected "to improve their living conditions, make their homes clean and comfortable, provide wholesome surroundings, good air and light, and to keep their households for themselves and immediate families."[26] Workers, in short, should become homeowners. "The Ford Co. urges its workmen to build and settle down," stated *Automotive Industries*, adding, "The Ford Motor Co. has solved the housing problem as far as Highland Park is concerned by the inauguration of a realty department and a building and loan association, where Ford employees are encouraged to borrow and build on the easy payment plan. . . . At Dearborn, Henry Ford is duplicating his Highland Park housing program."[27] The connection between home-ownership, citizenship, and nationalism may have been of special concern because of the number of Ford Motor Company workers in Dearborn, of which a little over a fifth (22 percent) were boarders and about one-half (51 percent) were foreign born. Significantly, foreign-borns made up close to

Ford Motor Company Workers in Dearborn
Tables 5 through 8

TABLE 5

WORKERS OF ALL LEVELS - *Managerial, Skilled, Semi-Skilled, Unskilled*

Household Heads	67%
Secondary Breadwinners	11%
Boarders	22%
Married	73%
Household Size	5.6 people
Native	49%
Foreign-Born	51%

TABLE 6

WORKERS - *Skilled*

Household Heads	75%
Secondary Breadwinners	9%
Boarders	16%
Married	72%
Household Size	4.9 people
Native	41%
Foreign-Born	59%

TABLE 7

WORKERS - *Semi-Skilled*

Household Heads	69%
Secondary Breadwinners	3%
Boarders	28%
Married	75%
Household Size	5.7 people
Native	53%
Foreign-Born	47%

TABLE 8

WORKERS - *Unskilled*

Household Heads	58%
Secondary Breadwinners	22%
Boarders	19%
Married	72%
Household Size	5.9 people
Native	39%
Foreign-Born	61%

Source: US Bureau of the Census, *1930 Manuscript Census.*

half of all "owner families," even though they were only about one-quarter of Dearborn's population.[28]

Another Americanism Henry Ford wished to instill was automobile ownership, a value important enough to him that in the early 1920s he initiated a marketing program encouraging employees to buy a Ford Motor Company car. Again, it was a somewhat revolutionary idea to expect the average working-class person to own a car. In a company newsletter, an article claimed the automobile "gives each that independence necessary to complete enjoyment," thus furthering the archetypal American characteristic of individualism.[29] Ford's advertisements for his automobile also emphasized its role in nation building, first in terms of producing healthy citizens by getting them outdoors. "No other nation is more definitely awake to the benefits of life in the open air than America today," commented one advertisement. "The Ford car, which provides reliable motoring at a cost millions can afford, is one of the big and vital factors in this turning to the out-of-doors."[30] The automobile would unite the country by breaking "barriers of time and distance," and another advertisement observed, "Good roads followed close behind the automobile and the isolation of country districts disappeared."[31] According to Ford, the automobile promoted a "wider circulation of right ideas [which] breaks down prejudices and helps secure universal understanding. . . . Such an interchange of social contacts, such a broadening of all people's geographical horizons will ultimately bring about a redistribution [of people]. The automobile has done for this country what the airplane and radio may do for the world."[32] Technology that bridged time and space, Ford believed, would "soon bring the whole world to a complete understanding" and result in a "United States of the World."[33] Finally, Ford used automobile ownership as an incentive for employees to work harder, and in doing so, he conveyed a work ethic that was particularly American.[34]

Throughout the 1910s and 1920s, as Ford refined his practice of welfare capitalism, his vested interest in doing so became more apparent. After all, by providing increased income and leisure, he could transform workers not only into good Americans but also into consumers of his own product, the automobile. With more time and money, Ford noted, "workmen go out of doors, go on picnics, have time to see their children and play with them. They have time to see more, do more—and, incidentally, they buy more. . . . This stimulates business and increases prosperity, and in the general economic circle the money passes through industry again and back into the workman's pocket."[35] In his opinion, "the country is ready for the five-day work week. . . . It is bound to come through all industry. . . . The industry of this country could not long exist if factories generally went back to the ten-hour day because people would not have the leisure, the desire, or the means to consume the goods produced."[36] He was also quite conscious of his own role in this, stating that the employer has to use "ingenuity" in creating customers from workers.[37] He commented in a *Dearborn Independent* editorial that "all are members of the consuming class," and on another occasion that "the people who consume the bulk of goods are the people who make them."[38]

Standard of Living for Workers

The new standard of living for Ford workers attracted much attention during the 1920s, and Dearborn was the showcase for this lifestyle. For instance, the headline in the *Detroit News Tribune*, "Living Standards of Ford Men Improving with Profit Sharing," expressed a commonly enthusiastic reaction.[39] According to company literature about the five-dollar day, worker homeownership had increased by 99 percent in the first year and a half, and bank deposits increased by 205 percent.[40] Although the evidence certainly points to some improvements for the condition of wage earners, a question is raised as to how great and lasting this change was and whether all workers benefited equally. A common critique was that, although Ford workers now enjoyed higher rates of homeownership and car ownership— as well as an increased participation in consumerism more generally— they were also living rather marginally. These workers increasingly relied on credit to get by and were susceptible to falling into debt or even losing their assets. Thus, the combination of uncertain employment and the gap between wages and prices meant that, even when autoworkers lived well, they remained financially insecure. The account by the following worker was typical. "Although I had worked steadily and my income was above average for the kind of work I did, life was still a real struggle," recalled autoworker Wyndham Mortimer. "Mortgage payments, taxes, and insurance put a strain on my income. . . . We had gotten rid of the landlord, but now were in the clutches of the mortgage holder."[41]

Other commentators complained of financial pressures created by the cyclical nature of the automobile industry. During the 1920s alone, there were two periods of severe layoffs: one in 1920–1921, when a postwar recession hit, and another in 1926–1927, when Ford Motor Company shut down the River Rouge plant to retool for conversion from the Model T to the Model A. "[The industry] has grown rapidly, but it has also grown spasmodically," observed Myron Watkins as early as 1920. "The history of the trade is a history of great 'rushes' and chronic 'lulls.'"[42] In 1933, Thomas Wright wrote for *Christian Century*, "Work in the Ford factory is essentially 'seasonal' work. . . . Even during the times when Ford was paying wages of $7 per day, most men were losing from four to six months a year from work, and their average earnings did not run above one thousand dollars a year. For most workers it averaged around eight hundred."[43] Fear of layoffs was pervasive, according to Cyril Arthur Player, writing for the *New Republic* in 1927. "The Ford tempo dominates the community: each man for himself, Adam's curse in the form of routine mechanical labor, and the black fear of unemployment which haunts, day and night, the peace of industrial communities. . . . To be out of work is inefficient, to be inefficient is to thwart life; a machine is fool-proof, and when it is no longer efficient it is, or should be, discarded. . . . A stern gospel . . . but one that rules the lives of several hundreds of thousands of families."[44]

Meanwhile, during upswings, rising wages struggled to keep up with the spiraling cost of living. "There's a curious compensation in these things," stated Webb Waldron in *Century*. "High wages draw swarms of people; a congestion of people brings profiteering in food and property values and rents." Waldron then quoted a die maker at Ford Motor Company who complained, "It's harder to live on seventy dollars a week now than on thirty-five before the war."[45] Local historian Pound observed, "Men work shorter hours and get more money per hour; but at the end of the year they are little ahead. . . . Increasing population brought increased living costs; family and social life are more complicated, more demanding. Time has erased the great dream from many minds, and doused the vision of success that lured the working force in the infancy of the industry."[46] High prices, however, were difficult to eliminate. This was the case even in the automobile industry, whose chiefs strained to push down prices so their products would be affordable to the workers who made them.[47] Altogether, it was difficult for workers to get ahead. "Automobiles and washing-machines and sealskin coats [may be] antidotes for Bolshevism," Waldron quipped. "But is labor any better off in Detroit with the soaring wages?"[48]

African American wage earners, of course, had even higher obstacles to overcome. One such Ford Motor Company worker lived in the Eight-Mile District, a community straddling the northern boundary of Detroit. Superficially, he was successful, earning thirty-five dollars a week, which matched the average for the company's workers, including white ones. His wife supplemented the household income by earning from ten to twelve dollars a week as a laundress. Their children ranged in age from six to fourteen. The worker had placed one hundred dollars down on a fourteen-hundred-dollar house and was paying the rest off at thirteen dollars a month. His house, though, was described by social workers as a "six-room shanty"—the outside was covered with tar paper, the inside walls were decorated with scrap paper, the rooms were partitioned with quilts, the sole heating source was a cooking stove, and lighting came from kerosene lamps. All the same, the aspiration of this family for respectability was perhaps evident in their furnishings, which included three iron beds, a kitchen table and chairs, a dining room suite, and last but not least, a piano.[49]

Both the high standard of living and the marginality of Ford Motor Company workers were confirmed by two independent surveys: one conducted by Yale industrial psychology student Chen-Nan Li and the other by the Bureau of Labor Statistics (BLS).[50] According to Li, "The Ford employees live under all sorts of conditions, from indecency to exquisite taste and refinement," although he qualified this by adding, "The majority of them maintain a fairly high standard of living." Li then differentiated between married Ford workers and those who were single. The married Ford man, he stated, was between thirty-five and forty years of age with a wife who was a little younger and together they had two or three children. Li commented, "He owns his house, or is paying for it on an installment basis. If he does not own a house, he probably rents a whole flat. He has not only enough rooms for his household, but often one or two extra rooms to let." Li described the furnishings of the home:

> He has for furniture, carpets, davenports, comfortable chairs. He has a few pictures on the walls and a few books on his shelf. He probably has a piano or a Victrola. He has a telephone and sometimes even a radio. Of course his house is supplied with modern conveniences, such as water, gas, and electricity. He owns a car, most probably a Ford. . . . He and his family have three square meals every day. . . . They rarely have delicacies; but their food is substantial and fairly well-balanced. . . . When he puts on his street clothes, he is hardly distinguishable from an average American business man.[51]

As for the unmarried worker, Li stated that he was most likely between twenty-three and twenty-eight years of age. "He is probably rooming in a private boarding house, sharing a double room with some other workman. . . . The room costs each of them from $3 to $4 a week. He eats in a restaurant, spending from $1 to $1.30 a day on his board. He has some savings in a bank. He contemplates getting into some business or getting married or both."[52]

Meanwhile, a survey commissioned by Ford Motor Company and conducted by the Bureau of Labor Statistics (BLS) had slightly different measurements and results. This study focused on one hundred Detroit families headed by Ford Motor Company workers, which eliminated any single men. At variance with Li's observations, the labor statisticians found that most families (68 percent) rented their housing rather than owning. Typically the families occupied a separate house (61 percent) or an entire flat (32 percent), and only 7 percent lived in an apartment. On average, there were 4.5 people in each household, and the homes contained two or three bedrooms, a bathroom, a living room, and a kitchen that served the multiple functions of food preparation, dining room, and meeting area for the family. Generally the houses had one or more room per person; all the rooms had outdoor exposure so they were well-lit; and the houses were located on improved streets (meaning they were paved and possibly had sidewalks and streetlamps). Additionally, the majority of houses featured running water, hot water, a kitchen sink, sewer connection, stoves for heating, and an inside toilet (although 14 percent had privies).[53]

The major expenses of the families were categorized as food (32.3 percent) and housing (22.6 percent), followed by clothing (12.2 percent) and utilities (6 percent), with "other expenses" making up the remaining 26.9 percent. Almost half (47 percent) the families owned automobiles, and in the category of "other expenses," cars were the largest-costing item. In fact, one family's installment payments on a new car accounted for 27 percent of their entire yearly budget. As for other household goods and appliances, electric irons were owned by 98 percent of the families, sewing machines by 80 percent, washing machines by 51 percent, phonographs by 45 percent, radios by 36 percent, vacuum cleaners by 21 percent, pianos by 13 percent, and telephones by 5 percent. Among new items purchased in the last year by more than half the families were sheets, brooms, towels, tablecloths, dishes, pots and pans, and curtains, while a quarter or more of families bought linoleum, blankets, silverware, stoves, and lamps. Also within the last year, about a fifth of the families bought mattresses, and roughly a tenth bought refrigerators. Almost all families (89 percent) bought toys as part of their discretionary items.[54]

Significantly, one point upon which both studies agreed was that most households could not be supported only on the earnings of a sole, male breadwinner, and this finding could be extrapolated equally to Detroit or Dearborn or any nearby suburb. This was an important finding, since an explicit goal of Henry Ford's welfare capitalism was to encourage the formation of nuclear families headed by such men. In such a family, women were not to work remuneratively, either within or outside the home. Ideally, households were not to take in boarders, as this meant that women were working for money. Nor were households to become home to extended family members, employed or not, as this disrupted the nuclear model.

The failure of Ford's expectation is not so surprising, considering the times: women of different classes were increasingly working outside the home; taking in boarders was a common way for working-class families to subsidize their housing costs, and finally, there was no lack of boarders or extended family members as Detroit's economy continued to attract wage earners who traveled in search of work and needed a place to live. Here, Ford Motor Company workers were no exception since they also survived by taking in boarders or having more than one family member earn money. Running a boarding business was fairly common, and Li noted that most married Ford Motor Company workers lived in a home with "one or two extra rooms to let."[55] The BLS study, which screened out any families taking in boarders, noted a variety of ways in which families nonetheless supplemented their income: the husbands took on odd jobs in their time off, doing carpentry, painting, automobile repair, cobbling, or working in stores; wives raised money by sewing and washing; and together, couples cultivated truck gardens and raised chickens.[56]

Alternatively, families relied on credit, more widely available than ever before due to the rise of installment purchasing, which now extended to everyday goods as well as to cars and houses. According to the BLS study, 59 percent of the families bought some household goods on the installment plan. One family, for instance, was still making payments on a living-room suite, a dining-room suite, and a phonograph purchased five years earlier. Overall, close to half (44 percent) of the families lived beyond their means, with about one-fifth (19 percent) breaking even, and only a little over one-third (37 percent) setting aside savings. As a result, the average family studied by the BLS was living in a state of deficit. The gap between their incomes ($1,711.87) and their expenditures ($1,719.83) was not too great, however—only $7.96.[57]

Organized Labor Responds

Henry Ford's desire to provide workers with a high standard of living fit for Americans appeared to place him on the same side as labor advocates. After all, these activists had long been fighting for the same thing through the standardization of hours and wages and the passage of protective legislation. They had begun to call for the establishment of a connection between wages and the cost of living. This was a change from the past when wages had been tied to the productivity of workers rather than to their consumption.

In other words, organizers argued for a living wage, one that enabled workers to obtain more than the bare necessities of survival, giving them instead
a chance at prosperity.[58] The standard they fought for on behalf of American
wage earners was often pitted in contrast to that for workers from abroad:
"The American workman won't get down on his knees to thank an employer
for decent surroundings, but he appreciates them none the less," observed
one welfare worker. "He is now developed to the point where he demands
them. His standard, both in shops and home, is so much higher than it used
to be and so much higher than standards are elsewhere, that he accepts
things as a matter of course which once would have amazed us and which
would still amaze the residents of foreign countries."[59] This is reminiscent
of a statement, reprinted by Ford Motor Company, that a high standard of
living is something "the American workman takes as a right, won by honest and strenuous labor, and gladly given by those with and for whom he
works."[60] On this topic, capital and labor seemingly converged during the
1920s.

Organizers of automobile manufacturing, like labor leaders elsewhere,
rallied around this issue. In fact, since they were employed in an industry portrayed as an economic miracle, automobile workers saw a singular
chance to bring about change. "There is a very great danger," predicted one
advocate, "that the American worker will demand some portion of industrial democracy. . . . A great movement toward higher wages, shorter hours,
and beter [sic] conditions is due."[61] Another activist clarified these demands,
stating that a living wage should assure workers an automobile, homeownership, education for children, savings for old age, and freedom from debt,
as well as daily amenities such as adequate food and clothes, labor-saving
household appliances, and recreational activities.[62] The article contrasted
this standard of living with that of "the toiler who swings a pick and shovel
all day long, who must be satisfied with a hunk of rye bread and cheese
and who finds dissipation in a cup of home-made wine and an occasional
photoplay." The themes expressed here were echoes of declarations made
by earlier laborites. "The American laborer," stated one advocate, "should
not be expected to live like the Irish tenant farmer or the Russian serf. . . .
His earning ought to be sufficient to enable him to live as a respectable
American citizen."[63] Altogether, workers in the automobile industry increasingly viewed as un-American the prospect of children denied an education,
mothers taken away from their role as homemakers, households reliant on
debt, and workers with too little leisure to participate fully as citizens.[64] They
hoped to make history, taking up the call from other organizers to replace
the feudal working conditions of the past with a more progressive model.

Frequently, however, these workers found themselves shortchanged by the failed promises of their employers. "The standard of living, the standard of wages, and the standard of working conditions enjoyed by those working in the automobile industry has been much over-rated," claimed one activist. "The automobile workers, tho having a higher standard than a great many industries, are not having the prosperity and luxury which the bosses would make it appear that they have."[65] As early as 1919, one advocate complained, "Wages have not kept pace with the raise in the cost of living."[66] A particular sore point was how the cyclical nature of employment in automobile manufacturing rendered homeownership a risky venture. The savings wage earners invested in their homes could be instantaneously wiped out if they missed a few payments causing their properties to be repossessed, especially given the gray-market mortgages available to them. With little regulation in place to protect consumers from fraud or misfortune, workers time and again found themselves losing the homes in which they had invested hard-earned equity. As one journalist reported, many families who had invested all their savings in small houses lost everything after years of regular payments for the lack of one month's rent, dispossessed of "not only the houses" but also "every stick of furniture. . . . From thrifty, saving, contented citizens they have been reduced to penniless dependens [sic] on city aid, helpless and disheartened and desperate."[67]

Automobile workers also became skeptical of the ulterior motives of welfare capitalism, despite the fact that its goals and theirs seemed identical, namely, bringing about a higher standard of living for Americans. Even so, labor leaders began to question the validity of worker benefits such as homeownership, insurance plans, and stock participation, recognizing their potential for coercion. For example, an editorial entitled "Welfare and Hel-fare" noted that workers who were obliged to stay at jobs in order to make mortgage payments or see their stock dividends returned became dependent upon their employers. The author explained that "the employer wants satisfied sheep, and at a cost as low as possible, [resulting in] slavery for the worker, the more far-reaching the scheme, the more enslaved he is. . . . What little independence the worker has left the employer hopes to crush by welfare work."[68] A somewhat more wry author observed, "The motto they are using is 'Contented Workers.' Sounds like the advertisement of Carnation Milk. . . . The wildest eyed wobbly if given a load of responsibility soon tones down and becomes comparatively conservative."[69] The author is likely referring to Carnation Milk's use of a cow image in its advertisements; workers would soon be as contented as cows. Cynicism about welfare capitalism reached a new low in 1928, when an article entitled "Auto Bosses Join

'Welfare Offensive'" asserted, "Ford, once the lord of welfare, has given up all pretense in recent years. . . . Ford takes less interest in the workers than any of the auto companies."[70]

Conclusion

In the automobile industry, the apparent similarities between the goals of labor leaders and those of welfare capitalists resulted in an uneasy truce. After all, both sides wished to raise the standard of living for American wage earners, leading to the spread of suburbs like Dearborn. This consensus was made possible by Henry Ford's success in transforming welfare capitalism by connecting mass production and mass consumption through high wages. In doing so, Ford stripped away many of the most paternalistic aspects of his previous management practices: high wages were made universally available to all workers, workers enjoyed more leisure as well as more income, and ultimately they were entrusted with greater freedom to make economic choices. Overall, Ford's reforms were able to deliver many improvements for the living conditions of workers, including opening the suburbs to wage earners. As the decade of the 1920s wore on, however, many promises of this new policy—also known as "Fordism"—went unfulfilled or were understood as attempts to coerce workers. The resulting tensions contributed to a growing unrest among wage earners, one that added momentum to the organization of the automobile industry in the following decade.

5

The Lives of Automobile Workers

OVERALL, HENRY FORD WAS remarkably successful in raising the standard of living for workers, who enjoyed relatively high rates of home- and car ownership and gained the reputation of being a "de luxe" labor force.[1] In doing so, Ford undertook the bourgeoisification of native white workers, the assimilation of immigrant workers, and the industrialization of Great Migration black workers. On the surface, this action by Ford appears to position him as a modernizer. As part of the package, though, he promoted a type of conservativism that was a throwback even at the time, encouraging nuclear families headed by a male breadwinner and discouraging drinking and jazz dancing. Ford considered Prohibition a moral issue, comparing the abolition of alcohol to the abolition of slavery. In referring to the prohibition of alcohol as a trend particularly American, he appeared to pit "dry" nativists against immigrants who brought their cultures of drinking with them. As for smoking, Ford believed it, too, had a "detrimental effect upon job performance."[2]

In addition, Ford maintained a system of racial segregation, both residentially and within his factory. African Americans were precluded from living in Dearborn, and Ford's proposals for company-built housing did nothing to change this. Ford also ordered that black workers were placed in menial jobs, which paid less, and these low wages increased the barriers to homeownership already in place. Thus Ford contributed to a cycle of impoverishment and exclusion for African Americans.

As might be expected, his reactionary values were not always embraced by the wage earners employed by him, even those who lived in Dearborn and who became homeowners and car owners because of him. After all, this was the decade of the 1920s, when American culture experienced radical changes in morals and manners. The rise of consumerism, popular culture,

and commercialized entertainment emphasized an increasingly instant grat-
ification of individual desires. Technological inventions affected mass communication, resulting in a better-informed and more sophisticated society; with
film and radio becoming commonplace, everyone could partake in news,
sermons, soap operas, sports, comedy, and music. For many citizens, greater
geographical mobility was made possible by newly affordable automobiles
and other transportation improvements such as airplane travel. Women
obtained the right to vote, and they enjoyed widening freedom in education,
leisure, and careers. As for African Americans, the National Association for
the Advancement of Colored People (NAACP) and the Urban Leagues of
various cities reached milestones on legislative and judicial fronts. Meanwhile, the Harlem Renaissance produced dazzling contributions in art,
music, and literature.[3]

Naturally, these trends extended to Dearborn and the workers who lived
and labored there, even if it meant countering Henry Ford's mandates. For
example, African American workers aspired to the same standard of living as that of their white counterparts: through resourcefulness and political organizing, they were sometimes able to become homeowners in the
neighboring suburb of Inkster. It was a frequent practice among Ford Motor
Company workers of all backgrounds to support a household through
the collective remunerative work of multiple family members rather than
through a sole breadwinner. In other words, many wives living in Dearborn
found a way to make money, often by bringing in boarders or even fibbing
that they were single in order to get a job at the automotive plant. Finally,
workers sought pleasure in drinking and dancing, often in Dearborn's own
vice district known as the South End. Altogether, Dearborn demonstrates
both the failures and the successes of Ford's new welfare capitalism, in terms
of the adoption of these values by workers themselves.

Rise of a Slum

Residential decentralization meant mobility for only a select number of Detroit's citizens. Many new arrivals, especially those who ranked
as unskilled workers, because of both economic and social barriers were
trapped in an inner-city slum. Before 1920, many downtown residents were
foreign-born whites who continued to add to Detroit's population even
after immigration restrictions were put in place. They moved there from
other American cities—Chicago, for instance, was an important source of
the city's Polish population. The 1920s also witnessed the Great Migration

from the South, which brought large numbers of African Americans to Detroit. As more African Americans and foreign-born whites moved into the downtown, taking the place of residents who were moving outward, the city center experienced a severe housing shortage. Detroit in 1920 had some of the highest rents of any city in the country, and the downtown was no exception, with the result that, despite its deteriorated housing stock, the neighborhood was nonetheless expensive and exploitive. Between 1920 and 1940, the inner city remained Detroit's poorest, most densely settled, and most outmoded residential section, a place of densely built, deteriorated housing with paradoxically high rents due to the demand created by a continuing influx of newcomers who chose, or were compelled, to live there. It featured high rates of crime and juvenile delinquency, welfare dependency, infant mortality, and deaths from tuberculosis.[4]

The rise of a slum in the center of Detroit was not entirely new, but its scale was larger than before both in geographic area and in numbers of inhabitants, and its persistence in the 1920s stood in marked contrast to the prosperity the city was experiencing overall. Detroit's slum was perpetuated, furthermore, by the concentration, both voluntary and involuntary, of the city's newcomers there.[5] On one hand, the downtown offered immigrants connections to their ethnic and racial communities, which helped them survive, so locating there was to some extent an active choice. Moving elsewhere was also not always practical or even possible. For immigrants, their lack of the English language, of job skills, and of savings made the downtown the first place to call home until they assimilated and moved elsewhere. Great Migration blacks experienced obstacles similar to those of foreign-born whites since they, too, lacked job skills and savings. In addition, they faced racial discrimination that restricted their ability to move elsewhere, and so the housing problem was more severe for them.

In fact, as early as 1911, decline was already apparent in the downtown district in which the Great Migration blacks were destined to live. Myron Adams writing for *Survey* identified the "steady exodus to the suburbs" of people from this port-of-entry neighborhood where "practically every family lived then in its own house, with grass and flowers in the yard." Left behind in their wake was a "dreary district [of] cheap boarding houses, many in bad repair." Side by side with the "infrequent homes of long-time property holders" were buildings taken over for prostitution. The rapid influx of newcomers drove rents up, and families began to double up within the same house in order to cover costs.[6] Conditions worsened in the late 1910s as the first wave of the Great Migration crested. A 1919 study by the Research Bureau of Associated Charities reported that the severe housing shortage meant that "three or four families in an apartment" was common-place and "homes have so many lodgers that they are really hotels." To create more space, landlords attempted ramshackle remodeling, converting attics or cellars into bedrooms and alleyside barns and outbuildings into houses. According to charity workers, nightclubs began charging for the privilege of sleeping on poolroom tables overnight.[7]

Activists spoke out repeatedly against the deplorable conditions of Detroit's "black belt," accurately identifying racial segregation as the cause of this worsening slum. The residential restrictions for African Americans inflated rents and caused families to take in boarders, observed a *Detroiter* editorial. The author commented, "Hence, in this area, hundreds of such 'homes' are literally covered from cellar to garret with 'flops' and, in many cases, those 'flops' are used by night workers in the daytime and by day workers at night. . . . It is impossible . . . for a Negro man or woman to secure decent quarters for self or family. His presence as a resident is not tolerated in many sections of the city. He is compelled to live in the slum districts."[8] According to journalist Len Shaw, Great Migration blacks living in Detroit were the victims of a housing shortage "more acute locally than in any other Northern center of population." They were a "human population" stuffed into "tumbledown shacks" because "they have no other place to go. . . . A European, be he ever so ignorant . . . can find localities where it is possible for him to rent or buy a home on easy terms. In the same district a Negro would be turned away, however worthy he might be."[9]

In general, the outward movement of residential development in the Detroit metropolis indicated a mobility that was social as well as physical. When African Americans and immigrants were able to escape the inner city, it was because they had the means to become home- and car own-ers, which in turn gave them new status. Since this trend increased with time during the interwar years, the ability of newcomers to move outward probably depended on how long they had lived in Detroit. "There is a steady drift out of all these groupings of foreign whites and native blacks," observed local historian Arthur Pound, as "succeeding generations" became acclimated to American culture and individuals rose in "wealth and social ambition."[10] Dearborn, for instance, was portrayed as a destination for "fore-men and skilled mechanics and artisans [as well as] plant executives," attract-ing a class of "industrial employes [*sic*] . . . [insistent] upon homes removed from the objectionable features of industrial propinquity" but who nonethe-less wanted to be no farther away from their jobs than a fifteen- or twenty-minute trolley ride.[11] This pairing of outward physical movement and upward social mobility caused scholar Olivier Zunz to state that, "for the first time,

Detroit's spatial arrangement began to resemble the classic zones of succes-
sive settlement—which newcomers entered in a set order—described by the
Chicago sociologists."[12]

African American Automobile Workers

Black workers at Ford Motor Company were often excluded from living
in Dearborn simply through intolerance and discrimination enforced by de
facto means. This racism was further institutionalized, however, through the
use of restrictive housing deeds enacted by real estate subdividers in the
spreading suburbs, resulting in de jure segregation.[13] When African American newcomers from the South arrived, they were bound to face trouble
finding a place to live in Detroit's long-saturated housing market. Worse
still was the fact that although Henry Ford hired more African Americans
than his colleagues, initially he provided no aid for their housing.[14] In fact,
in the three-hundred-house subdivision he sponsored in Dearborn, not a
single African American resided (although no deed restrictions were found
on record for this subdivision, a screening process by the company was in
place, which likely excluded blacks).[15] In the late 1930s and early 1940s, when
the Ford Foundation developed the Springwells Park subdivision, also in
Dearborn, blacks were excluded again (in this case, restrictive deeds were
actually placed on record). In the depths of the Great Depression, Ford did
subsidize some housing for African Americans living outside Dearborn in
the community of Inkster, but this was a stopgap measure only.

Most African Americans working for Ford Motor Company resided in
Detroit, in segregated neighborhoods whose boundaries were vigilantly
enforced by whites. In the downtown slum ironically known as Paradise
Valley, where many blacks were concentrated, a randomized sample of the
1930 manuscript census showed not a single African American Ford Motor
Company worker who owned his home. In fact, most were boarders in
households headed by other people, and these households averaged ten people in size. Of the rest, some were household heads who rented rather than
boarded while others were secondary breadwinners of a household, who
contributed income to a family but did not serve as its head. In comparison,
white Ford Motor Company workers living in Dearborn had a homeownership rate of 57 percent and a median house value of $7,200. Typically the
worker was married and served as the sole breadwinner for a household of
5.6 members.[16]

This problem was to some extent engineered by Henry Ford himself,
whose views on race were biased even by the standards of the day. Most

glaringly, he tended not to give African American workers the same opportunities as others: they were steered into unskilled jobs that earned them no
more than the minimum wage; white workers, meanwhile, were brought
into skilled and semi-skilled jobs, sometimes given training in the process,
and they were eligible for wages above the minimum.[17] Of course, without
earning the same money, African Americans could not obtain housing comparable to that of their white counterparts. To Ford (a self-professed segre-
gationist), this was as it should be: African Americans, in his opinion, might
be more assimilable into the mainstream than other groups, but they would
never blend completely. In 1925, he declared, "Race lines are fixed. Nature
punishes transgression with destruction."[18] In 1921, he had claimed that "racial
differentiation" makes "assimilation" impossible for the African American
population.[19] He also believed segregation was desirable also for the African
Americans: "The Negro does not want to crowd in among the whites; what he
does want is the air, sunlight, space and sanitation which are to be had in white
residential sections. He should have all these things in his own quarter."[20]

On the other hand, since Ford thought blacks were characterized by a
childish dependency, he also claimed it was up to the white race to help
them, and this belief motivated him to place African Americans in a token
way at various high occupations within his organization. As he stated in
1922, "The Negro is a human being, capable of integrity, loyalty and domestic peace and prosperity. . . . The Negro needs a job, he needs a sense of
industrially 'belonging,' and this it ought to be the desire of our industrial
engineers to supply."[21] The opportunities Ford provided African Americans
were arguably an improvement over those in the South, and they were even
better than many alternatives in the North. Boxer Joe Louis, for example,
described conditions in the slums of Detroit as better than what they had
left behind in the South:

> I was twelve years old when Pat Brooks heard about the money Ford was pay-
> ing. He went up first, then brought us up to Detroit. We moved in with some
> of our kin in MacComb Street. It was kind of crowded there, but the house
> had toilets indoors and electric lights. Down in Alabama we had outhouses
> and kerosene lamps. My stepfather got a job with Ford, and we got a place of
> our own in a frame tenement in Catherine Street.[22]

Nonetheless, Ford's commitment to preserve a hierarchy based on race ultimately limited the advancement of African Americans.[23]

A few of Detroit's African Americans in search of a better life moved
into white neighborhoods—with confrontations, even violence, following.

NAACP officer Walter White reported that "a colored woman and her family were notified by certain white people to vacate the home which they had recently purchased." After not one but two stonings on the house, "the colored women fired at the mob." She was later acquitted. A black physician was threatened when he moved into a new house on King Avenue, but after announcing "he was going to protect his home and his family, if necessary, [he received] no further trouble." In an incident with a less fortunate outcome, a home on Spokane Avenue bought by an African American man was attacked by a mob, which "broke into his home, smashed a great deal of the furniture, loaded the rest of it on a van and carried it back to this man's former home." According to White, "nothing was done by the police to prevent this attack."[24]

These incidents culminated in the 1925 case of Ossian Sweet, an African American doctor and graduate of Howard University, who bought a house with a racially restrictive deed attached.[25] The white woman who sold him the house received threats, which prompted Sweet to notify the police of his moving-in date and to arm himself.[26] When he moved in, a mob formed outside his house, and on the second night, its members, now up to six hundred strong, became violent, stoning the house.[27] The ten police officers present did nothing to intervene. Then, from the Sweet house, gunfire was shot into the crowd, killing one and wounding another, which resulted in the arrest of everyone inside.

The Sweet case became a lightning rod for racial issues in Detroit, as evident in the letter that Mayor John Smith sent to the *Detroit Free Press* in which he pointed the finger of blame in all directions. The rise in prejudice he attributed to a "revival of the Ku Klux Klan," which he referred to as a "cowardly campaign." The police, meanwhile, had failed to provide "legal protections to all persons, regardless of creed or color." At the same time, however, he faulted African Americans who moved into predominately white neighborhoods, declaring, "I believe that any colored person who endangers life and property, simply to gratify his personal pride, is an enemy of his race as well as an incitant of riot and murder."[28] Smith also appointed an interracial committee to study the condition of African Americans in Detroit. Their findings, published a year later in a report entitled "The Negro in Detroit," consisted of only cautious remarks about residential integration. For instance, they offered the tepid observation that "if such white neighbors are tolerant and civil, the resulting situation is not bad, [but] if a particular colored family offends against the established standards of the neighborhood, friction is inevitable."[29] Ultimately the case attracted the attention of Clarence Darrow, who defended Sweet and managed to get him acquitted. Still, little changed for Detroit's blacks as a result of the case, however. Racially restrictive deeds continued to be used, and in the meantime periodic disputes over housing continued in Detroit, with legal aid provided by the NAACP.

However, many African American Ford Motor Company workers managed to find a housing alternative on Detroit's West Side, one of the few neighborhoods in the city that was not subject to racially restrictive deeds. This area, centered on the intersection of Tireman and West Grand Boulevard, was convenient to two Ford Motor Company plants: the River Rouge plant (in Dearborn just over the border from Detroit) and the Lincoln plant, which was nearby within the city limits. Ford Motor Company workers tended to move to the West Side more so than other African Americans because their high wages made them more mobile, both geographically and socially. Here they lived side by side with members of the black bourgeoisie who had settled in the neighborhood before the Great Migration began.

By 1930, the typical black Ford Motor Company worker residing on the West Side was a married household head who was 50 percent likely to own a house, and when he did, its median value was $8,250 and the household size was an average of 6.4 members. In almost all cases, homeownership was achieved because the income of the main breadwinner was supplemented by the earnings of relatives or by taking in boarders. Although about half of all black Ford Motor Company workers in the neighborhood were household heads, two-fifths (42 percent) were boarders, and about a tenth (9 percent) were secondary breadwinners, that is, relatives of the household head such as sons, brothers-in-law, nephews, and so on.[30] About three-quarters of the West Side's black Ford workers were unskilled; of the remainder, 15 percent were skilled, 7 percent were semi-skilled, and 4 percent were low-level managers such as foremen. The living standard of these black Ford Motor Company workers was impressive, since it tended to beat the average for Detroit, where the homeownership rate was 41 percent and the median house value was $7,986 (although the average household size was only 4.2).[31]

According to commentators, residents claimed that "the West Side is the best side," and they created "an attractive neighborhood [and] took pride in their achievement, [vowing to] keep their homes on a high level."[32] A 1920s survey referred to the West Side as "the best type of large Negro area in the city. . . . The West Side has fewer lodgers and relatives per family but it has a larger number of children." According to this survey, "financial independence [and the] fact that many of the West Siders belong to established families" accounted for this disparity.[33] A recent film documentary about the West Side also emphasized the aspirations of the neighborhood during this period. "There was a lot of pride among the residents of the West Side," stated resident Marguerite Massey, who was interviewed for the film. "It showed because of the way property was maintained, the lifestyle of the residents, the good schools, the fraternization at the churches. It was a very good place to live." Narrator Jerry Blocker noted, "Even now, as we view the West Side, you get a special feeling of pride and independence, a feeling of no matter how unfair and unjust things may be, I'll get my piece of the American pie."[34]

Meanwhile, in response to the lack of adequate housing for African Americans in the suburbs, Detroit Urban League head John Dancy initiated the development of a subdivision called Inkster Gardens, which neighbored Dearborn to the west.[35] Because Inkster Gardens was connected to the River Rouge plant by interurban, it attracted a large number of Ford Motor Company workers among its African American population. These residents, like anyone else, were drawn to the suburbs for the improved standard of living usually offered there. This sentiment is expressed in a real estate advertisement for Inkster Gardens, which called it "beautifully situated, . . . just far enough out to be free from the noise and dirt of the crowded city, yet convenient to all the large factories of the west side." The ad emphasized a typically bourgeois aspiration for every "one to have his own vine covered bungalow." Finally, developing such a respectable community was something in which to take civic pride, and the ad described the many beautiful homes built there as "a credit to the community but also to the city of Detroit" and noted that "those who buy property are the ones who really decide the policy of the nation and here will be found some of America's most noble and respected citizens."[36]

Conditions for African American Ford Motor Company workers in Inkster Gardens were tangibly better than for those in Detroit's downtown slum. If anything, Inkster Gardens represented an inversion of the situation in inner-city Detroit: while in Inkster Gardens most residents were married household heads who owned their houses and served as sole breadwinners for their families, those downtown rented, usually as boarders in crowded households. More specifically, in Inkster Gardens, the homeownership rate among black Ford Motor Company workers was notably high (86 percent), about twice as high as either the rate in Detroit (41 percent) or the national rate (46 percent). The median value, however, was only $3,000, which was less than half the median for Detroit ($7,986). It was also lower than the national median ($4,778), but not by as much. Of the Inkster Gardens Ford Motor Company workers, 94 percent were head of household, 3 percent were secondary breadwinners, and 3 percent were boarders; 93 percent were married, and the average household size was 4.8 people. Only about a third

(36 percent) of the workers lived in homes where the income of the household head was supplemented by the presence of boarders or secondary breadwinners. This was remarkable since virtually all Inkster Gardens Ford Motor Company workers were unskilled and therefore made only the company's minimum wage, which was six dollars a day. Overall, Inkster Gardens was clearly an improvement over living in downtown Detroit, where none of the African American Ford household heads owned their homes, only 68 percent of the workers were married, and almost all (96 percent) lived in households where the income of the household head was supplemented by taking in boarders or relying on secondary breadwinners.[37]

Despite the example of Inkster Gardens, African Americans generally remained underrepresented in the suburbs of Detroit. In 1940, they made up about 7 percent of Detroit's urban population but only 3 percent of the suburban, and within the central city a majority of African Americans were compelled to live in the downtown slum.[38] Still, communities like Inkster Gardens—and others such as Ecorse and River Rouge—demonstrate the yearnings of African American Ford workers for suburban homeownership. As stated by reformer Marvel Daines on the topic of black suburbanization in Detroit: "They wanted a place to live—unhampered by the congestion of conditions of the rapidly deteriorating downtown slum. They wanted sunlight and fresh air, and they wanted a space for gardening."[39] It can be argued that the pursuit of the American dream promoted by Henry Ford prompted African American workers to challenge the hierarchy he intended for them, at least in the arena of housing.

Women and Work

Henry Ford was motivated by a desire to turn working-class people of all kinds into good citizens, yet he believed women were to have a different destiny than men. Supposedly, their role was not to set aside time to think about civic issues but to make their homes happy by transforming them into a site of consumption and leisure, which in turn contributed to the performance of male workers.[40] Ford believed that it was only with women as homemakers that workers could make the transition "from poor and squalid to healthy, sanitary quarters, with [an] environment conducive to health, happiness, and comfort."[41] In other words, the role of women in households was crucial to Ford's reform of workers and their quality of life in terms of wages, hours, and assimilation into American culture. An article discussing the wife of a Ford Motor Company worker—who had improved her home after the implementation of the five-dollar-day policy—elaborated upon her role. The author noted that the family (a man, his wife, and their baby) were now alone in their four-room apartment, as they no longer had boarders. The homemaker had taken care to provide rugs, a tablecloth, and a bookcase, as well as several clean shirts for her husband. Following this attentive housekeeping, they were now prepared to enjoy a day off on the upcoming weekend.[42] Clearly evident in this anecdote was the assertion that increased consumption and leisure should exist for all members of society, including the working class. Ford had a double reason to promote consumption and leisure within the home: they increased his workers' productivity and it encouraged families to be the consumers of his own product.[43]

Henry Ford recognized the work that women performed as homemakers and how that contributed to the productivity of his industry. He actually considered the high wage he paid their husbands to be compensation for the women's labor, stating that "the shop must pay them both. . . . Otherwise, we have the hideous prospect of little children and their mothers being forced out to work."[44] Certainly, such a sight would not do in Dearborn, Ford's model of industrial reform. Through the presence of female homemakers, the households of workers would be made not only more bourgeois—offering greater material comfort—but modernized. Ford's prediction that technological improvement would make housework as efficient as the assembly line indicates an awareness of the need for change: "Although a man's actual working hours a week have decreased, hardly anything has been done to eliminate the fundamental drudgery of housekeeping." He emphasized, "Well, the modern young woman who maintains a household and brings up several children is going to change this. She is refusing the drudgery . . . and as a consequence it will disappear."[45] In fact, working-class households were now more likely than ever to feature updated amenities such as gas, electricity, and running water, as well as appliances such as washing machines and connections to the outside world via telephones and radios.

Henry Ford's belief that women should not work outside the home was a theory he expounded upon in his essay "Should Married Women Work?" and that he put into practice by not hiring them unless under extenuating circumstances.[46] A 1916 article about Ford reported that one of his female employees recently quit her job to marry a fellow worker, and in response he told the department head, "Put a man in her place, give him a chance to earn five dollars a day and maybe he will marry another of our girls." Ford then referred to women as "cheap labor" necessary "to tap typewriters," and he continued, "I can't fire our girls, but I certainly would like to buy a carload of wedding presents for them."[47] For Ford, hiring women was a necessary evil, something to be done when a woman supported a family and when the company needed inexpensive labor, but ultimately it was preferable to hire a man and pay him well. In the cases when Ford did hire women, he preferred widowed or unmarried women, and originally he excluded all female employees from eligibility for the five-dollar day, paying them instead as little as half as much or even less. In the end, criticism from feminists resulted in a mediation by President Woodrow Wilson so that Ford was forced to change his policy.[48] Despite this gain, however, women employed in production at the River Rouge plant represented no more than 1 percent of its workforce throughout the 1920s. In this regard, Ford was an exception among automakers, who counted on women to play an important role in the industry.[49]

In Dearborn, wives employed in factories were rare, but that does not mean they were not working. As observed by sociologist Chen-Nan Li, they had households to run, and this was not easy, especially when a family's schedule had to be tailored to the hours of an autoworker breadwinner. The wife of a typical Ford Motor Company worker, commented Li, "works hard at house-keeping." Of all family members, she was affected the most by her husband's shifts, especially the midnight shift, which was the most detrimental to the health of workers. Li noted, "She has to attend to his food and to see to it that he gets up in time and to control the children in such a way that noise in the house may be minimized."[50] In addition, about a fifth of all wives took in boarders, which added to their workload.[51] The situation of these wives is particularly intriguing because it shows how the homes of working-class people had not yet evolved entirely into places of consumption and leisure rather than production, even though this was a long-term trend of the times. After all, when a worker's wife had to attend to her husband's needs in meeting a schedule, her actions can be interpreted as an extension of the production taking place in the factory—her job is to get the husband ready for work, just as a worker might grease a machine that is about to be operated.

Although Henry Ford acknowledged the home as a place of production, he believed it should be a place of unremunerative labor only, objecting to the practice of boarding, which was used to bring in money.[52] Perhaps he found it acceptable for workers in the central city to do this, but it would be unseemly in Dearborn, his ideal suburb. In regard to the criteria for the five-dollar day, he declared, "We had to break up the evil custom among foreign workers of taking in boarders—of regarding their homes as something to make money out of rather than as a place to live."[53] Little was he aware that boarders continued such a commonplace occurrence, found throughout Dearborn. In general, Ford did what he could to maintain separate roles for men and women, assuring the home remained predominately a place of consumption and leisure, a situation that best suited the needs of his business.

In actuality, finding remunerative employment was essential to many working-class women in Dearborn and in the rest of the Detroit metropolis— whether it was taking in boarders or finding work outside the home. According to one female autoworker, Henry Ford's policy caused some women to live with their partners without marrying so they could stay eligible for employment—ironically creating the opposite effect intended by Ford, who concerned himself with legitimating domestic arrangements as well as ensuring that families were headed by a sole male breadwinner.[54] Instead, his policy simply encouraged women, desperate for a job, to lie about their marital status.[55] On the topic of whether married women should be excluded from factories, Irene Young Marinovich, an autoworker in her own right, stated, "Most of the married women working in the plant would be darn glad to get out of it. . . . These women are whole-heartedly in favor of going back home and taking care of their families. But they don't intend doing it at the expense of having their children without proper food and shoes, and a decent standard of living." It was a problem that would remain unsolved, she believed, until "the men are guaranteed a sufficient hourly wage [or] the government can give the women some security." Besides, she added, under any condition, "women have as much damn right to work as a man does."[56]

Life for female autoworkers was harder than for their male counterparts, Marinovich asserted. They did the same job for less pay, often under the same dangerous conditions. Marinovich herself was a heavy press operator, a milling machine operator, and a drill press operator who worked "side by side" with men. At the Briggs plant, where she first worked, the presses lacked safety devices, and as a result "very few people in there didn't have two or three fingers off or half a hand or whole hands."[57] Meanwhile, the women had housework and child care to do when they got off from the factory. "All the women were so anxious to get home at night," remarked Marinovich. "Of course women had, you know, triple jobs, . . . they held a job during the day, they had to get home and cook and they had to clean house, they had to wash nights, Saturday and Sunday." For care of their children when they were at their jobs, the women relied on relatives or older children, or they worked opposite shifts of their husbands. Women were also subject to sexual harassment. "[The foreman] tried to pinch me one day," remembered Marinovich, "and I'd threatened to wrap a piece of steel around his neck if he ever done it again."[58]

In addition, women were crucial players in the fight to organize labor, taking the same risks as men, especially at factories containing a high proportion of women. At the General Motors Ternstedt plant in Detroit, women made up 50 percent of the workers, and they were key to the effectiveness of a slowdown strike that lasted for ten days. "This thing really caught on fire. . . . The company was really taken by surprise," Marinovich commented. Regarding applications for union membership, she remembered, "Girls would come up, and they'd hand me a dollar and their name, and I'd have my pockets stuffed full, my purse stuffed full. And go home at night and try to, hope that the dollars and the names, you know, added up. . . . By the time that 10 days was over, Ternstedt was organized," she concluded. "We called for an election, and we won it."[59] At another point, when working for the Briggs plant in Highland Park, Marinovich faced violence on the picket line. "That was my first encounter with the Detroit Police Department," she recalled, "and they were strike breaking. . . . I missed getting my head knocked off by a quarter of an inch. Because he swung at me, and I ducked, you know. The club went over. It would have killed me."[60]

Recreation for Workers

Finally, Henry Ford was a conservative when it came to the recreational activities of his workers. His policies, of course, proved easier to implement inside the workplace than outside. Upon the grounds of his plant he was able to control alcohol and tobacco by simply banning them, but speakeasies (or "blind pigs") as well as places for gambling and prostitution clustered around the factory gates. This neighborhood was known as the South End, and although it was primarily a residential neighborhood for Ford Motor Company's immigrant workers, it was also Dearborn's vice district. In recalling the South End, former mayor Joseph Karmann stated that there were frequent troubles requiring the intervention of the police.[61] As reported in the paper, South End was "where shooting and stabbings have occurred." Full of "rooming houses, hotels, coffee shops," it was populated by "racketeers and aliens."[62] Iris Becker, a local teacher, recalled that "it became a rather famous section of town . . . sometimes infamous, because bootlegging was involved. The Italians and some of the other people made their wine . . . and made it despite prohibition because they brought that custom from the old country."[63] Becker also remembered the prostitution rings run by organized criminals. This problem, she noted, received a hypocritical response from citizens in the more upscale sections who failed to enforce laws as long as the practice was contained within a low-status neighborhood. Residents who lived nearby, however, objected to the prostitution as it threatened the family-oriented character of their community.[64] Sociologist Li confirmed that Ford Motor Company workers found a "perverted form of recreation" in "visiting the so-called 'sporting houses'" that were located plentifully in Detroit, and likely in Dearborn as well.[65]

In Ford's crusade against jazz dancing, smoking, and drinking, he had the law on his side for the latter as it was the era of Prohibition. The blind pigs of the South End were the target of sporadic raids by Dearborn police throughout the 1920s. More typical was a rather innocuous complicity on the part of the police, as revealed by officer William Henson:

> It's Saturday night and as usual there is a wedding at Romanian Hall. Well, then that was supposed to be dry. That was prohibition, you know, but they'd have plenty of beer and plenty of moonshine. But the boss would tell you to cover these, you know. Naturally if you covered them, a policeman didn't drink on the job. You'd get coffee or they'd give you cake or whatever.

He concluded, "They liked it, the cops."[66]

Then the raids escalated in the spring of 1930, when a tabloid exposé of Prohibition violation in Dearborn was reprinted in *Time* magazine. Henry Ford, infuriated and embarrassed at the national coverage, partnered with local police and, later, federal agents to increase enforcement.[67] Tips were exchanged between Dearborn Chief of Police Carl Brooks and the head of Ford's security department, Harry Bennett, with the result that violators faced both arrests by the police and disciplinary actions by the company, which included being fired. "In making raids," said one newspaper, "Brooks and his men would report to Bennett the names and badge numbers of Ford workmen found in places where liquor was kept or sold, and in return the Ford service department [which handled labor relations and security] would supply the police with such information regarding blind pigs as came into its hands." Drinking in Dearborn consisted of more than moonshine made from homemade stills, however, as the community, located on the border with Canada, was the site of rum-running by organized-crime members. Even Bennett doubted if bootleggers had been entirely scoured from Dearborn after the raids, and he admitted, "Whether the bootleggers have been licked or are just waiting until things quiet down, I don't know."[68]

Meanwhile, Henry Ford's revival of square dancing was something he took on as part of a "war on jazz dancing."[69] A dance manual put out by Ford denigrated modern dancing, calling it utterly lacking in "grace, style, and skill," and declared it would soon to go out of vogue because of "its lesser demand for skill and spirit, tuneless music, tendency to jazz and essential unsociability."[70] Ford's racism was also a factor in his crusade. One newspaper noted, "The Detroit manufacturer does not think very much of the 'negroid' or 'animal' dances," and concluded, "He would have our youngsters touch fingers in a minuet rather than touch cheeks in a bunny hug."[71] Ford's square dancing revival started with such dancing a regular feature at the parties he held at his estate. Ford's parties were quirky in themselves as Dearborn was considered to be out-of-the-way compared to the Grosse Pointes where the "gasoline aristocracy" and other members of Detroit's high society were centered. Having square dancing at a Dearborn party was thus doubly out of fashion, but as Henry Ford was averse to hobnobbing, it is not too surprising he did this. Many company executives did not know how to do the outdated dances, so Ford imported a full-time dance instructor to live in Dearborn. The executives had no choice but to learn, as the paths of their careers depended on showing up at Ford's parties.[72] Next, Ford funded square-dancing classes at all the public schools in Dearborn, so the children of the community were square-dancing, too.[73] Eventually, Ford made the music for square dancing a part of his radio advertising campaign, and the music was also played in the dealership showrooms.[74] Square dances were also held at his country club.

Although square dancing was something Ford could foist upon executives, dealers, and schoolchildren, there is little evidence it took off with his workers, who preferred more contemporary entertainment.[75] "First of all, the majority of the Ford employees have cars," stated sociologist Li on the topic of recreation. "Many of them drive out in the late afternoons or go away for week-ends. Many of them go fishing and swimming on holidays. They play tennis, baseball, golf and billiards." The younger men frequented parks, poolrooms, drugstores, theaters, and dancing halls, attending concerts, burlesque, vaudeville, and films on a weekly basis. "The average Ford employee, like the average American workingmen, is almost destitute of any academic interest," commented Li, and he added that workers with educational levels beyond the eighth grade were rare. Li asserted this left Ford Motor Company workers with little interest in reading, music, or art. They seldom attended sermons or lectures or visited the library.[76] Ammerman, another sociologist, confirmed Li's research: "The type of recreation [in] which the people of Dearborn participate the most appears to be the movies. Figures show that in one month (March 1939) the five theaters in Dearborn had an attendance of over 42,500 people a week." Ammerman also noted that dance halls, beer gardens, and theatrical venues were also favored by residents. Dearborn's six bowling alleys were also very popular, especially during the winter months.[77]

According to labor historian Joyce Shaw Peterson, a transformation in the recreational tastes of Ford Motor Company workers from less to more commercial can be traced from the 1910s through the 1920s, and this has proved as true in Dearborn as any place else. In this regard, "autoworkers' recreational habits were much like those of other urban workers of the Midwest." Peterson then compared two studies of these workers. "A 1914 poll of more than 1,250 male Ford workers," she stated, "revealed the following recreational preferences. Outdoor sports, especially football and cricket, led the list as the favorite of 452 men; then came walking, 227; cycling, 178; bowling, 157; gardening, 82; reading, 63; homelife, 35; music, 32; and none, 30. Daily newspapers were consumed with avid interest as was neighborhood news." By the 1920s, however, commercial recreational facilities (such as movie theaters, burlesque and vaudeville shows, dance halls, and pool halls) were more frequented. A 1930 study "revealed that 86 percent of the families spent some money on motion pictures. In addition, 2 percent reported expenditures for plays and concerts, . . . 9 percent for excursions, 7 percent for vacations outside the city."[78] Newspapers continued to be popular, with all the families buying them. About half the families bought magazines, but rarely were books bought (the average was one book for every five families). At variance with the findings of Li, pianos were found in 13 percent of the households, and music lessons were paid for by 9 percent of the families.

Thus the South End automobile workers participated in many typically American forms of leisure as observed by Li, Ammerman, and Peterson. Still, they maintained their immigrant cultures through other forms of recreation, with coffeehouses, churches, and ethnic community centers functioning as gathering places. In fact, according to the aforementioned 1930 study, 79 percent of Ford families belonged to a religious organization, and 9 percent joined lodges, clubs, or societies. "They all had their own customs," recalled police officer Henson. "They'd drink *mastica* and they'd have their native dances. They'd have a dance nearly every night in the Romanian Hall on Salina. There were the Turks, the Syrians, the Armenians and everybody. . . . They all had their own coffee houses."[79] Becker commented, "Later on it became fashionable to be interested in different things, the 'in thing'! But the [South End] of Dearborn always tended to have an interest in a wide variety of customs because that was indigenous to the area." She continued, "It was also a chance to get acquainted with different nationalities and different kinds of food."[80] It was, remembered resident Michael Adray, "Heinz 57, everybody of every nationality, the melting pot. It was a typical melting pot of the U.S.A."[81]

The many ethnic differences in the neighborhood contributed to its solidarity and tolerance, and to some extent, its safety. Of the South End residents, Adray declared, "You didn't have to lock your doors. You didn't have to worry about somebody stealing your bicycle."[82] Even Henson, who fought crime there, declared, "Everybody talked about what a terrible [place] but I found more kind personal friends down there. Just treat them decent and they were your friends for life."[83] So, in spite of the South End's reputation as a vice district, community activities contributed to the building of a safe, tightly knit, family-oriented neighborhood. If anything, the cohesiveness within the South End may have benefited from the neighborhood's detachment from the rest of Dearborn.

Conclusion

Well before momentum was gained in efforts to organize labor through unionization, wage earners found ways to resist Henry Ford's new welfare capitalism, even while attaining a suburban lifestyle. For instance, Dearborn residents went ahead with supplementing the family income through the earnings of women, and they were unabashed in seeking commercial entertainment, in the community's movie theaters and bowling alleys. African Americans organized politically through the formation of the Detroit Urban League and other associations, and they gained greater equality through the development of their own suburban community on the border of Dearborn. Ford himself, as an industrialist, had helped to bring about these very changes—once workers had more money and time, they had no reason to restrict themselves to nuclear families headed by sole male breadwinners, or to square dancing instead of jazz dancing, or to abstinence versus drinking, or for that matter to living in a central-city slum instead of the suburbs. Actually, Ford Motor Company workers made changes in their lives that in many aspects restructured society, especially while wage earners suburbanized and aspired to middle-class levels of leisure and consumption, immigrants became Americanized, and African Americans lost their Southern deference. It was, therefore, only a matter of time until Ford's attempt to keep the Dearborn community in a mold of his own making was halted by a rising labor movement.

6

The Transformation of Fordism

THE HIGH STANDARD OF living that Henry Ford helped his workers achieve was a product of "Fordism," conventionally defined as the linking of mass production and mass consumption through high wages. Ford was compelled to do this not just because it was good business but also from an imperative to share profits with workers, which he believed was accorded them by their rights as citizens. As stated in a company newsletter, high wages were something "the American workman takes as a right, won by honest and strenuous labor, and gladly given by those with and for whom he works."[1] Ford explained, "We want our people to desire more and better things, and demand a higher standard of living."[2] In other words, he wanted his workers to achieve the "American dream." In turn, automaker competitors were forced to match Ford's wages, and soon other American industries, who also drew upon a labor pool of semi-skilled operatives, followed suit, causing this standard of living to become prevalent throughout the country.[3] On this point Ford declared exuberantly, "The American way . . . is to pay wages sufficient to guarantee the workingman not only subsistence, but the comforts and some of the luxuries of life. Let him buy a car, a radio, and an American home!"[4]

The onset of the Great Depression, however, undid many of the gains of workers in the previous decade. Wage earners started losing jobs, possessions, and homes, all things brought to them by Fordism. It was the prospective collapse of this system that motivated workers at Ford Motor Company to unionize—shop floor conditions had been a longtime aggravation, but it was the threat of losing a whole way of life that pushed workers over the edge. Ultimately, Ford Motor Company workers succeeded in unionizing, winning a contract unprecedented in its favorability to labor and assuring themselves continued access to an American standard of living.[5]

Furthermore, when the Great Depression arrived, it struck harder in the Detroit area than in any other part of the country because of a number of factors: the gigantic scale of its production and consumption, which was now disrupted; the lack of diversity in the area's economy; the inflexibility of vertical integration; the fractionalization of its tax base; the lag between philanthropy and welfare needs; and the decision, taken during the previous decade, to increase its debt load as tax revenues were decreasing. Of particular relevance was the metropolitan trend that had allowed Dearborn and surrounding suburbs to thrive throughout the 1920s, sometimes at the expense of the central city. During this decade, in the Detroit area and throughout the nation, the growth rate of suburbs outpaced that of the city, although the urban population was still increasing.[6] The consequences for Detroit were evident in the rise of an urban slum, the decline of the downtown, falling tax revenues, and increasingly unsound management of municipal finances. The arrival of the Depression naturally exacerbated these problems. Still, it is important to emphasize that the Depression was not so much the cause of these issues as it revealed extensive weaknesses that already existed. Also, although Dearborn had long experienced a trend of prosperity that was counter to that of the central city, at last the two localities were both headed in a downward direction as neither was immune to the collapse of the national economy.

Great Depression Arrives

Even before the Great Depression, Detroit was rather shaky financially. Throughout the 1920s, it was subject to an increased demand for public expenditure brought on by multiple annexations and a spiraling population. Millions of dollars were allocated for capital improvements such as streets, water, sewers, schools, and parks and for services like police and fire protection, social work and welfare, and education.[7] The Detroit Bureau of Government Research, a citizens' advisory group whose role was to monitor budget and other issues, noticed the unusual problems that prosperity had brought to Detroit: "Automobiles, higher standards of living, and increased population have thrown unusual burdens upon this generation of city taxpayers." They listed a number of improvements now necessary: water must be filtered, and sewage could no longer be released untreated; narrow cobble streets needed to be widened, then paved with asphalt and lined with streetlamps; parks, playgrounds, schools, and libraries would replace the meadows and open spaces in which children had played. To cope with growth, city leaders resorted to bonded debt at a greater rate than they increased taxes. The researchers were worried about this trend, remarking that Detroit was paying a high rate for access to credit: "from 1920 to 1929, per capita debt has multiplied by five," while revenues lagged, with an increase in per capita taxes factoring at only one and a half.[8] They also noted how the tax base was being undermined by the suburban migration of industry: "Industry [is] always choosing between big cities with transportation facilities, labor supply and high taxes, and little cities with little taxes."[9] Clearly, the city was headed for disaster if it took on more debt than could be paid off with existing levels of tax revenue. These concerns prompted the Detroit Bureau of Government Research to call for action from the city's politicians: "The needs of the community are so many and funds so limited that the time has come to plan public works for a few years ahead."[10]

When the Depression came, the Detroit economy was arguably hit much harder than that of any other major American city because of its lack of diversification. The whole environment of Detroit was geared to produce no fewer than 4 million cars per year. People of all professions organized themselves around this single quota, including those outside the automobile industry such as merchants, landlords, banks, contractors, employees, borrowers, and lenders. Over a period of three years, that quota fell to 25 percent of 1929 volume, and this affected everyone participating in this economy, resulting in fewer profits and less money circulating.[11] Detroit's jobless rate reached the highest in the country, and this played out in a staggering increase of welfare relief: in February 1931, there were 211,000 applicants in comparison to 17,000 on average in the 1920s, and during the same period, welfare expenditures increased from about $100,000 a month to $1.5 million.[12] The Depression reached its worst point in the early weeks of 1933, when close to one-third of the labor force was unemployed.[13] Automobile workers amounted to anywhere from 14 to 20 percent of the relief load for the entire city.[14]

As the freefall continued, the problems afflicting Detroit soon escalated to mind-boggling proportions. Construction projects fell from a total of $100 million in 1929 to only $4 million in 1932. More than five hundred businesses per year declared failure between 1930 and 1932. Within a span of six months, from April to October of 1930, the unemployment rate rose from 12.3 percent to 17.8 percent, representing a total of 76,011 people and 127,200 people, respectively. By June 1931, close to a third of the city's workforce was unemployed (32.4 percent or 223,000 people). Normally, Detroit provided a welfare program to its citizens: yet at exactly the same time that the need for social services was increasing, the city's revenues dropped because of tax delinquency. The city's financial problems were made worse by the reliance on bonded debt it had established in the previous decade, whose payments were coming due. From 1929 to 1932, the percentage of the city budget allocated for debt service rose from 21.6 percent to 42.6 percent.[15]

Soon, the welfare system was collapsing under the weight of hundreds of thousands of unemployed automobile workers and their dependents. The most obvious problem was that, while most of the automobile manufacturing jobs were in the suburbs, a majority of the workers lived in Detroit. This in turn meant that, when those in the automobile industry were laid off, they went on welfare in Detroit, where social services were, of course, not supported by the taxes of suburban employers. Detroit's mayor, Frank Murphy, was all too aware of this injustice and noticed the discrepancy between the location of the employers versus the employees. He began to criticize publicly the irresponsibility of metropolitan industrialists who had located to the suburbs.[16] It should be emphasized that the relief provided by the Department of Public Welfare was extremely minimal, in part due to pressure brought about by bankers to keep the city solvent. Thus, many people legitimately in need were turned away and told to find work or to ask for help from relatives. Meanwhile, the aid that was given consisted of the barest amount of food and cash thought necessary, and it was often inadequate for a family to survive upon. As the ranks of the unemployed grew, organizing took place in the form of soapbox gatherings in city parks.[17] Probably nothing provided more incentive to agitate than the repeated attempts of the city council to decommission municipal homeless shelters. Although Murphy fought to keep the facilities open, he was opposed by conservative aldermen who did not share his political outlook. As a result, during two entire seasons, one in 1931 and another in 1932, existing shelters were made inaccessible to the thousands who needed them.[18]

Here it is relevant to look at the role Henry Ford played in Detroit's experience of the Great Depression. Not only was he the single largest employer in the metropolis but he led the way in the suburbanization of its industry, which now functioned as an obstacle to providing taxes for welfare relief. Thus, Ford's response to the Depression was important, even crucial, to local recovery. Yet the position he took throughout the early 1930s was at best mixed. Like many businessmen, his immediate reaction to the Depression was to be optimistic, even boosterish, and to declare that the dip was only temporary. Like other manufacturers, however, he was soon slashing the labor force, scaling back production, and outsourcing work to relatively cheap suppliers. Between 1930 and 1933, Ford reduced the number of his workers to less than a third of what it had been in 1929, laying off approximately sixty thousand people. As if that were not bad enough, for a period of about six months in 1931–1932, he shut down production in order to retool for a changeover to a model with an eight-cylinder motor. Wages were also falling: at the River Rouge plant, wages were 92 cents per hour in 1929 and dropped to 59 cents per hour in 1933. Plus, workers were employed for few hours. By the summer of 1931, there were only thirty-seven thousand in the workforce, and about one-half of those laborers were working only three days a week.[19] Edmund Wilson, writing for *Scribner's,* analyzed the city's one-industry economy, stating, "You can see here, as it is impossible to do in a more varied and complex city like New York, the whole structure of an industrial society: almost everybody in Detroit is dependent on the motor industry. . . . When the industry is crippled, everybody is hit."[20] Yet even among the major automakers, Ford Motor Company had a pervasive and insidious effect in leading Detroit into its downward spiral.

The consequences for Ford Motor Company workers were made clear in various commissioned studies and journalistic investigations. In 1932 the Labor Research Association issued a report that provides a stark contrast to the 1930 study undertaken by the Bureau of Labor Statistics (BLS).[21] Like the BLS study, the report by the Labor Research Association focused on Detroit autoworker households, with a sample of one hundred families averaging 4.5 people, mostly headed by a sole, male breadwinner who worked for Ford Motor Company. The biggest change identified by the follow-up study was that, during 1931, a fifth of the autoworkers earned nothing at all. Among those who were working, the average income was only $757, which compared to $1,711.87 in 1929. Autoworkers, in other words, were now living on less than half of what they had earned a few years prior. Workers were making less money because they had fewer hours of employment: the average time worked in 1931 was only two and a half days per week. Meanwhile, many workers complained of speedups that were more than double or triple in scale. Almost all the workers studied by the Labor Research Association reported being in debt to stores, individuals, or organizations.[22] The case of a Ford Motor Company worker presented in *Christian Century* cites similar figures: "In 1929, I made $800. In 1930, working three days a week at $7 per day, during the working time, I made $900. In 1931 working four days a week, when I worked, [I] made $500. In 1932, I worked from March to September and made $750 for the year." However, the trend worsened, and in 1933, the worker reported, "At $4 per day I worked from March to September and have made about $450 to date."[23] Witnessing the long lines at the welfare office and the gates of automobile plants, *Survey* writer Helen Hall described the thousands of people gathered as "one disconsolate lump," adding, "The only worse thing I've ever seen, was the look of the faces of a company of French poilus who had been in the trenches four years."[24] The scale of problems faced by Detroit-area automobile workers is evident in their many testimonials. Most emphasized their earnest attempts at frugality and responsibility. At the beginning of the Depression, one autoworker after being laid-off stated that he did not require "any help from the Community Fund [as] by economy I have a comfortable home nearly paid for," but he also prophesied, "Unless the factories open up before long there will be dire suffering in Detroit."[25] Many workers were put in a bind by the obligations of homeownership, since their mortgages were not yet paid off. According to a report by the Detroit Mayor's Unemployment Committee, which surveyed 145 families who were paying off mortgages, 77 were in arrears or had already experienced foreclosures. In one Detroit factory alone, 40 percent of those owning houses had lost them. In addition, approximately one-third of all homeowners were delinquent in their taxes.[26] "Hardly a day passes," declared the mayor of Dearborn Clyde Ford, in 1932, "without some bewildered and worried home owner comes to my office seeking information and advice on how he can save his home."[27]

This was not the first economic downturn to threaten the ability of autoworkers to be homeowners. During the recession of the early 1920s, one worker chastised Henry Ford in a letter, saying, "Very many of your employees attempted to buy houses at high prices with big payments and interest, figured on roomers and tenants to help. And now between layoffs and loss of roomers many cannot make their payments, have no funds for fuel and winter clothing."[28] Some Detroit wage earners were now out on the streets, with no other option than to fend for themselves as best they could. Ford Motor Company worker Dave Moore recalled "shanties out in the boondocks [built] for whole families to live in, [as well as] people living in cars."[29] Homeless men were everywhere throughout the city, noted writer John Dos Passos, in waterfront "shacks and shelters, [along] wharves and alleys, [and] in the back rooms of unoccupied houses. . . . Unemployed men lie out on the grass in a hundred helpless attitudes of sleep."[30]

Throughout, the all-too-familiar gap between wages and cost of living continued to create a dilemma. The wife of autoworker John Rogers nostalgically recounted their life in 1928, when her husband made thirty dollars a week to support her and the baby. "We lived that year," she stated. "We went on the boat and I went to the library and got books. We furnished our rooms, too. We didn't spend our money foolish." She added, "But then came the black year [1929]."[31] Another family was plunged into financial trouble, and not for the first time, and the wife stated, "We have struggled for ten years and we are still in deep water." They had "no movies, no fancy clothes, no radio," and no other foolishness, "just saving for our house." While they had paid down eight hundred dollars on their current house and bought all the furniture, they feared losing it like the last house—in which they had invested five thousand dollars of equity but lost it all because of a six-month stint of unemployment. Now, she predicted, "it looks as though we were going to lose this one." And she concluded, "It's the insecurity that kills you, not the work or the saving."[32]

Complained Anthony Lombardo, who worked for Ford, "Everybody say here, 'Why don't you save when you work?' But how can you save when you no work steady? . . . You work, you make something, you stop. You spend what you got save. You getta the debts. Then you get a job. You pay the debts. You save a little. You stop. And now I stop too long this time."[33] Wage earners also despaired of the cyclical nature of industrial production. "The trouble is you just can't plan ahead," stated one Detroit citizen. "Ford gets a new model out," noted autoworker Thomas Karekin, "and I think everything will be fine, but it ain't."[34] According to one 1932 survey, Detroit's population was now caught in a "process of pauperizing, that is rapidly reducing the . . . American citizen to . . . insecurity and want, and destroying what had once been known as the American standard of living."[35]

In the meantime, Mayor Frank Murphy had exhausted the local resources available for fighting the Depression in Detroit. He was unable to gather adequate political support to merge the city and county welfare agencies into a single metropolitan one that would not only have combined urban and suburban tax revenues but also have saved costs through the efficiencies gained. He was also turned away by Henry Ford and other industrialists when he appealed to them to expand their own welfare programs for aid to current and former employees. Then, when Murphy asked for state assistance for Detroit, he was rebuffed by Governor Wilber Brucker whose constituency, naturally, was mostly rural. Finally, Murphy came up with the iconoclastic idea of asking for direct federal aid in the form of a 1932 amendment to the Reconstruction Finance Corporation (RFC) act. His logic was simply that, if the federal government could provide loans to bail out businesses through the RFC, why not for cities as well? On this point, he was backed by the mayors of all major cities, now organized under the US Conference of Mayors, which he had founded. In the end, Murphy succeeded in getting Congress to agree to this, and the RFC program became the single greatest factor in getting Detroit through the Depression. Of course, even with aid from the RFC, Detroit had a rocky period in the 1930s, characterized by the usual Depression-era experiences of bank closures, reliance on scrip to pay public employees, tax delinquency, and defaulting on bonds. Still, the RFC provided more money than any single alphabet-soup agency such as the WPA or CCC, which followed under Franklin Roosevelt's New Deal. Incidentally, Murphy's innovation in making cities eligible for direct federal aid in the form of loans forever changed city-federal relations and set the foundation for the urban renewal policies of the post–World War II period.[36] More succinctly, the *Detroit News* referred to Murphy's demand for direct federal aid as the "revolt of the cities."[37]

Relief Efforts in Dearborn

Although autoworkers living in Dearborn fared slightly better than those in Detroit, the situation was still difficult there, especially for the less skilled or immigrant workers, who mostly lived in the South End. The fortitude demanded of South End residents even during periods of economic stability was discussed in a newspaper article: "These people, generally industrious and simple livers, are able to subsist on much less than the native-born American. Again as a general rule, they are people who save from whatever earnings they acquire."[38] Yet now they found themselves "asking the help of city officials to get back their jobs" at Ford Motor Company. Although conditions in the South End were tougher than ever, most residents were slow to realize just how bad times were. For instance, proprietors of rooming houses and workingmen's hotels in the South End continued to support unemployed workers, covering the cost of their food and lodging in the expectation of being paid back when hiring was revived. These generous business owners, however, soon found themselves in debt as economic recovery receded into the future.[39] People living only marginally well before the Depression were pulled under by the economic low tide. "There were also things going on in the South End, I mean the prostitution, the things that often grow out of Depression years, things that make a community grow worse," recalled Iris Becker. "Most of the people in the South End were concerned about what was happening to them and a large part of them, of course, [went] on welfare."[40]

The deepening downturn throughout Dearborn was attested to by deputy city clerk Joseph Cardinal. "The council was armed," he recounted. "They feared for their lives from these people who were so upset to be deprived of a livelihood. . . . [People today] wouldn't realize how desperate people were and actually our councilmen, and the mayor, had trouble meeting through."[41] The mounting scale of problems is revealed by a 1930 report stating that, while only 1,500 applications were made at the welfare department in 1928–1929, the number shot up about ten times that amount in the next year, reaching a total of over 15,000.[42] This was quite phenomenal, given that Dearborn had a population of 50,000 residents of which 20,300 were normally in the labor force—likely, the community was attracting unemployed people migrating from elsewhere.[43] Nevertheless, the degree of aid offered by Dearborn officials was fairly limited. Of the more than 15,000 applicants, only 1,657 were placed in a job of any sort. For families lacking a potential breadwinner, such as a mother with dependent children, relief was provided in the form of food, fuel, rent, and hospital care or some other measure. In 1929–1930 alone, 562 families qualified, on the grounds of illness, accident, insanity, alcoholism, and wife desertion.[44] Also, the city council established a soup kitchen (which fed 168 people the day it opened in 1931), issued vouchers for lodging in rooming houses and hotels, and coordinated thrift gardens.[45] Still, the Depression did not abate, and by 1932, the city council was buying food for welfare cases by the carload, causing them to rent an entire warehouse for storage.[46] In the same year, wages for public employees were cut.[47] Drives for private charity were stepped up, and the Dearborn Community Chest raised twenty thousand dollars in 1931.[48] City officials began lobbying for federal aid in the form of loans from the Reconstruction Finance Corporation (RFC),[49] created programs to address the prevention of mortgage foreclosures,[50] and eventually applied for Works Progress Administration (WPA) funds.[51]

Less well off were the African American Ford Motor Company workers living in the outskirts of Dearborn, especially since their community, Inkster, lacked the resources to create effective aid. In fact Inkster, all throughout the 1920s, was less established than Dearborn, featuring minimal development, infrastructure, and municipal services. Historian Howard Lindsey asserts, "It seems that in the rush to flee the over-crowded and dilapidated living conditions in Detroit, the Inkster residents created the same situation they were fleeing. Some people bought existing homes on land plots. Others bought plots with the expectation of building their own homes . . . In the latter case, people built dwellings that were little more than shacks of scrap wood, sheet metal, and tar paper."[52] Lindsey recounted, "One can gauge the desperation of those first settlers to Inkster after Dancy announced the availability of land in the community. . . . Remember that before 1926, Inkster was little more than the name on the map. There was no government as such, because officially the community was not yet incorporated."There were no central water or sewer systems, no streetlamps, perhaps not even streets, and certainly no local police or fire service. "Indeed, this could have been a community of the non-urban South," he concludes. "Except Inkster stood in the shadow of the fourth largest city in the country."[53]

Henry Ford, meanwhile, made some attempts to provide relief for work-ers, especially those concentrated in Dearborn and Inkster. For instance, he donated land for thrift gardens in which workers grew their own food. In Inkster, he ordered housing renovated and had clothing donated. Both former and current employees were eligible for aid dispensed by company social workers. Ford also cooperated with Dearborn's welfare department to hire unemployed workers it referred to him. Actually, in 1932, he insisted that Dearborn remove a proposal for a welfare bill so that needy cases could instead be placed on the company's own relief rolls. Of course, Ford often got something in return for his policies. In the case of the removal of Dear-born's welfare bill, he was assured lower taxes. As for current employees who received subsidies, they paid off this so-called charity through docks on future wages.[54]

In the end, the response by Henry Ford as well as by public officials was simply inadequate, causing frustration among Ford Motor Company wage earners, which resulted in their increased solidarity and desire to agitate. For example, riots at the gates of the River Rouge plant were possible when announcements of hirings were made, as happened in early 1929 and again in the spring of 1930, when the plant was stormed by thousands of job seekers.[55] According to a *New Republic* article, in 1929 men stood in line in zero-degree weather night after night, only to be turned away with fire hoses; in 1930, job seekers smashed the hiring offices. After these incidents, "the police inaugurated a policy of repression. Men were not allowed to start fires to warm themselves; they were prohibited from gathering in groups; they were required to keep moving; if they were in line they had to move quickly to avoid being beaten."[56]

Unemployed workers also began showing up at Dearborn's city council meetings in greater numbers, at first making their demands politely, and later with more force. In 1930, the Polish Citizens' Club, which had a membership of 7,500, sent a request to the city council urging them to get residents hired at local factories; in 1931, a crowd of 200 showed up at a council meeting; and in 1932, this number grew to 800, to the irritation of Mayor Clyde Ford.[57] A newspaper reported that South End resident Michael Milton, affiliated with an unnamed "Detroit worker's organization," stepped forward as spokesper-son at the 1931 meeting, stating that he and his friends had been out of work for over a year. While the hotels and rooming houses had taken care of them so far, they were now on the verge of eviction as they could not pay their accumulated rent debt. He was asking only that the elected officials help find honest work and a place to sleep and eat, and he questioned how could it be that Dearborn's own citizens living outside the factory could not obtain work. On a more inflammatory note, he declared, "It was a shame the richest city in the United States could not do something for them."[58] When Mayor Clyde Ford interrupted him to say relief had been promised the week before, Milton replied, "But we cannot live on empty promises." After the meeting, the mayor complained of the militancy expressed by labor organizers, and he showed reporters a handbill being distributed in Dearborn, stating, "If Henry Ford won't give us jobs, we must take them."[59] A 1931 editorial in one of Dearborn's normally conservative newspapers took on a rather radical tone, stating that, in spite of leading the way with job opportunities at high wages, Dearborn "did not escape the pangs of hunger and destitution." The editorial continued, "The wage earner today is facing a situation unparalleled in American history. . . . Any attempts to cut wages should be discouraged, as it is bound to be reflected by strikes and lockouts as labor, and rightly so, will use whatever means they consider necessary to maintain the present day living standard of the American people."[60]

In the spring of 1932, frustrated workers decided to march on the River Rouge plant to voice demands for rehiring and relief.[61] Although the protest was organized by Communists, the slogans on the signs of most marchers were actually far from revolutionary, calling for pragmatic, commonsense actions: "Open the Rooms of the Y's for Homeless and Youth," "Sign Workers' Unemployment Insurance Bill," "Punish Rich Tax-Dodgers," and "Fight against Dumping of Milk While Babies Starve."[62] As the unarmed protesters crossed over the Detroit border, Ford Motor Company security guards and Dearborn police blocked their way, and a conflict ensued in which four demonstrators were killed by gunfire, mostly at point-blank range, while a few dozen others were injured, with one dying later. A common funeral for the marchers who had been killed followed within a few days. The procession was attended by a massive turnout, with onlookers filling Detroit's streets. This gathering of outraged citizens, though, was only a foreshadowing of the huge AFL- and CIO-led strikes that would overwhelm the automobile industry by the end of the decade.[63]

1941 Walkout at Ford

Labor organizing among Detroit's autoworkers can be said to date from this pivotal incident, the 1932 Hunger March. From this point on, attempts at unionizing Detroit's major industry were characterized by an increasing militancy that became a hallmark of the 1930s everywhere. Now the stage was set for the singular year that turned Detroit into a "union town"—with the notable exception of Ford Motor Company. In late 1936, the city's first sit-down took place at Midland Steel, a supplier of car body frames, where a strike of twelve hundred workers resulted in abolition of piecework wages, a pay raise of ten cents per hour, and recognition of the United Autoworkers (UAW) and its grievance committee. Soon afterward Kelsey-Hayes, a West Side factory of five thousand workers that made automotive brakes, became the next plant organized by the UAW, again using a sit-down, led this time by rising star Walter Reuther of Local 174. After city and county officials refused to send in police, the company reached an agreement with the union, agreeing at first to a seventy-five-cent-an-hour minimum wage and later to overtime pay, seniority rules, and a 20 percent reduction in the speed of the assembly line.[64]

The UAW then turned its sights to automotive giant General Motors (GM), the first of the Big Three to become one of its targets. GM was the most decentralized of the three, so any strike would have to be a coordinated affair—in this case across different states, since the dies for the current model had been placed in two locations, Cleveland and Flint. Once the die shops were closed, dozens of other plants that depended upon them would be compelled to shut down in a domino effect. At the end of December 1936, UAW organizers in the Detroit region received word that a sit-down was underway in the Cleveland die shop; within two days, they kicked off a sit-down at the Flint plant, Fisher One, that would turn out to be of incredible duration and intensity. Quickly, strikes spread to other GM plants, including Fisher Two in Flint; Cadillac in Detroit; Guide Lamp in Anderson, Indiana; Chevrolet and Fisher Body in Janesville, Wisconsin; and Chevrolet in Toledo and Norwood, Ohio. As predicted, the strikes in turn forced the closing of plants dependent on supplies from others, such as Chevrolet, Buick, and AC in Flint; Pontiac in Pontiac; Oldsmobile in Lansing; Ternstedt in Detroit; and Delco-Remy in Dayton, Ohio.

Within the Detroit region alone (Detroit, Pontiac, Lansing, Flint), nine plants and tens of thousands of workers were now under the sway of the UAW. The first thirteen days of the sit-down were peaceful in Flint, as the UAW worked successfully within the legal system to delay an injunction to evacuate the plant. At last, however, police arrived at Fisher Two to evict the strikers and caused a rout in which strikers brought about a retreat of the police by defending themselves with improvised weapons while the police resorted to teargas and eventually guns. Finally, it was time to bring in state troops—but Governor Frank Murphy made the startling decision to deploy them *between* the police and strikers, in order to maintain calm. After weeks of standoff that became the subject of national attention, GM eventually agreed to negotiate, thus bringing an end to the forty-four-day protest by recognizing the UAW as a collective bargaining agent in all seventeen plants where workers had struck.[65]

Labor organizing in Detroit's auto industry was now at a point of high momentum. A month after the GM agreement, the UAW struck Chrysler, pulling off with military precision a simultaneous sit-down in nine plants that again resulted in recognition of the union as a collective bargaining agency. In the meantime, the UAW won agreements at Hudson, Packard, Studebaker, Briggs Body, Murray Body, Motor Products, Timken-Detroit Axle, L.A. Young Spring and Wire, and Bohn Aluminum. The UAW had gained formal recognition from two of the Big Three manufacturers as well as from many smaller car companies. In a matter of months, its membership grew in leaps and bounds, climbing from 3,000 to 35,000 after the GM strike and reaching 245,000 after the Chrysler one.[66]

Then it was time for the UAW to focus its attention on unionizing Ford's Rouge plant in Dearborn.[67] In the spring of 1937, organizers Walter Reuther, J. J. Kennedy, Robert Kantor, and Richard Frankensteen arrived to distribute leaflets at the Rouge. In anticipation of the shift change, they gathered on an overpass at the main entrance of the plant, ready to hand them out to the workers coming and going. They were confident and relaxed, since they had a permit to be there. Nonetheless, Harry Bennett, the head of security at Ford Motor Company, put out an order for the unionizers to be stopped. It was, after all, part of his job to do so, but he had ulterior motives to be vigilant since unionization threatened the racket he was running at the plant—losing control over hirings and firings would mean the end of lucrative bribes for him. As the four activists paused to be photographed by the press, they were approached by a group of Ford Motor Company security guards who outnumbered them. After cursorily ordering them off the property, the guards attacked the organizers by kicking and punching them, even throwing them down the stairs. As Frankensteen testified, four or five men repeatedly knocked him down, then picked him up to knock him down again, eventually bouncing him down the steps of the stairs.[68] Kennedy was so severely beaten he was hospitalized immediately and died four months later.[69] The entire incident was witnessed by the reporters who were there to cover the story. Although the guards tried to grab the photographers' film, one set of photographs was salvaged and published in *Time*. Henry Ford, in a fit of outrage, withdrew his advertising from the magazine. The incident became known as the Battle of the Overpass.

Thereafter, labor organizing within Dearborn faced a unique obstacle since the community now functioned as an increasingly repressive company town.[70] Dearborn was still not a company town in a traditional sense: unlike Pullman or Gary, there was no single patron who owned or developed housing in a monopolistic way. Dearborn was also different from its contemporary, Flint—where wage earners lived and worked in the same place—since those working in Dearborn generally commuted in from Detroit. All the same, Dearborn's city council could be counted on to comply with the requests of Ford Motor Company. Meanwhile, although Henry Ford had formerly run Dearborn from behind the scenes, it appears that by the 1930s, he relinquished such backroom dealings to Bennett, who in turn crossed a line in the continuing relationship between town and company by making the Dearborn council complicit in his own schemes for graft and corruption. For instance, Bennett had the police department hire his own goons from Ford Motor Company, which facilitated his skimming profits from vice operations in the South End. Bennett was able to do this with total impunity—the police were not going to catch him since he had gotten them their jobs and they received kickbacks from these underworld proprietors.[71]

To control the mayor's office, Bennett crudely attempted to manipulate elections by sending thugs on his payroll into neighborhoods to intimidate voters.[72] Bennett was now in a position to exert his influence within the Dearborn government to inhibit labor organizing through legislative means. Shortly after the Battle of the Overpass, the council outlawed the distribution of handbills, which severely limited the efforts of labor organizers. One can only wonder at the role of Henry Ford or Harry Bennett in convincing city hall to propose and pass this illegitimate bill.

Close to four years passed before a drive to organize the River Rouge plant again appeared propitious. Ever since April 1937, when the Wagner Act survived a constitutional challenge, the National Labor Relations Board (NLRB) had ruled repeatedly against the abusing of union activists by Ford Motor Company. Also around this time, Ford Motor Company lost a $10 million defense contract to build trucks because the government refused to condone the company's poor labor record.[73]

At the end of 1940, local judge Lila Neuenfelt bucked the Ford-Bennett political machine to repeal Dearborn's anti-leafleting ordinance. The UAW now had leverage for another campaign on the River Rouge plant, one revived in late 1940 when they brought in Michael Widman from United Mine Workers (UMW) and gave him a local base for operations, with a budget and a staff. This effort was given the boost it needed in February 1941 when Ford Motor Company workers who had been fired for labor organizing were reinstated under an order by the US Supreme Court. Soon after, workers at the River Rouge plant signed up for the union at an exponential rate and began openly wearing their membership buttons at work.[74]

A few months later, on April 1, 1941, an action by Bennett incited what became the turning point at Ford Motor Company when he fired eight members of a grievance committee in the rolling mill. In protest, fifteen hundred workers in that unit initiated a wildcat stoppage. By now a walkout was the only option for the UAW—the US Supreme Court had outlawed the sit-down in 1939, although it upheld the right to picket under a 1940 decision in which Frank Murphy, now a justice, was instrumental.[75] In any case, the stoppage compelled the UAW to make a decision, and within a few hours, they went ahead with an order for a plant-wide walkout of forty thousand workers; workers arriving for the next shift were directed to join the strike; and a picket line was formed by ten thousand workers. In the meantime, about two thousand or so strikebreaking workers, mostly African American, remained inside the plant. Then a multiple-day standoff ensued, in which workers inside the plant, urged to violence by management, emerged twice to attack the picketers.

Overall, though, the strike was peaceful. It was well coordinated by the UAW, which deployed a huge amount of resources quickly and effectively. The strike also attracted tremendous support from the community—a soup kitchen was formed, with many local businesses donating food. The Dearborn police, riddled with Bennett appointees, were replaced by state troops who took over controlling the crowd. The troops were ordered to guard the plant rather than break up the law-abiding picket line. At last, after ten days, Henry Ford capitulated to the union and ended the strike.[76]

In the following weeks, the UAW won a contract that was favorable in many ways, even compared to the groundbreaking agreements already standing between it and other major automakers. For the first time ever, the UAW was allowed to serve as representative of all the plants of a single automaker, even for factories that did not previously have much of a union presence. The UAW was given immediate and exclusive recognition as a collective bargaining agent; as a result, all plants were made closed shops, with dues checkoffs; committee representatives were set up at a ratio of one for every 550 employees, and they were paid full-time by the company with the sole responsibility of working for the union; and finally, security guards that had served under Bennett were curtailed in their powers and required to wear uniforms at all times.[77] Henry Ford was the last of the Big Three automakers to resist unionization. Although his about-face on the issue of the union can never be fully explained, it is likely he accepted that change had become inevitable. Ford, however, did not live to see much of what followed from the rise of the union, as within six years he died at age eighty-four.

Conclusion

At the center of the Ford Motor Company strike was not just the empowerment of wage earners to demand better working conditions but also their right as Americans to a decent standard of living. The sense of entitlement that spread among workers is clear in the slogans on the signs carried by picketers—such as "Unionism is Americanism," "Make Dearborn a part of the United States," "Union way means higher pay," and "Happy homes for our children." These signs asked not just for a living wage but for one that conformed with the aspirations of an exceptional nation.[78] That unionization was seen as connected to the American dream is also apparent in the rhetoric of UAW leaders, especially as expressed by Walter Reuther, who became president in 1946. As he pointed out, the purpose of the UAW extended beyond the shop floor to bring workers a high standard of living, advancing "the interests and welfare of its members and their families," working as "a responsible member of the community," and attempting to "improve the quality of life for all the people."[79] It must, Reuther concluded, "set an example for the nation and people everywhere of the democratic promise in a free society." Generally, Reuther connected the individual rights of workers with the need to make communities stronger. He referred to the need for a steady income as "more than a matter of economic justice to the wage earner . . . it is a matter of economic necessity to our nation, for freedom and unemployment cannot live together in democracy's house."[80] In fighting for a high standard of living, Reuther was motivated by the vision of a new social contract that would turn America into a true democracy.

On this topic, Reuther was not too far away from the philosophy of Henry Ford, who decades earlier had observed that democracy cannot operate where there is widespread inequity—that without economic freedom, there can be no political freedom. In Ford's own words: "The principles upon which we live together as a nation and out of which we have reared our great free institutions shall operate in industry also."[81] Of course, to Ford, "economic liberty" meant not just high wages but also the right to work, free of unionism. Still, Reuther and Ford were on the same page in terms of the need to give workers a right to consumption, leisure, and ultimately economic security if they were to contribute to, rather than undermine, a democratic society. They both recognized that democracy requires a citizenry that is informed and able to participate, which is not possible if every waking hour of one's life is concentrated on survival; that the equality promised by democracy rang hollow while extreme differences in income prevailed; and finally, that workers disgruntled by poverty could easily be seduced by authoritarian political systems that promise security in place of freedom.

In addition, this high standard of living was reinforced by recently created federal entitlement programs that became the basis of a modern welfare state. Thus, Fordism was forced to transform, and from now on, business partnered with labor and government to maintain living standards for workers. As a result, wage earners were able to resume similar patterns of earning, consumption, and leisure as before, and high-end laborers again merged with an expanding middle class. This trend was clearly evident in Dearborn, whose indicators of well-being soon exceeded the national average. From 1940 to 1950, the population doubled, reaching ninety-five thousand, while homeownership approached 75 percent and car ownership stood at close to two automobiles per household.[82] In the process of buying houses and cars and moving to the suburbs, however, workers continued to change American patterns of settlement, hastening the abandonment of Detroit and other cities, whether intentionally or not.

Dearborn itself had changed during this time. For more than two centuries this had been a pioneer settlement of early explorers that later became a small farm-market community, and it eventually added some low-level industries, all overshadowed by the nearby city of Detroit. Its growth was incremental, and for much of its history it belonged to a preindustrial age. With the arrival of Henry Ford, Dearborn grew overnight into a world-renowned center of manufacturing. Its residential section prospered, establishing Dearborn as a new kind of all-American hometown, with middle-class comfort for everyone. Prior to the Great Depression, Dearborn was the last place one would expect the massive labor action that resulted in unionizing the Ford Motor Company, or any of the unrest leading up to it, including pleas at town hall meetings demanding assistance for the unemployed using federal aid, if needed. After all, these problems seemed like ones that should be contained to major cities. So, although Dearborn recovered more quickly than Detroit after the Depression, it would never again be the same. In the decades to come, it would confront the rise of civil rights, the entry of women into the workplace, the decline of the nuclear family, an influx of non-European immigrants, and rising tensions between cities and suburbs as the urban crisis escalated—among the many social issues facing it and the rest of the country.

7

Detroit Metropolis after Henry Ford

FOR THE MOST PART, the UAW succeeded in assuring automobile workers a standard of living fit for Americans, and in doing so its leaders hoped
to set an example that would help wage earners all over the world. In fact,
Detroit became one of the most prosperous cities in the nation during the
postwar period, with soaring wages and high rates of home- and car ownership. Of course, the UAW did not do this alone, as by now it was aligned
with policies adopted by both government and business. In this tripartite
arrangement, capital and labor, mediated by the state, worked together to
create not a socialized economy but a planned one in which the extreme
cycles of boom and bust were softened and both profits and wages followed
somewhat predictable courses. This relationship was possible because of
some longtime trends. For instance, the desire to create a planned economy
was one of the motivations behind the New Deal, whose leaders wished to regulate capitalism in order to save it. New Dealers also claimed for Americans
a standard of living that was the basis for Roosevelt's critique of one-third of
a nation "ill-nourished, ill-clad, ill-housed" as well as his promotion of the
Four Freedoms and an Economic Bill of Rights.[1] Meanwhile, the programs
that came out of the New Deal—such as mortgage standardization, unemployment compensation, and pensions—formed the foundation of the new
welfare state. These policies also served to reinforce the bargaining strength
of the UAW when negotiating for wages and benefits.[2]

As for the incentive for business to partake in a partnership for a planned
economy, business leaders felt that fewer unexpected expenses would make
their enterprises more profitable in the long run. On this point, they supported unionization because it was a form of containing labor. Bargaining
with representatives over contracts, for example, was easier than dealing
with disruptive wildcat strikes. Industrialists had their own Fordist reasons

to improve conditions for workers on and off the job, which was also helpful. After all, they wanted to continue linking mass production and mass consumption through high wages in order to assure performance and profitability. As Alfred Sloan, head of GM, wrote of his company's relationship with the UAW, "I think the fact that our workers benefit on a definite and prescribed basis, resulting in an increase in their standard of living, gives us a more sympathetic cooperation."[3] Henry Ford and the other carmakers likely agreed.

Surely Dearborn and other working-class suburbs benefited tremendously from the partnership of capital, labor, and government. Dearborn was never quite the same after the 1930s, however, at least on a political level. As the suburb entered the postwar period, it would soon face challenges as tensions over residential integration grew stronger, and while it never became home to many African Americans, it eventually welcomed non-European immigrants, becoming one of the largest Muslim-dominated Middle Eastern communities in the United States. Among its autoworker residents, labor activism remained part of the social fabric, which was another break from the area's demographic profile of previous decades. However, in the immediate aftermath of the Depression, Dearborn recovered well economically, taking on a quick resemblance to its previous self as the prosperous community envisioned by Henry Ford, where all residents could aspire to the middle class. As early as 1939, the Ford Foundation announced plans for Dearborn in the form of Springwells Park, a subdivision like the Ford Homes, intended to create middle-market housing with ownership opportunities. Given that Edsel Ford, Henry's son, was granted the lead on this project, it can be interpreted as a preservation of Dearborn as an ideal community for a new generation of workers pursuing high standards of living.

Implications for Cities and Suburbs

Largely because of the tripartite relationship between labor, capital, and the state, Detroit experienced a period of relative peace and plenty from 1945 to 1965.[4] In 1953, the city reached its all-time peak in population, totaling close to 2 million inhabitants.[5] This was due in part to the arrival of a second wave of Great Migration African Americans, which caused blacks as a percentage of the Detroit population to vault from 9 percent in 1940 to five times that by 1970.[6] The downtown experienced a construction boom, as the first new buildings were put up since before the Depression. Publicly subsidized projects that helped transform this area included the city-county building, the Ford Auditorium, the Cobo Hall and Arena, a veterans' memorial, and

Lafayette Park, a middle-class housing development. A network of modern expressways was overlaid on the metropolitan landscape, cutting silver paths through dense urban neighborhoods and stretching uninterrupted into outlying communities. The *National Observer* reported glowingly on the "freshness and vitality" in the Detroit metropolis, noting the "acres of slums" that had been razed and replaced by "steel-and-glass apartments," while "severely rectangular skyscrapers [jostled] uncomfortably with the gilded behemoths of another age." Regarding the purchases of new cars and houses, the author remarked, "Accustomed to years of adversity, to decades of drabness and civic immobility, Detroiters are naturally exhilarated."[7]

The automobile industry shifted into high gear to satisfy pent-up consumer demand that had not been met during war rationing: in 1949 automobile sales topped 5 million, shattering the record set twenty years earlier, and in 1955 the breakneck production pace contributed to sales cresting at 8 million.[8] Auto manufacturing became the most prosperous of major industries, with annual rates of return at least twice as great as in all manufacturing corporations and lasting from 1947 to 1967.[9] Throughout Detroit, unions played an important role in passing on to workers a share of the economic miracle; the percentage of union households in the city was 60 percent in 1945, double the national average. Aggressive negotiating, particularly by the UAW, meant that workers now enjoyed wages 40 percent higher in real dollars than at the end of the war, plus gains continued to be made in non-wage benefits like pensions, health plans, sick pay, life insurance, disability coverage, and paid vacations. Overall, Detroit workers took home an average wage of $98 a week, well above the national average for manufacturing, which was only $75.[10]

One of the most dramatic changes brought about by the new tripartite alignment was a cresting wave of suburbanization. The government contributed to this trend through policies that widened the population eligible for mortgages; business gave incentives to move out of the city by decentralizing its plants; and the union demanded wages that enabled its members to become homeowners. Actually, this pattern paralleled the one from the 1920s, as again it was the migration of industry, the mobility of automobile drivers, and the empowerment of high wages—combined with the privilege of race—that provided incentive for relocation. As a result, the Detroit metropolitan district came to include seven counties, as its boundaries were expanded by a spreading, and ever larger, population (see figure 13).[11] Within this region, the suburbs of Wayne, Macomb, and Oakland Counties alone (referred to hereafter as the tri-county area) witnessed a 225 percent increase in population as the number of residents leapt from 1.2 to 2.7 million between 1950 and 1970.[12]

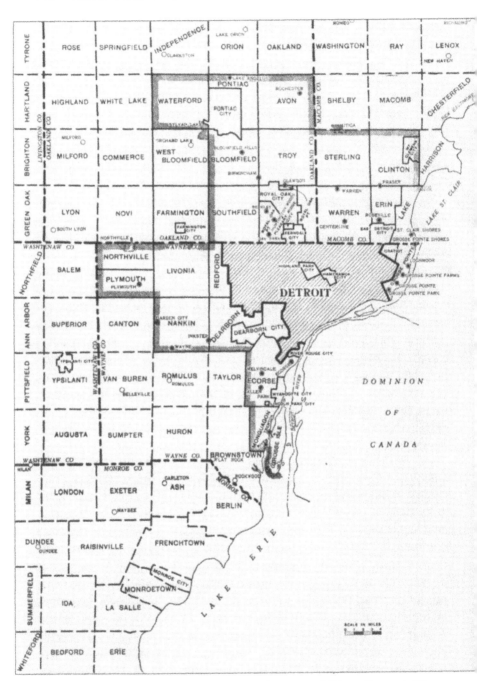

FIGURE 13. Map of Detroit Metropolitan Area, 1940 (University of Chicago, Regenstein Library, Map Collection)

Working-class whites were moving to the suburbs in greater numbers than ever before. From 1947 to 1955, the Big Three built twenty new factories in the Detroit area employing seventy thousand workers, all outside the city. Workers resettled near the plants, their ability to buy houses boosted by the G.I. bill and VA mortgages and their commutes eased by hundreds of miles of newly constructed highways. Relocation away from the downtown was led by ethnic groups who migrated along corridors of urban development as they followed opportunities for jobs and housing: Italian and German Americans moved outward along Gratiot into Harper Woods and East Detroit; Polish Americans from Hamtramck moved north into Warren and surrounding communities; and members of the Jewish community moved north and west from the Dexter–Davison–12th Street area into Southfield and Oak Park. Of the 260,000 new homes built in the metropolis in the 1950s, nearly all were built in the suburbs, contributing to a massive population shift. At the center of this suburban construction boom was the 1950 Northland shopping mall, billed as America's first "regional" shopping center.[13] Suburban communities that attracted the most residents were those with factories from World War II or later, such as Warren, Birmingham, Livonia, and Centerline, and the townships of Sterling and Romulus.[14] As an example of the scale of this migration, Warren alone grew from 700 residents to 179,000 from 1950 to 1970.[15]

Jobs as well as housing opportunities were relocating to the suburbs in this period, and this shift was especially evident in the industrial sector: while manufacturing employment outside Detroit grew from 295,800 to 329,700 between 1958 and 1963, the amount of manufacturing within the city as a percentage of the metropolis fell by half between 1948 and 1967.[16] The wartime development of suburban factories had demonstrated the advantages of moving to locations where taxes and wages were lower. These sites also showed how much easier it was to assemble large parcels of land outside the city for building sprawling single-story facilities that better accommodated modern production methods, including automation. As early as 1940, the *Detroit Free Press* reported enthusiastically on the prospects of this brave new world, crediting the "migration of thousands of families from blighted urban areas to more attractive home sites [to] federal loaning agencies and liberal private financing institutions." The reporter continued to comment on "gigantic manufacturing industries," some with defense contracts, that also located to the suburbs. After all, "beyond the city limits [there is] little traffic congestion, land is cheap, and taxes low."[17] Eventually, many manufacturing jobs left the Detroit metropolis altogether, headed for the other Rust-belt cities, where they would be close to steel production, or for the Sunbelt, where unions were either less likely or less militant. Later in the 1970s and 1980s, some jobs formerly located in the Detroit metropolis left the country entirely to go overseas.

Corridors of Growth By 1940, the outward migration of Detroit residents leaving the city to follow jobs in the automobile industry and other sources of employment meant the metropolitan area outside the central city now featured nineteen incorporated communities of four thousand people or more in size. These suburbs were clustered in four major corridors: (1) Woodward Avenue to the north, which contained Birmingham, Royal Oak, Berkley, Ferndale; (2) Michigan Avenue to the west, which contained Dearborn, Inkster, and Plymouth; (3) Downriver, which contained Melvindale, Lincoln Park, Trenton, Ecorse, River Rouge, and Wyandotte; and (4) the Northeast Shore, which contained Grosse Pointe, Grosse Pointe Park, Mt. Clemens, St. Clair Shores, Roseville, and East Detroit.[18]

These corridors can be further subdivided by land use and by the status of residents in terms of class and race. For example, the residential blue-collar suburb was a place that in terms of population had more blue-collar residents than white-collar ones, yet as its land use was primarily residential instead of industrial, the blue-collar residents there commuted to jobs elsewhere. This type of suburb was by far the most common, comprising ten of the nineteen metropolitan communities: Royal Oak, Berkley, Ferndale, Mt. Clemens, St. Clair Shores, Roseville, East Detroit, Plymouth, Melvindale, and Lincoln Park. The residential blue-collar suburb could be found in each of the four corridors.

In comparison, Woodward Avenue and the Northeast Shore corridors contained the only white-collar suburbs. By definition, the white-collar suburb contained more white-collar residents than blue-collar ones and land use was predominately residential, and there were three of these: Grosse Pointe, Grosse Pointe Park, and Birmingham.

Meanwhile, the other two corridors, Michigan Avenue and Downriver, were characterized by a mixture of industry and residences. Also, only these corridors held industrial blue-collar suburbs and African American suburbs. The industrial blue-collar suburb had a majority of blue-collar residents, but it was different from the residential suburb in that it contained a significant amount of industry within its boundaries. This suburban type was also distinctive in having a relatively high percentage of foreign-born whites and industrial workers, averaging 28 percent and 16 percent respectively. There were three industrial blue-collar suburbs found outside Detroit: Dearborn, Wyandotte, and Trenton. Their land use and population composition made them comparable to the suburbs within the city, Highland Park and Hamtramck. So in total, there were five industrial blue-collar suburbs. Dearborn made the Michigan Avenue corridor further remarkable as its population contained the highest percentage of foreign-born whites at 21 percent.

Finally there was the African American suburb where, although they were never the majority, African Americans made up a noteworthy percentage of the population, ranging from 14 to 39 percent, as exemplified in Ecorse, River Rouge, and Inkster. The population of the African American suburb furthermore had the greatest percentage of industrial workers at an average of 32 percent. As the land use of the African American suburb varied from primarily residential (as in the case of Inkster) to primarily industrial (Ecorse and River Rouge), these workers were either employed within their community or commuted elsewhere.

The residential blue-collar suburb was the most common in Detroit's metropolitan area, with a total of ten suburbs, more than twice as many as any other. The frequency of this type resulted from the relocation from the city to the suburbs of industrial workers who, more often than not, chose communities without industry instead of those with it. On the other hand, suburbs that contained industry generated the largest communities in terms of population size. In 1940, four of the industrial blue-collar suburbs had fairly substantial populations—Highland Park (50,810), Hamtramck (49,839), Wyandotte (30,618), and Dearborn (63,584)—while the fifth, Trenton, had a relatively small population (5,284). In contrast, the residential blue-collar suburb averaged a population size of approximately 12,000. Taking together the residents of all Detroit's industrial blue-collar suburbs, their population (200,135) totaled more than one and a half times the number who lived in residential blue-collar suburbs (119,612). As during the 1920s, the movement of industry, as much as the migration of workers, was an important factor in the suburbanizing of the metropolitan area. Also like previous decades, patterns of segregation by class and race were established anew.

Despite much progress, the suburbanization of housing and job opportunities in the postwar period meant the increasing exclusion of African Americans. Although racially restrictive housing deeds were struck down by the US Supreme Court in 1948, new barriers arose, such as the redlining policies by the Federal Housing Administration (FHA), which prevented many blacks from qualifying for mortgages.[19] Despite this, African Americans were able to migrate outward to some extent, as long as it was to neighborhoods within the city limits, and by 1960 they formed a significant presence in twice as many of the city's census tracts as they had in the previous decade.[20] Still, the housing they obtained was often outdated or in disrepair.

This problem was made worse by wartime shortages, and one 1944 study revealed that over half of all dwelling units occupied by African Americans was substandard, while only 14 percent of white-occupied housing was in this classification. The situation persisted even after the war was over, and a 1948 report stated that 43 percent of black veterans' families lived "doubled-up or in rented rooms, trailers or tourist cabins."[21] Meanwhile, although housing was better in the suburbs, there was a long list of outlying communities from which African Americans were effectively barred: Dearborn, Royal Oak Township, Troy, East Detroit, the Grosse Pointes, Hazel Park, Ferndale, Madison Heights, Sterling Heights, Southfield, Redford Township, Westland, Farmington, Allen Park, Melvindale, Lincoln Park, Birmingham, Livonia, Fraser, Warren, Oak Park, and others.[22]

The hardship faced by many African Americans in finding transportation to suburban jobs was also combined with discriminatory hiring practices that prevented their employment opportunities from expanding in accordance with the economic upswing.[23] It was still difficult for black automobile workers to break into the skilled trade positions, where they made up only 3 percent or less of workers.[24] The relationship between the UAW and its African American constituency was an imperfect one. The union was less than competent at making civil rights a reality throughout its organization, and although racial equality was always highlighted in the policies of union leaders, bigotry was commonplace among rank-and-file members. Part of the problem was the distinct culture that existed at each Detroit auto manufacturing plant: depending on the hiring strategies of employers before unionization, some factories relied on a labor force that was almost entirely white, while others, like the Rouge, had a notable African American presence. During wartime mobilization, when a second wave of Great Migration from the South took place, blacks and whites came into more contact on the shop floor, which heightened tensions, and the worst conflicts took place in plants that had been historically white. A typical problem was the "hate strike," whereby white workers walked off the job when blacks were assigned to work with them, a practice the union condemned and eventually managed to stop. After the war was over, however, many blacks were displaced from their jobs by returning white veterans, and in contending with these discriminatory practices, UAW leaders were often ineffectual.[25] Finally, although African Americans made strides in climbing the ladder within union leadership, overall they remained underrepresented well into the postwar period, and for this they criticized the UAW.[26] Overall, the black unemployment rate stayed consistently higher than that for whites. Between 1948 and 1985, the unemployment rate for black males ranged from a low of 1.5 times that of white males to as much as 4.0 times as high. This trend was even more evident among the autoworkers.[27]

Springwells Park

Even as working-class communities became more common throughout the Detroit metropolis, benefiting from the decades-long trend of suburbanization, Dearborn remained both typical and exceptional. It was the prototype of this trend as well as its epitome, and in the postwar period, it remained as strong as ever. It recovered quickly from its stint experiencing the nation's economic downturn and a period of historic labor unrest, taking on again its previous qualities as an all-American hometown for workers. For example, looking back to the decade of the 1920s, Dearborn had doubled its physical size and multiplied its population ten times over, increasing from five thousand to fifty thousand. During the same decade, the number of Ford Motor Company workers living in Dearborn started as three hundred residents, then expanded to half the employed residents throughout the whole community. Dearborn featured the greatest number of manufacturing jobs compared to nearby suburbs, constituting close to a quarter such job in the whole metropolis.[28] This astonishing rate of growth was attempted again in the postwar period, but on a smaller scale. Dearborn's population doubled from 1940 to 1950, totaling ninety-five thousand residents—not quite the tenfold increase of the 1920s but still ranking it as one of Detroit's largest suburbs. Autoworkers remained a large component of the population, with sixty-five thousand workers at the River Rouge plant, of which twenty thousand lived in Dearborn. Also in this decade, more than eleven thousand houses were built, and the homeownership rate was higher than ever, approaching 75 percent. Dearborn's automobile registrations grew by 60 percent, and the car ownership rate measured close to two automobiles per household. Lastly, Dearborn's assessed valuation leapt from $215 million in 1940 to $376 million in 1950, compared to $163 million shortly after consolidation in 1929.[29]

To strengthen Dearborn further Edsel Ford stepped forward to continue the legacy of his still-living father, Henry, who overshadowed him professionally. At the time Edsel Ford was kept as nominal president of Ford Motor Company, where despite Edsel's passion for all things automobile-related, Henry still controlled everything. However, Edsel managed to find an identity for himself as head of the Ford Foundation (started in 1936), where he gained greater latitude in this family-run foundation, collaborating with both his parents, Henry and Clara, on charity interests that they shared. In 1939, the Ford Foundation announced its plan for Springwells Park, and since Edsel headed the foundation, there is no doubt he favored this project (see figure 14). It would be sited on land that had been in the Ford family since 1915. The plan was for a large-scale development of 132 acres accommodating sixteen hundred people that would contain a variety of residences and a shopping center, located on the road to the local airport. The housing stock was to be a mix of owner-occupied lots and rental units, designed at a fairly high density, with an assortment of single-family and two-family houses, townhouses, and multi-unit apartment buildings. A total of 230 owner-occupied lots and 450 rental units was projected, to be built in multiple phases, with the first lots offered for sale in 1940. In step with modern

FIGURE 14. Aerial Photo of Springwells Park ("Philanthropy Starts a Subdivision," *Freehold*, June 1941)

times, all apartment units came with air conditioning and electric garbage disposals, and single-family houses came with garages. Housing of all sorts would be clustered together on winding cul-de-sacs to preserve open space and leave room for gardened landscapes and walkways. Undeveloped Ford-owned land surrounded the subdivision, further serving as a buffer of wildlife and nature. In 1955, an elementary school was added, through the successful petitioning of residents.[30]

As an indicator of what had changed in Dearborn, it is useful to compare the Springwells Park subdivision with the Ford Homes district from nearly two decades earlier. To start, the site planning of Springwells Park—with its picturesque curves and pastoral appearance—purposefully picks up details of Leonard Willeke's predecessor plan for the Ford Homes district, called Fordson Village, which at the time was deemed infeasible (see figure 15). The Fordson Village plan, as first proposed, was to include single-family, double-family, and four-family houses; open space was to be preserved by setting aside no more than half the land for houses; the village center would feature a mix of municipal and commercial buildings; and transportation would be provided by automobile boulevards and a railroad station. In contrast, houses in the Ford Homes district were square, blocky, and solid, laid out in an evenly spaced grid, with little room for landscaping along the street or room for public parks and playground. While charming and cozy as individual houses, the Ford Homes do look somewhat urban when taken together. The return to Willeke's plan must have been some kind of decision worked out together by members of the Ford family: Edsel was only twenty-five around the time that Willeke was first hired, and there is no evidence he was in charge of the Ford Homes the way Henry was. Despite the years that had passed, Willeke's holistic approach to community planning—creating an instant neighborhood with a mix of residences and commercial uses—was now even more on trend.[31] However, Willeke was not directly involved any more, and the task of site planning was taken up by Ford Motor Company engineer Ralph Taylor, who became one of Springwells Park's first homeowners.[32]

Another difference was the mix of housing options. Springwells Park offered a majority of rental units while Ford Homes offered none, as the houses were intended to be owner-occupied only. Springwells Park offered much smaller housing units, some as modest as two-room studios, while the Ford Homes houses were consistently larger, averaging two stories and containing three bedrooms. In other words, the Ford Homes houses were intended for large, stable families taking up long-term, possibly permanent, residence in Dearborn while Springwells Park could accommodate various

FIGURE 15. Map of Fordson Village (University of Michigan, Bentley Historical Library, Willeke Collection)

configurations of households that were small in size. Aesthetically, the housing in Springwells Park featured a stripped-down, boxy Colonial style repeated in a somewhat monotonous way across the subdivision, lacking the beautiful finishes, textured materials, and architectural details that made the Ford Homes so attractive and different from each other. As for the audience to which these neighborhoods were marketed, Springwells Park advertised to the general public while the Ford Homes were initially available only to Ford Motor Company employees. In both places, the owner-occupied housing was intended for middle-class residents seeking affordability and value in a private-sector market and was not intended to provide subsidized housing for poor people. In Springwells Park, the apartment buildings remained under the ownership and management of the Ford Foundation, and a homeowners association formed in 1941 maintained a strong relationship with the foundation.[33] Also, in both Springwells Park and the Ford Homes, the residential demographic was entirely white, which was in keeping with the rest of Dearborn. In the example of the Ford Homes, this was ensured through a screening process undertaken by Ford Motor Company as it handpicked the employees eligible for buying houses. As for Springwells Park, the houses came with racially restrictive deeds attached, likely mandated by the Ford Foundation, which barred races other than whites from living there.[34]

The 2010 population data for Springwells Park feature many of the demographic trends nascent when the project was first proposed by Edsel Ford.[35] The population is about 85 percent white, which is not surprising given the tone that was set early on with restrictive deeds and the racial tensions that ensued in Dearborn during the Civil Rights period. Although this kind of deed was later struck down in a landmark Supreme Court case, it was not easy to reverse in one instant a longtime trend of discrimination, so Springwells Park remained majority white even after integration began its deliberate pace.[36] Today, the 15 percent of residents who are not white are split about equally between African American, Asian American, and Hispanic American. Households in size are a little smaller in Springwells Park (2.2 people) than in the rest of Dearborn (3.1 people), and they are more likely to consist of married couples with children in Springwells Park (over a third) than in Dearborn (about a quarter), suggesting that these are starter homes. The variety of housing stock is remarkably preserved, with the same ratio of rentals and owner-occupied units as originally. The availability of rentals also implies households that are a little less established, as does the frequency of small-sized units, consisting of one-, two-, or three-room apartments.[37] Altogether, the Springwells Park of today is not completely dissimilar to the one envisioned in 1939, a conclusion based upon analyzing the housing stock and the sort of residents who needed this. The original residents of the community were likely to be a mix of single people and young families, and the single people were either living alone in the smallest of units or were in roommate arrangements. Either way, the community of Springwells Park as envisioned by Edsel Ford was intended to serve a different purpose from that of Ford Homes, conceived by Henry Ford. It seemed targeted to a more transient, mobile generation of workers, overall more like the residents of Dearborn to come.

Mixed Legacy

The suburbanization of Detroit first advocated by Henry Ford was now being furthered by a new generation. Nonetheless, it is worth asking how differently this was done in the postwar era, especially by the three major actors involved: labor, capital, and the state. It is clear what the government and business gained from the suburbanization of residences and jobs—a docile and productive workforce, whose members were assured of a major investment in the homes they owned and would be averse to any unrest because of their dependence upon a single, somewhat isolated, employer. The racial segregation of the central city and its suburbs was actually seen as an advantage to those in power—especially real estate lenders—since they perceived it as ensuring stability. It also provided a handy excuse for employers who did not want the effort of integrating workplaces. Plus, taxes were lower in the suburbs, which appealed to business, and there were fewer municipal services to provide, which made the job of politicians easier.

Less obvious is what the UAW gained in promoting suburbanization, which in turn raises the question of whether its members did this at all actively or consciously. On one hand, the high standard of living for which the union negotiated certainly empowered workers to afford locating in suburbs. During World War II, the union proposed a program of satellite cities to manage suburban growth and to enable workers of all races to live near plants that were decentralizing.[38] A reference to this is made in a 1944 policy statement that acknowledged the trend for people "of all income levels to move to outlying areas for convenience to their employment in industry," noting the improvements that made it "possible for city dwellers to escape from the increasingly bad living conditions within the city."[39] Also, despite controversy over reliance on mechanization rather than craft, the union considered promoting prefabricated housing that was more affordable for wage earners.[40]

For the most part, however, the UAW was dedicated to a sharp critique of the unplanned metropolitan growth responsible for uneven housing and job opportunities in the suburbs and divestment in the central city. The same policy statement declared this "one of the major problems facing the country in the post-war period." Its authors explained, "The twin processes of rapid unplanned growth and unorganized decentralization [result in] large areas of blight and slum. . . . As the movement from the cities takes place the new areas develop, become congested, and repeat most of the old maladies of the city. . . . The character of the areas is usually so weak and unstable as to create belts of incipient blight around our cities. . . . They are also the source of slums for the future."[41] The solution was the creation of an "economically sound and socially desirable living environment for millions of our own citizens."[42]

A more extreme example of the UAW's skepticism about suburbanization was its opposition to "Operation Runaway," as it dubbed the Ford Motor Company's plan to decentralize its plants.[43] By 1955, the company's total labor force was two hundred thousand, but increasingly these jobs were at factories other than in Dearborn, its center of production since the mid-1920s. During this time, Ford Motor Company, at a cost of $2.5 billion, developed new plants in the Detroit suburbs of Birmingham, Livonia, and Ypsilanti; in the Rustbelt cities of Cleveland, Buffalo, Canton, and Cincinnati; and in the more far-flung cities of St. Louis, Atlanta, Kansas City, and Los Angeles.[44] As a result, employment at the Rouge fell from eighty-five thousand in 1945 to fifty-four thousand in 1954 to only thirty thousand in 1960.[45] In order to draw public attention to the issue of decentralization and the job losses entailed, UAW's Dearborn chapter, known as Local 600, repeatedly confronted Ford Motor Company, at times without the support of the international union.[46] In 1951, in an effort to reduce layoffs through job sharing, the local chapter called for a thirty-hour week at forty hours' pay and filled the lobby of the international union's headquarters with thirty thousand petitions to this effect but their concerns were dismissed.[47] In the same year, Local 600 gained the symbolic support of many blue-collar suburbs who passed resolutions against the decentralization of plants—among these communities were Dearborn, Ecorse, Garden City, River Rouge, and Melvindale. Also around this time, in an otherwise festive and light-hearted Labor Day parade, members of the local carried militant signs such as "Support Our Fight against Job Runaway."[48]

Finally, later on that year, in its most quixotic attempt to stem the loss of jobs, Dearborn's Local 600 brought a lawsuit against Ford Motor Company, claiming breach of contract. The case was thrown out.[49] Members of the local chapter were, however, able to mobilize the international union on their behalf in some minor ways, whose leaders "negotiated areawide transfer rights for workers displaced by plant closures and made certain that new job classifications generated by new technology did not erode the general wage structure."[50] In the end, Local 600 was a "lonely voice against deindustrialization," in the words of historian Thomas Sugrue.[51] Without major backing from the international union, the metropolitan business community, and locally elected officials, there was little the Dearbornites could do to reverse the stream of job losses as plants relocated.

Regarding the UAW's stance on suburbanization, perhaps the most accurate assessment that can be made is simply that it lacked a consistent policy on such a complex issue. After all, the union had to respond to more than one constituency among its members. The leaders themselves were of different persuasions, and progressives among them worried less where the housing was located than whether it was affordable. Toward this end, they promoted anything from public housing to cooperatives to privately owned houses, from multi-unit buildings to row houses to single-family detached houses, as well as housing built by traditional methods or prefabricated—all were up for discussion and often hotly debated.[52] In the meantime, at the rank-and-file level, white workers voted with their feet by moving to the suburbs in droves, while black workers were relegated to the central city by means both de facto and de jure. In the end, the suburbanization of Detroit remains one of the mixed legacies of the UAW.

Conclusion

Ultimately, the rise of suburbs like Henry Ford's Dearborn was on many levels to the detriment of Detroit, for it created a permanent rift in black-white relations, hastened residential flight and economic divestment, and demoralized many citizens in the city and suburbs alike. Still, it is worth stating that the 1967 riot was a symptom rather than a cause of the city's plunge into dysfunctionality during the 1970s and 1980s. After all, the reason for Detroit's decline was multifaceted, with many components in place long before the 1960s, and although not all factors can be analyzed here, a few obvious ones can be named. One factor was the lack of planning for the Detroit metropolitan area that resulted in the much-cited lack of diversity of the central city's economic base, focused almost exclusively on automobile manufacturing. A city with little to balance out its dependency on a single industry was bound to experience disruptions just from the cyclical nature of production alone. These downturns, although inevitable, were nonetheless difficult to anticipate, which in turn made it challenging to manage the city in a proactive way. The harsh impact of the economic cycle became evident in the periodic recessions that struck Detroit even during the height of its prosperity in the postwar period.

More important, the lack of a diverse economy meant that, when manufacturing increasingly left the city and eventually the region, there was little to take up the slack. Even going back to the 1920s, the growing presence of Ford Motor Company and the rest of the Big Three outside Detroit meant that the central city not only lacked economic diversity but was losing out on future opportunities for jobs and housing. Although the trend to deindustrialize did not manifest until the 1950s and 1960s, the interwar period can be seen as a time of *underindustrialization:* industrialization was still taking place in the central city, but its pace began to lag behind that of the suburbs. The ongoing flight of capital attracted concern from officials and activists, who time and again called for intervention. Although comprehensive metropolitan plans were repeatedly proposed by citizens' groups—and at one point, by the UAW and its Dearborn chapter—nothing was implemented successfully.[53] On the other hand, some policies put into place only made matters worse, such as redlining by the mortgage lenders; government subsidization of suburban factories; and urban renewal and highway development that, notoriously, destroyed neighborhoods.

During the postwar period, a complex relationship among the automobile industry, its unions, and various urban development policies determined the fate of Detroit and its suburbs, including Dearborn. The intersection of these forces—first set in motion by Henry Ford and his peers—brought about unprecedented prosperity for the white working class, who gained new access to social and economic upward mobility, symbolized by the prize of suburban residence. African Americans, however, were denied these opportunities, even as they became an ever-increasing portion of the population. Dearborn is a case in point, since many African Americans worked there yet were excluded residentially from the Ford Homes, Springwells Park, and the rest of the community. Meanwhile, the decrease in manufacturing jobs through relocation and automation meant that all workers, regardless of race, were bound to experience some hardship. Yet, as Detroit lost residents and employers and a new pattern of racial segregation emerged, these disturbing trends were ignored since their consequences were not yet costly.

Initially, suburbs like Dearborn benefited from this trend, but eventually their tax base shrank as well, once jobs began leaving under "Operation Runaway." In the meantime, opportunities to enforce existing guidelines for fair housing and employment, to implement metropolitan planning, to diversify the economy, and to develop a model for cooperative rather than competitive regional industrial growth were all lost. Also missed was a chance for management and labor to work together with policy makers on these issues. So, even during its golden postwar period, the Detroit metropolitan area was simultaneously a "blue-collar El Dorado" and a place of "slippery gains," where superficial prosperity masked deepening economic divides and where the tokenist advancement of African Americans hid an endemic injustice.[54] By the 1970s and 1980s, these problems only worsened, bringing about a scale of devastation reminiscent of wartime to a city once known as "Detroit, the Dynamic."

Notes

Epigraph quotation is from Henry Ford, "An Ideal Realized," *Ford Times* 6, no. 9 (June 1913): 366.

Introduction

1. For the high wages of the Ford Motor Company, see Stephen Meyer, *The Five Dollar Day* (Albany: State University of New York Press, 1981); Hooker, *Life in the Shadows*; Asher and Edsforth, *Autowork*; Nelson Lichtenstein and Stephen Meyer, eds., *On the Line: Essays in the History of Auto Work* (Urbana: University of Illinois Press, 1989); Roediger, "The Limits of Corporate Reform"; Peterson, *American Automobile Workers*; David Gartman, *Auto Slavery: The Labor Process in the Automobile Industry, 1897-1950* (New Brunswick: Rutgers University Press, 1986).

2. Nevins and Hill, *The Times, the Man, the Company*, 452.

3. Ibid., *Expansion and Challenge*, 200–216.

4. "Prices Cut on All Ford Houses in Dearborn," *Ford News* 1.16 (June 15, 1921): 4, 8.

5. "The Ford Plan," advertisement (box 24, acc. 572, Benson Ford Research Center's Ford Archives at the Henry Ford Museum [hereafter BFRC]), 11–12.

6. Henry Ford, *Ford Ideals* 1, *Being a Selection from "Mr. Ford's Page" in The Dearborn Independent* (Dearborn Publishing, 1926), 157.

7. Henry Ford, quoted in Tarbell, "Every Man a Trade," 79.

8. By "de jure" segregation, I mean racism that has been institutionalized through legislative or judicial means; for example, the use of housing deeds to dictate the race of persons ineligible to purchase a house, which was common in the Detroit area. By "de facto" segregation, I refer to the everyday practice of discrimination perpetrated by individuals. In extreme examples, this might result in the harassment of racial minorities who moved into residential neighborhoods that were predominantly white. Detroit's Ossian Sweet situation is a case in point, in which a black family had their house surrounded by neighbors threatening violence. For more on Ossian Sweet, see Boyle, *Arc of Justice*.

9. US Bureau of the Census, *Fifteenth Census of the United States, 1930*. Refer especially to the Sanborn maps, city directories, tax assessment rolls, subdivision plats, and real estate deeds.

10. Joseph Arnold, *The New Deal in the Suburbs* (Columbus: Ohio State University Press, 1971), 11–12.

11. US Bureau of the Census, *Metropolitan Districts*, 3. See also US Bureau of the Census with Warren Thompson, *Population: The Growth of Metropolitan Districts*. "Metropolitan" as a category of urban development was first used by the US Bureau of the Census

in 1910. Metropolitanization was of immediate interest to many social scientists, such as McKenzie, author of *The Metropolitan Community*, as well as Harris, "Suburbs"; Douglass, *The Suburban Trend*; Mumford, "The Fourth Migration"; and Graham Taylor, *Satellite Cities*.

12. Leo Schnore, *The Urban Scene: Human Ecology and Demography* (New York: Free Press, 1965), 80. See also Blake McKelvey, *The Emergence of Metropolitan America, 1915–1966* (New Brunswick: Rutgers University Press, 1968); Charles Glaab, "Metropolis and Suburb: The Changing American City," in *Change and Continuity: The 1920s*, eds. John Braeman et al. (Columbus: Ohio State University Press, 1968); Amos Hawley, *The Changing Shape of Metropolitan America: Deconcentration since 1920* (Glencoe: Free Press, 1956).

13. Robert Fishman, "The Metropolitan Tradition in American Planning," in *The American Planning Tradition*, ed. Robert Fishman (Baltimore: Johns Hopkins University Press, 2000).

14. This process is known as "embourgeoisement." For related literature, see Lizabeth Cohen, "Encountering Mass Culture at the Grassroots: The Experience of Chicago Workers in the 1920s," *American Quarterly* 41.1 (March 1989): 6–33; Ronald Edsforth, *Class Conflict*. See also T. J. Jackson Lears, *Fables of Abundance: A Cultural History of Advertising in America* (New York: Basic Books, 1994); Clair Brown, *American Standards of Living*; James R. Barrett, "Americanization from the Bottom Up," 996–1020; Martha Olney, *Buy Now, Pay Later: Advertising, Credit, and Consumer Durables in the 1920s* (Chapel Hill: University of North Carolina Press, 1991); Robert Whaples, "Winning the Eight-Hour Day," 393–406; David Roediger and Philip S. Foner, *Our Own Time*; Roland Marchand, *Advertising the American Dream: Making Way for Modernity, 1920–1940* (Berkeley: University of California Press, 1985); Martha May, "Bread before Roses."

15. Kenneth Jackson, *Crabgrass Frontier: The Suburbanization of the United States* (New York: Oxford University Press, 1985). For the expansion of the working class into suburbs, see Borchert, "Cities in the Suburbs," 211–27; Kruse and Sugrue, *The New Suburban History*; Wiese, *Places of Their Own*; Lewis, *Manufacturing Suburbs*; Becky Nicolaides, *My Blue Heaven*; Harris and Lewis, "The Geography of North American Cities," 262–93; Wunsch, "The Suburban Cliché," 643–58; Barbara Kelly, ed., *Suburbia Re-examined* (New York: Greenwood Press, 1989); Richard Harris, "American Suburbs: A Sketch of a New Interpretation," *Journal of Urban History* 15 (1988): 98–103; Carol O'Connor, "The Suburban Mosaic: Patterns of Land Use, Class, and Culture," in *American Urbanism: A Historiographical Review*, eds. Howard Gillette and Zane Miller (New York: Greenwood Press, 1987); Joel Schwartz, "The Evolution of the Suburbs," in *American Urban History*, ed. Alexander Callow (New York: Oxford University Press, 1982).

16. Rupert, *Producing Hegemony*. For more on Fordism, see Richard Florida and Marshall Feldman, "Housing in U.S. Fordism," *International Journal of Urban and Regional Research* 12.2 (June 1988): 187–88; Charles Maier, *In Search of Stability* (Cambridge University Press, 1987); Hounshell, *From the American System*; Piore and Sabel, *The Second Industrial Divide*; Michel Aglietta, *A Theory of Capitalist Regulation* (London: New Left, 1979); Antonio Gramsci, "Americanism and Fordism," *Selections from the Prison Notebooks of Antonio Gramsci* (New York: International, 1971).

17. Harvey, *The Condition of Postmodernity*.

18. For the increasing population of postwar suburbs as well as resultant social, economic, and political issues, see Bruegmann, *Sprawl: A Compact History*; Nicolaides and Wiese, *The Suburb Reader*; Freund, *Colored Property*; Lassiter, *The Silent Majority*; Kruse, *White Flight*; Harris, *Creeping Conformity*; Gregory Randall, *America's Original GI Town*:

Park Forest, Illinois (Baltimore: Johns Hopkins University Press, 2000); Barbara Kelly, *Expanding the American Dream: Building and Rebuilding Levittown* (Albany: State University of New York Press, 1993); Barry Checkoway, "Large Builders, Federal Housing Programs, and Postwar Suburbanization," *International Journal of Urban and Regional Research* 4.1 (March 1980): 21–45; Herbert Gans, *The Levittowners: Ways of Life and Politics in a New Suburban Community* (1967; New York: Columbia University Press, 1982); Bennett Berger, *Working-Class Suburb: A Study of Auto Workers in Suburbia* (Berkeley: University of California Press, 1960); Harold Wattel, "Levittown: A Suburban Community," in *The Suburban Community*, ed. William Dobriner (New York: G. P. Putnam's Sons, 1958).

19. Cowie and Heathcott, *Beyond the Ruins*.

20. The best overviews of Detroit are Zunz, *The Changing Face of Inequality*; and Robert Conot, *American Odyssey* (New York: William Morrow, 1974). See also Sharoff, *American City*; Thompson, *Whose Detroit?*; Woodford, *This Is Detroit*; Thomas, *Redevelopment and Race*; Eckert, *Buildings of Michigan*; Thomas, *Life for Us Is What We Make It*; Fine, *Violence in the Model City*; Joe Darden et al., *Detroit: Race and Uneven Development* (Philadelphia: Temple University Press, 1987); Steve Babson, *Working Detroit: The Making of a Union Town* (New York: Adama, 1984); Ticknor, "Motor City"; David Allan Levine, *Internal Combustion: The Races in Detroit, 1915–1926* (Westport: Greenwood Press, 1976); Melvin Holli, ed., *Detroit* (New York: New Viewpoints, 1976).

21. Ticknor, "Motor City," 201–4. Ticknor bases this and the following statistics on census data for population and manufacturing.

22. The population of the metropolis in 1920 was 1,252,909; in 1930, it was 2,104,764; and in 1940, it was 2,295,867. Thompson, *Whose Detroit?* See also US Bureau of the Census (Batschelet); US Bureau of the Census, *Sixteenth Census of the United States, 1940*.

23. Ticknor, "Motor City," 201–4.

24. In 1940, 36 percent of Detroit's manufacturing was in its suburbs, and 23 percent of its residential population was suburban (ibid., 204).

25. US Bureau of the Census, *Fifteenth Census of the United States, 1930*; Nevins and Hill, *Expansion and Challenge*, 687; Paul Reid, *Industrial Decentralization, Detroit Region, 1940–1950 (Projection to 1970)* (Detroit Metropolitan Area Regional Planning Commission, 1951), 3–4.

26. Ticknor, "Motor City," 198–205.

27. Ibid., 185–205.

28. Vertical integration simply meant that new economies of scale could be attained because a single company owned everything in its supply chain, from semi-finished products to the rawest of materials. Thanks to vertical integration, mass production of unimaginable proportions was suddenly possible. This streamlining was further facilitated by the creation of a standardized product (in which parts were interchangeable) and by use of the assembly line (in which workers performed repetitive tasks). The cost savings achieved through this process simultaneously raised the wages of workers and lowered the price of consumer products. Ultimately, this meant that mass production was now connected to mass consumption—the defining characteristics of "Fordism."

29. Nevins and Hill, *Expansion and Challenge*, 202–10, 687.

30. Brinkley, *Wheels for the World*.

31. Nevins and Hill, *Expansion and Challenge*, 459.

32. Thomas Sugrue, "'Forget about Your Inalienable Right to Work': Deindustrialization and Its Discontents at Ford, 1950–1953," *International Labor and Working-Class*

History 48 (1995): 112–30; Kent Trachte and Robert Ross, "The Crisis of Detroit and the Emergence of Global Capitalism," *International Journal of Urban and Regional Research* [Great Britain] 9.2 (1985): 186–217; Dan Luria and Jack Russell, *Rational Reindustrialization: An Economic Development Agenda for Detroit* (Detroit: Widgetripper, 1981); Richard Child Hill, "At the Cross Roads: The Political Economy of Postwar Detroit," *Urbanism Past and Present* 6 (1978): 1–21; Melvin Holli, "Detroit Today: Locked into the Past," *Midwest Quarterly* 19.3 (1978): 251–59.

33. US Bureau of the Census, *Sixteenth Census of the United States.* The population of the city in 1900 was 285,704; in 1920, it was 993,675; and in 1940, it was 1,623,452.

34. Melvin Holli, ed., *Detroit* (New York: New Viewpoints, 1976), 119.

35. *Detroit City Directory, 1925–1926*, in *Detroit and the Great Migration, 1916–1929* (Ann Arbor: Bentley Historical Library, 1993), 4.

36. Ticknor, "Motor City," 287–88. Some automotive jobs were lost from Detroit to other states as well as to the city's suburbs.

37. "Dearborn Michigan Market Report: Growth and Population," Vertical File, Dearborn Historical Museum (hereafter VF.DHM).

38. I use the term "American dream" as a way to connect concerns from the period about standard of living and Americanization among workers. The term also comes up frequently in literature about the automobile industry, its workers, and its product. See Ely Chinoy, *Automobile Workers and the American Dream* (Garden City: Doubleday, 1955); Stevenson, *Selling the Dream*; Richard Feldman and Michael Betzold, *End of the Line: Autoworkers and the American Dream* (New York: Weidenfield and Nicolson, 1988); Emma Rothschild, *Paradise Lost: The Decline of the Auto-Industrial Age* (New York: Random House, 1973). See also Bennett Berger, *Working-Class Suburb: A Study of Auto Workers in Suburbia* (Berkeley: University of California Press, 1960).

39. Katie Turner, "Henry Ford: A Life," review of *Henry Ford* by Vincent Curcio, H-SHGAPE, H-NET Reviews, October 2013, https://www.h-net.org/reviews/showrev.php?id=39607.

40. Roger Lowenstein, *The Crank That Set the World Rolling*, review essay, *Wall Street Journal*, May 10, 2013.

41. Dimitry Anastakis, review essay, *Business History Review* 82.1 (April 2008): 119–26. For more, see the seminal trilogy written by Allan Nevins and Frank Ernest Hill in the 1950s and 1960s, which provided the fundamentals for any scholarship that followed: *Ford: The Times, the Man, the Company* (New York: Scribner, 1954); *Ford: Expansion and Challenge, 1915–1933* (New York: Scribner, 1957); and *Ford: Decline and Rebirth, 1933–1962* (New York: Scribner, 1963).

42. Of the Big Three automakers, Ford Motor Company was the only one to decline a federal bailout in the 2008 recession.

43. Watts, *The People's Tycoon*; Bak, *Henry and Edsel*; Neil Baldwin, *Henry Ford and the Jews: The Mass Production of Hate* (New York: Public Affairs, 2001); Carol Gelderman, *Henry Ford: The Wayward Capitalist* (New York: The Dial Press, 1981).

44. Nevins and Hill, *Expansion and Challenge*, 202–10, 500–507, 687.

45. For more on the history of the automobile industry, see Brinkley, *Wheels for the World*; David Farber, *Sloan Rules: Alfred P. Sloan and the Triumph of General Motors* (Chicago: University of Chicago Press, 2002); Rubenstein, *Making and Selling Cars*; Davis, *Conspicuous Production*; John B. Rae, *The American Automobile Industry* (Boston: Twayne, 1984); Richard Crabb, *Birth of a Giant: The Men and Incidents That Gave America the*

Motorcar (Philadelphia: Chilton, 1969); Alfred Chandler, ed., *Giant Enterprise: Ford, General Motors, and the Automobile Industry* (New York: Harcourt Brace, 1964).

46. Nevins and Hill, *The Times, the Man*, 117, 169, 175–90, 206–14, 235–48.

47. Ibid., 387, 470–73, 496–97, 512; Nevins and Hill, *Expansion and Challenge*, 202–10, 687.

48. Nevins and Hill, *Expansion and Challenge*, 270–79.

Chapter 1: The Urban Plans of Henry Ford

1. Martha Banta, *Taylored Lives: Narrative Productions in the Age of Taylor, Veblen, and Ford* (Chicago: University of Chicago Press, 1993); David Nye, *Henry Ford: "Ignorant Idealist"* (Port Washington, NY: Kennikat Press, 1979); David Lewis, *The Public Image of Henry Ford: An American Folk Hero and His Company* (Detroit, Wayne State University Press, 1976); Reynold Wik, *Henry Ford and Grass-Roots America* (Ann Arbor: University of Michigan Press, 1972); Keith Sward, *The Legend of Henry Ford* (New York: Rinehart, 1948).

2. For interwar suburbs, see also Robert Fogelson, *Bourgeois Nightmares: Suburbia, 1870–1930* (New Haven: Yale University Press, 2005); John Stilgoe, *Borderland: Origins of the American Suburb, 1820–1939* (New Haven: Yale University Press, 1988); Michael Ebner, *Creating Chicago's North Shore: A Suburban History* (Chicago: University of Chicago Press, 1988); Margaret Marsh, *Suburban Lives* (New Brunswick: Rutgers University Press, 1990); Marc Weiss, *Rise of the Community Builders: The American Real Estate Industry and Urban Land Planning* (New York: Columbia University Press, 1987); William H. Wilson, *Coming of Age: Urban America, 1915–1945* (New York: Wiley and Sons, 1974); Joseph Arnold, *The New Deal in the Suburbs* (Columbus: Ohio State University Press, 1971); Paul Conkin, *Tomorrow a New World: The New Deal Community Program* (Ithaca: Cornell University Press, 1959).

3. Drew Pearson, "Ford Predicts the Passing of Big Cities and Decentralizing of Industry," *Motor World* 80 (August 28, 1924): 9.

4. Recent works about this appeal to a general audience: Vincent Curcio, *Henry Ford* (Oxford University Press, 2013); Richard Snow, *I Invented the Modern Age: The Rise of Henry Ford* (New York: Scribner, 2013); *Henry Ford*, American Experience documentary film, PBS, 2013. All were released in 2013 to coincide with the centenary of the assembly line.

5. Within this work, Henry Ford will sometimes be referred to by his last name only, as "Ford." Ford Motor Company, however, will always be called just that. So to clarify, when readers see the word "Ford," they should assume this means Ford the man, not the company. At times a discussion about Henry Ford will also delve into policies he created within the company or communication channels he controlled, such as company newsletters, marketing pieces, or journalistic publications. Because Ford was in a position of power, it seems logical to assume that company policies or communication channels under his influence expressed his own values and beliefs—even when the authorship of these ideas is only indirectly attributed to him or for publications that were ghostwritten. After all, who would presume to oppose him? For more on this problem of attribution, see Gib Pettyman, "Criticism, Business, and the Problem of Complicity: The Case of Henry Ford," *Interdisciplinary Literary Studies: A Journal of Criticism and Theory* 2 (Fall 2000): 49–66.

6. Captains of industry had long justified their actions by arguing for the greater good they created, in a system called "paternalism." See Sanford Jacoby, *Masters to Managers* (New York: Columbia University Press, 1991); Nikki Mandell, *The Corporation as Family: The Gendering of Corporate Welfare, 1890–1930* (Chapel Hill: University of North Carolina Press, 2002); Marc Eisner, *From Warfare State to Welfare State: World War I, Compensatory State-Building, and the Limits of the Modern Order* (University Park: Pennsylvania State University Press, 2000); Roland Marchand, *Creating the Corporate Soul: The Rise of Public Relations and Corporate Imagery in American Big Business* (Berkeley: University of California Press, 1998); Andrea Tone, *The Business of Benevolence: Industrial Paternalism in Progressive America* (Ithaca: Cornell University Press, 1997); H. M. Gitelman, "Welfare Capitalism Reconsidered," *Labor History* 33.1 (1992): 5–31.

7. US Bureau of the Census, *Fifteenth Census of the United States, 1930.* Refer especially to the Sanborn maps, city directories, tax assessment rolls, subdivision plats, and real estate deeds.

8. *Ford News*, a company newsletter for workers, is a good example of a publication controlled by Henry Ford. The purpose of this newsletter was to educate and inform workers about company policies, including programs to make cars and houses affordable. The newspaper *Dearborn Independent*, in the period from 1919 to 1927, was owned by Ford and circulated nationally, which elevated it from its previous incarnation as just another local paper. As for other venues, Ford was able to commission some ghostwritten autobiographies that conveyed his views on the world, such as *My Life and Work*, co-authored by Samuel Crowther (Garden City, NY: Doubleday, Page & Co., 1922).

9. Ford Bryan, *Beyond the Model T: The Other Ventures of Henry Ford* (Detroit: Wayne State University Press, 1990); Carolyn Loeb, "Entrepreneurial Vernacular: Developers' Subdivisions in the 1920s" (PhD diss., City University of New York, 1990); Thomas Brunk, *Leonard B. Willeke: Excellence in Architecture and Design* (Detroit: University of Detroit Press, 1986); archival material (acc. 47, BFRC); David Good, "The Ford Homes," unpublished paper, 1975 (DHM), 5–7; "Builders with Brains Plus Courage Create an Ideal Colony for Workers," *Dearborn Independent* (Dec. 6, 1919): 8–9; "Rents Down! Savings Up! Homes Easy!" *Dearborn Independent* (Dec. 13, 1919): 12; "Prices Cut on All Ford Houses in Dearborn," *Ford News* 1.16 (June 15, 1921): 4, 8; "Ideal Suburban Home in Dearborn Ford Subdivision," *Ford News* 2.9 (March 1, 1922): 3.

10. US Bureau of the Census, *Sixteenth Census of the United States, 1940.* The population of the city was 285,704 in 1900, then 993,675 in 1920, and reached 1,623,452 in 1940.

11. Schnore, *The Urban Scene*, 80. See also McKelvey, *The Emergence of Metropolitan America*; Glaab, "Metropolis and Suburb"; Hawley, *The Changing Shape of Metropolitan America.*

12. For more on metropolitanism, see Fishman, "Metropolitan Tradition"; Jeremiah Axelrod, *Inventing Autopia: Dreams and Visions of the Modern Metropolis in Jazz Age Los Angeles* (Berkeley: University of California Press, 2009); Robert Lewis, *Chicago Made: Factory Networks in the Industrial Metropolis* (Chicago: University of Chicago Press, 2008); Richard Dennis, *Cities in Modernity: Representations and Productions of Metropolitan Space, 1840–1930* (Cambridge University Press, 2008); Jon Teaford, *The Metropolitan Revolution: The Rise of Post-urban America* (New York: Columbia University Press, 2006); Greg Hise, *Magnetic Los Angeles: Planning the Twentieth-Century Metropolis* (Baltimore: Johns Hopkins University Press, 1997); David Ward and Olivier Zunz, eds., *The Landscape*

of Modernity: New York City, 1900–1940 (New York: Russell Sage, 1992); William Cronon, *Nature's Metropolis* (New York: W. W. Norton, 1991).

13. Nevins and Hill, *Expansion and Challenge*, 202–10, 687.

14. For "Fordism" in urban development, see Harvey, *The Condition of Postmodernity*; Michael Storper and Richard Walker, *The Capitalist Imperative: Territory, Technology, and Industrial Growth* (Oxford: Blackwell, 1989); Mark Gertler, "The Limits of Flexibility: Comments on the Post-Fordist Vision of Production and Its Geography," *Transactions of the Institute of British Geographers* 13 (1988): 419–32; N. Albertson, "Postmodernism, Post-Fordism, and Critical Social Theory," *Environment and Planning D: Society and Space* 6 (1988): 339–65; Richard Florida and Marshall Feldman, "Housing in U.S. Fordism," *International Journal of Urban and Regional Research* 12.2 (June 1988): 187–210; E. Schoenberger, "From Fordism to Flexible Accumulation: Technology, Competitive Strategies, and International Location," *Environment and Planning D: Society and Space* 6 (1988): 245–62; Allen Scott and Michael Storper, eds., *Production, Work, Territory* (Boston: Allen and Unwin, 1986); Neil Smith, *Uneven Development: Nature, Capital, and the Production of Space* (New York: Blackwell 1984); Richard Walker, "A Theory of Suburbanization: Capital and the Construction of Urban Space in the United States," in Michael Dear and Allen Scott, eds., *Urbanization and Urban Planning in Capitalist Societies* (London: Methuen, 1981).

15. For deindustrialization, see Cowie and Heathcott, *Beyond the Ruins*; Steven High, *Industrial Sunset: The Making of North America's Rust Belt, 1969–1984* (Toronto: University of Toronto Press, 2003); Jon Teaford, *Cities of the Heartland: The Rise and Fall of the Industrial Midwest* (Bloomington: Indiana University Press, 1993); Roger Friedland, *Power and Crisis in the City: Corporations, Unions, and Urban Policy* (New York: Schocken Books, 1983); Barry Bluestone and Bennett Harrison, *The Deindustrialization of America: Plant Closings, Community Abandonment, and the Dismantling of Basic Industry* (New York: Basic Books, 1982).

16. For more on the urban crisis, see Thomas Sugrue, *Origins of the Urban Crisis: Race and Inequality in Postwar Detroit* (Princeton, NJ: Princeton University Press, 1996); Kevin Boyle, "The Ruins of Detroit: Exploring the Urban Crisis in the Motor City," *Michigan Historical Review* 27.1 (2001): 109–27; Eric Arnesen, Nancy Gabin, Jacqueline Jones, Judith Stein, and Joe Trotter, "Symposium on Thomas J. Sugrue: The Origins of the Urban Crisis," *Labor History* 39.1 (1998): 43–60; Robert Beauregard, *Voices of Decline: The Postwar Fate of U.S. Cities* (Cambridge: Blackwell, 1993); The Urban Institute, *Confronting the Nation's Urban Crisis: From Watts (1965) to South Central Los Angeles (1992)* (Washington: The Urban Institute, 1992); Jon Teaford, *The Rough Road to Renaissance: Urban Revitalization in America, 1940–1985* (Baltimore: Johns Hopkins University Press, 1990); M. Gottdiener, ed., *Cities in Stress: A New Look at the Urban Crisis* (Beverly Hills: Sage, 1986).

17. Susan Hirsch, *After the Strike: A Century of Labor Struggle at Pullman* (Urbana: University of Illinois Press, 2003); Eric Clements, *After the Boom in Tombstone and Jerome, Arizona: Decline in Western Resource Towns* (Reno: University of Nevada Press, 2003); Linda Carlson, *Company Towns of the Pacific Northwest* (Seattle: University of Washington Press, 2003); William Littmann, "Designing Obedience: The Architecture and Landscape of Welfare Capitalism, 1880–1930," *International Labor and Working-Class History* 53 (1998): 88–114; Margaret Crawford, *Building the Workingman's Paradise: The Design of American Company Towns* (London: Verso, 1995); Paul Krause, *The Battle for Homestead, 1880–1892: Politics, Culture, and Steel* (Pittsburgh: University of Pittsburgh Press, 1992);

Crandall Shifflett, *Coal Towns: Life, Work, and Culture in Company Towns of Southern Appalachia, 1880–1960* (Knoxville: University of Tennessee Press, 1991).

18. Bryan, *Beyond the Model T*; Loeb, "Entrepreneurial Vernacular"; Brunk, *Leonard B. Willeke*; archival material (acc. 47, BFRC).

19. Mumford, "The Fourth Migration"; Frank Lloyd Wright, *The Future of Architecture* (New York: Meridian, 1981), 191; Carol Aronovici, "Suburban Development," in *Housing and Town Planning*, ed. Carol Aronovici, *Annals of the American Academy of Political and Social Science* 51 (Philadelphia: American Academy of Political and Social Science, 1914); William Bailey, "The Twentieth Century City," *American City* 31.2 (August 1924): 142–43; *Slums, Large-Scale Housing, and Decentralization*, eds. John Gries and James Ford (Washington, DC: President's Conference of Home Building and Home Ownership, 1932), 197–98; President's Research Committee on Social Trends, *Recent Social Trends in the United States* (New York: McGraw-Hill, 1933), xxii.

20. For more on the company towns of Henry Ford, see David Lewis, "The Rise and Fall of Old Henry's Northern Empire," *Cars and Parts* (December 1973): 90–97; Howard P. Segal, *Recasting the Machine Age: Henry Ford's Village Industries* (Amherst: University of Massachusetts Press, 2005); Greg Grandin, *Fordlandia: The Rise and Fall of Henry Ford's Forgotten Jungle City* (New York: Metropolitan Books, 2009); Littell McClurg, "Seventy-Five Mile City," *Scientific American* 127 (Sept. 1922): 156–57.

21. For more on the industrial suburb, see especially the work of Robert Lewis (editor of the anthology *Manufacturing Suburbs*) who co-wrote the lead article in a special issue of *Journal of Historical Geography*; Richard Walker and Robert Lewis, "Beyond the Crabgrass Frontier: Industry and the Spread of North American Cities, 1850–1950," *Journal of Historical Geography* (Great Britain) 27.1 (2001): 3–19. See also Edward K. Muller, "Industrial Suburbs and the Growth of Metropolitan Pittsburgh, 1870–1920," ibid., 58–73; Richard Walker, "Industry Builds the City: The Suburbanization of Manufacturing in the San Francisco Bay Area, 1850–1940," ibid., 36–57; Richard Harris and Robert Lewis, "Constructing a Fault(y) Zone: Misrepresentations of American Cities and Suburbs, 1900–1950," *Annals of the Association of American Geographers* 88.4 (1998): 622–39; Borchert, "Cities in the Suburbs."

22. Nevins and Hill, *Expansion and Challenge*, 202.

23. In describing Dearborn prior to the consolidation of 1929, this study includes Springwells, which was later named Fordson. While the proposal for consolidation happened in 1927 and the vote took place in 1928, it was not put in effect until 1929.

24. Julia Moore, "History of the Dearborn Area" (unpublished paper, Bentley Library, University of Michigan, 1957).

25. Most workers of all races commuted in from either Highland Park (the site of Ford's previous plant) or Detroit, and to a lesser extent from other suburbs such as Royal Oak to the northeast, Melvindale and Lincoln Park to the south, and Inkster to the west. For more on the location of Ford workers, see a study conducted by the Detroit Street Railways in 1925 to determine the feasibility of future routes to the River Rouge plant. "5000 Workers Petition for Northwest Belt Line," *Detroit News*, Jan. 25, 1925; clippings, "D.S.R. Making Oakman Study," *Detroit News*, Feb. 1925, "Figures Show Where Ford's West Side Workers Live," *Detroit News*, April 1925, "Northwestern and Other Lines to Open May 1," *Detroit News*, 1925 (clipbook, BFRC); "New D.S.R. Line Nearly Done," *Detroit News*, March 8, 1925. For a comparison of where Ford workers lived in the 1910s, see a map assembled

by the company's Sociological Department in 1917, "Map of the City of Detroit" (box 31, acc. 572, BFRC).

26. Henry Ford, letter to public, *Dearborn News*, June 9, 1928.

27. Organization, "Dearborn Facts and Figures" (pamphlet, 1927), 1, City of Dearborn, History File (hereafter HF.DHM).

28. Julia Moore, "History of the Dearborn Area," 243.

29. Walt Clyde, "Henry Ford's Home Town," *Dearborn Magazine* 1.1 (1926): 2 (HF. DHM).

30. "The Inside Story of Henry Ford," *Dearborn Magazine* 1.1 (1926): 3.

31. "Greater Dearborn: The Consolidation Story," unpublished paper, n.d. (City of Dearborn, Consolidation, HF.DHM), 1–9; Saul Shiefman, "Ever Hear of Dearson?" unpublished paper, 1954 (City of Dearborn, Consolidation, HF.DHM), 1.

32. Julia Moore, "History of the Dearborn Area," 299–306; Fordson Board of Commerce, "Fordson, Michigan: Western Gateway to Detroit" report, 1927 (City of Fordson, HF.DHM), 2–11.

33. Joseph Karmann, oral history (DHM), 4.

34. Fordson Board of Commerce, "Fordson, Michigan," 2–11.

35. Iris Becker, oral history (DHM), 150.

36. Albert Ammerman, "A Sociological Survey of Dearborn" (master's thesis, University of Michigan, 1940), 57–58.

37. Becker, oral history, 74–75 (quote), 149.

38. Karmann, oral history, 4, 13, 17, 18.

39. Ford, letter to public, *Dearborn News*, June 9, 1928.

40. Joseph Cardinal, speech, Feb. 3, 1966 (DHM), 5.

41. "Consolidation Committee . . . ," *Fordson Independent*, Sept. 2, 1927; Julia Moore, "History of the Dearborn Area," 245.

42. "Greater Dearborn," 1–9.

43. Save Dearborn Association, editorial, *Dearborn Press*, May 17, 1928.

44. "Greater Dearborn," 1–9.

45. Consolidated Cities Association, pamphlet, City of Dearborn, Consolidation (HF.DHM).

46. "Ideal Suburban Home in Dearborn Ford Subdivision," *Ford News* 2.9 (March 1, 1922): 3.

47. "Rents Down! Savings Up! Homes Easy!" *Dearborn Independent* (Dec. 13, 1919): 12.

48. "Citizenship," *Ford News* 3.3 (Dec. 1, 1922): 2.

49. Ford, *Ford Ideals*, 296.

50. Henry Ford [attributed], *The International Jew: The World's Foremost Problem*, reprint of articles appearing in the *Dearborn Independent* (Dearborn Publishing, 1920), 175.

51. Ford, *Ford Ideals*, 157.

52. Ibid., 408.

53. Pearson, "Ford Predicts the Passing of Big Cities," 9.

54. "Prices Cut on All Ford Houses in Dearborn," *Ford News* 1.16 (June 15, 1921): 4, 8.

55. "Ideal Home Not in Crowded City," *Ford News* 1.9 (March 1, 1921): 1, 8.

56. "The Ford Plan," advertisement (box 24, acc. 572, BFRC), 11, 4.

57. Tarbell, "Every Man a Trade," 79.

58. *Ford Times* 6.9 (June 1913): n.p.

59. "Luxury or Necessity," *Ford News* 3.19 (Aug. 1, 1923): 2.

60. Ibid.

61. "Out Beyond the Car Lines," advertisement (file O, 1925, box 4, acc. 19, BFRC).

62. Susan Hirsch, *After the Strike: A Century of Labor Struggle at Pullman* (Urbana: University of Illinois Press, 2003); Eric Clements, *After the Boom in Tombstone and Jerome, Arizona: Decline in Western Resource Towns* (Reno: University of Nevada Press, 2003); Linda Carlson, *Company Towns of the Pacific Northwest* (Seattle: University of Washington Press, 2003); Littmann, "Designing Obedience"; Paul Krause, *The Battle for Homestead, 1880–1892: Politics, Culture, and Steel* (Pittsburgh: University of Pittsburgh Press, 1992); Crandall Shifflett, *Coal Towns: Life, Work, and Culture in Company Towns of Southern Appalachia, 1880–1960* (Knoxville: University of Tennessee Press, 1991).

63. Edward Greer, "Monopoly and Competitive Capital in the Making of Gary, Indiana," *Science and Society* 40.4 (1976–1977): 468.

64. Crawford, *Building the Workingman's Paradise*.

65. Segal, *Recasting the Machine Age*; John Mullin, "Henry Ford Field and Factory: An Analysis of the Ford Sponsored Village Industries Experiment in Michigan, 1918–1941," *Journal of the American Planning Association* 48.4 (1982): 419–31; Bryan, *Beyond the Model T*, 45–58.

66. Howard Segal, "'Little Plants in the Country': Henry Ford's Village Industries and the Beginning of Decentralized Technology in Modern America," *Prospects* 13 (1988): 181–223.

67. Mullin, "Henry Ford Field and Factory," 424–25.

68. Ibid., 422.

69. Nevins and Hill, *Expansion and Challenge*, 229.

70. *Ford News*, 16.4 (April 1936): 65–66, 75.

71. David Lewis, "The Rise and Fall of Old Henry's Northern Empire," *Cars and Parts* (December 1973): 90–97; Nevins and Hill, *Expansion and Challenge*, 218–20.

72. Grandin, *Fordlandia*, 61.

73. David Lewis, "Northern Empire," 91.

74. Bryan, *Beyond the Model T*, 118–29.

75. Brian Cleven, "Henry Ford's 'Tasty Little Town': Life and Logging in Pequaming," *Michigan History* 83.1 (1999): 18–23; David Lewis, "Northern Empire," 94, Bryan, *Beyond the Model T*, 122.

76. Preston Hubbard, *Origins of the TVA: The Muscle Shoals Controversy, 1920–1932* (New York: Norton and Vanderbilt University Press, 1961); Nevins and Hill, *Expansion and Challenge*, 305–11; Bryan, *Beyond the Model T*, 57; Grandin, *Fordlandia*, 65.

77. Littell McClung, "Seventy-Five Mile City," *Scientific American* 127 (Sept. 1922): 156–57.

78. Bryan, *Beyond the Model T*, 57.

79. Ibid.

80. Grandin, *Fordlandia*; Mary Dempsey, "Fordlandia," *Michigan History* 78.4 (1994): 24–33; Bryan, *Beyond the Model T*, 151–62; Nevins and Hill, *Expansion and Challenge*, 231–38.

81. Bryan, *Beyond the Model T*, 157.

82. Grandin, *Fordlandia*, 28–31, 233.

83. Ibid., 316–19.

84. Bryan, *Beyond the Model T*, 157–59.

85. Henry Ford, "Progress Reflected by City's High Standards," *Dearborn Press*, May 21, 1931.

86. For the connection of yeoman farmers and artisans to citizenship, see scholarship on the antebellum period: Paul A. Gilje, ed., *Wages of Independence: Capitalism in the Early American Republic* (Madison House, 1997); Howard B. Rock, Paul A. Gilje, and Robert Asher, eds., *American Artisans: Crafting Social Identity, 1750–1850* (Baltimore: Johns Hopkins University Press, 1995); Stephanie McCurry, *Masters of Small Worlds: Yeoman Households, Gender Relations, and the Political Culture of the Antebellum South Carolina Low Country* (New York: Oxford University Press, 1995); David Montgomery, *Citizen Worker: The Experience of Workers in the United States with Democracy and the Free Market during the Nineteenth Century* (Cambridge University Press, 1993); Jeanne Boydston, *Home and Work: Housework, Wages, and the Ideology of Labor in the Early Republic* (New York: Oxford University Press, 1990).

Chapter 2: Suburbs and the Working Class

1. Ford, *Ford Ideals*, 157.

2. E. G. Liebold, correspondence, 1919 (box 1, acc. 47, BFRC).

3. US Bureau of the Census, *Fifteenth Census of the United States, 1930*.

4. As noted by many scholars and contemporaries, Detroit was characterized by a distinct lack of tenements and featured instead a landscape of single-family detached houses. See Zunz, *Changing Face of Inequality*.

5. US Bureau of the Census, *Fifteenth Census of the United States, 1930*.

6. This observation is based on randomized sampling of the 1930 manuscript census. I also compared the list of managers and professionals appearing in Ford Bryan's *Henry's Lieutenants* (1993) against Dearborn and Detroit directories. Ford Bryan, *Henry's Lieutenants* (Detroit: Wayne State University Press, 1993).

7. These categories are based on how subjects self-identified in the 1930 manuscript census. Those listed in the census as laborers, I refer to as "unskilled"; those listed as machinists, machine operators, or operatives, I call "semi-skilled"; and anyone with a title that indicated a higher level of training, such as millwright, electrician, patternmaker, diemaker, toolmaker, or repairman, for example, I categorize as "skilled." I classified foremen as "managerial." These categories may be imperfect, but they produce very strong correlations with standard of living.

8. "They Know How to Get Along," *Dearborn Independent*, May 10, 1940.

9. John Baja to Orville Hubbard (Housing Department, City of Dearborn, DHM), in David Freund, "Making It Home: Race, Development, and the Politics of Place in Suburban Detroit, 1940–1967" (PhD diss., University of Michigan, 1999), 505.

10. Bob Biermann, *The Gang on Kendal Street* (Loudon, TN: St. Ben, 1999), n.p.

11. Michael Adray, oral history (DHM), 7.

12. Marcus Lathers, "The Rural Area around Detroit" (papers, 1945–1961, DHM), 3.

13. Ammerman, "Sociological Survey of Dearborn," 20.

14. Becker, oral history, 148–49, 150.

15. Ibid., 150.

16. The 1930 manuscript census, Sanborn maps, and Dearborn directories. This phenomenon of improvised housing is referred to by Olivier Zunz as the "informal housing

market," and it is discussed by Richard Harris as well, who calls it "self-built" housing. Zunz, *Changing Face of Inequality*; Richard Harris, "Self-Building in the Urban Housing Market," *Economic Geography* 67.1 (1991): 1–21. See also Bryan, *Beyond the Model T*, 82.

17. Another article observed, "Industrial executives realize that the employee who owns what is commonly known as 'temporary' or 'garage home' makes a much better employee than the one who owns nothing or pays rent. The rent payer is usually more shiftless and less reliable than the home owner." From "C. W. Treadwell O.K.'s Building of Small Homes," *Springwells Independent*, June 13, 1924.

18. The 1930 manuscript census.

19. On Sanborn maps, garage homes were identified as small residences on the rear of lots. Anything that was a garage for cars was labeled "A," for "automobile." Meanwhile, the actual phrase "garage home" appeared on building permits. This, I suppose, was to distinguish the permits from those taken for building a garage for cars. On some pieces of property, there were permits for both garage homes and garages for cars. Permits are located at City of Dearborn Department of Building.

20. The 1930 manuscript census.

21. Harold Vartanian, oral history (DHM), 31.

22. Ibid.

23. Ibid., 33, 34.

24. In the 1960s, the city of Dearborn demolished these houses under a policy they referred to as "Operation Eyesore."

25. In 1919, Willeke was replaced by architect Albert Wood, although it appears that Willeke's plans for the Ford Homes were by then complete and Wood's role was less to design the housing than to oversee its construction. See Bryan, *Beyond the Model T*; Loeb, "Entrepreneurial Vernacular"; Brunk, *Leonard B. Willeke*; archival material, acc. 47, BFRC.

26. David Good, "The Ford Homes," unpublished paper, 1975 (DHM), 5–7.

27. E. G. Liebold, correspondence, 1919 (box 1, acc. 47, BFRC).

28. "Builders with Brains Plus Courage Create an Ideal Colony for Workers," *Dearborn Independent* (Dec. 6, 1919): 8–9.

29. E. G. Liebold, correspondence, 1919 (box 1, acc. 47, BFRC).

30. "Builders with Brains Plus Courage Create an Ideal Colony for Workers," *Dearborn Independent* (Dec. 6, 1919): 8–9.

31. "Ideal Suburban Home in Dearborn Ford Subdivision," *Ford News* 2.9 (March 1, 1922): 3.

32. Henry Ford owned all but a few dozen lots in the Molony Subdivision where the Ford Homes were located. The Ford Homes, in turn, were not limited to Ford employees, and many other people lived there. Of the 260 households in the Molony Subdivision, 113 (44 percent) were headed by Ford employees. The 1930 manuscript census, Dearborn directories, tax assessment rolls, Sanborn maps, and Molony Subdivision plat.

33. The 1930 manuscript census.

34. Nevins and Hill, *Expansion and Challenge*, 202–10, 687.

35. Henry Ford, with Samuel Crowther, *Moving Forward* (Garden City: Doubleday, 1930), 113–14.

36. Ford, *Ford Ideals*, 324.

37. Bryan, *Beyond the Model T*; Segal, "Little Plants in the Country."

38. "Fordson and the City Beautiful," *Fordson Independent*, Nov. 18, 1927.

39. R. J. McLauchlin, "Dearborn Sighs and Lays Away Dream of Industrial Greatness," *Detroit Saturday Night*, Oct. 29, 1921.

40. "An Interview with Henry Ford," *Chicago Daily Tribune*, July 12, 1935.

41. William Simonds, "Rural Factories along Little Streams," *Stone and Webster Journal* 41 (Nov. 1927): 653, in Segal, "Little Plants in the Country," 184.

42. Edith Mae Cummings, "The Reason for My Faith in Dearborn," *Pipp's Weekly* (Aug. 8, 1925): 27.

43. "Dearborn Is Cynosure of National Interest," *Grand Rapids Press*, Sept. 23, 1923.

44. Donley Peddicord calls Dearborn an "ideal suburban city" in his "Henry Ford and His Home Town" pamphlet, 1924 (HF.DHM). An article on residential development named Springwells "the wonder city of Michigan." *Springwells Independent*, June 26, 1925. See also "City's Growth Is in Suburbs" and "Move Out in Ozone District," *Springwells Independent*, July 4, 1924; "Dearborn Throbs, but Without Smoke, Noise," *Detroit Free Press*, Nov. 25, 1923.

45. *Dearborn Star*, Nov. 15, 1929.

46. "Dearborn Is Called A Smiling, Happy City," *Detroit News*, Oct. 6, 1923.

47. Marion Arnold, "Dearborn, Child of Destiny and Fate," *Dearborn Magazine* 1.1 (1926): 2.

48. Judson Welliver, "Detroit, the Motor-Car Metropolis," *Munsey's* 67 (1919): 655.

49. Edmund Wilson, "The Despot of Dearborn," *Scribner's* 90 (July 1931): 34.

50. Arthur Pound, *Detroit: Dynamic City* (New York: D. Appleton-Century, 1940), 368–69.

51. Becker, oral history, 153–54. In the 1940s, Hubbard appointed John "Smokey" Parkhurst to head Dearborn's official antipollution efforts. Parkhurst, according to Becker, "kept pleading and working with the city for some kind of control of pollution. . . . He was . . . an interesting man, but he worked early on about environment in this town." Ibid., 152.

52. The number of building permits issued by Dearborn ranked it second in the state of Michigan in 1931, or twenty-seventh across the nation in 1929. "Dearborn Is 27th in U.S. in Building," *Dearborn Star*, Aug. 9, 1929; "Building Activities are Being Rushed; Hundreds of Apartments and Homes under Construction," *Springwells Independent*, Oct. 2, 1925; "Dearborn Again Tops Metropolitan Cities," *Dearborn Independent*, June 13, 1930; "Construction Here during Year Exceeds $8,000,000," *Dearborn Independent*, June 12, 1931.

53. Becker, oral history, 74–75.

54. "C. W. Treadwell O.K.s Building of Small Homes," *Springwells Independent*, June 13, 1924.

55. "The Joys, Pleasure, and Profits of Home Ownership in Springwells," ibid.

56. Speaking of the South End, Becker remarked: "You know that it grew up because the Rouge plant came there and farmland suddenly became a subdivision and [was] developed. The Miller farms, the Roulo farms, all of those farms that were there became housing." Becker, oral history, 149.

57. Henry Haigh, "Future Given in Address," *Dearborn Press*, May 21, 1931.

58. Karmann, oral history, 5–9.

59. Clyde Ford, memoir (acc. 1068, BFRC), 47–48.

60. Cardinal speech, 6.

61. Theodore Graham, oral history (DHM), 20.

62. Robert Erley, "The Enlargement of Dearborn," *City Manager Magazine* 8.7 (July 1926): 10.

63. Karmann, oral history, 12.

64. "City of Shacks or Fine Homes?" *Springwells Independent*, March 27, 1925; "Housing Facilities Are Lacking," *Dearborn Press*, June 14, 1918; "Realtors Pledge Aid for Better Homes," *Springwells Independent*, July 3, 1925.

65. Pound, *Dynamic City*, 354.

66. Jonathan Norton Leonard, *The Tragedy of Henry Ford* (New York: G. P. Putnam's Sons, 1932), quoted in *Henry Ford*, ed. John B. Rae (Englewood Cliffs: Prentice-Hall, 1969), 104.

67. Clyde Ford, memoir (acc. 1068, BFRC), 57.

68. Lathers, "The Rural Area around Detroit," 3.

69. Robert Duffus, "Detroit: Utopia on Wheels," *Harper's* 162 (Dec. 1930): 50–51.

70. "'F.O.B. Detroit': The Romance of the Wonder City of the Magic Motor," *Outlook* (Dec. 22, 1915): 979, 985.

71. Welliver, "Motor-Car Metropolis," 652.

72. "C.W. Treadwell O.K.'s Building of Small Homes," *Springwells Independent*, June 13, 1924.

73. Cyril Arthur Player, "Detroit: Essence of America," *New Republic* (Aug. 3, 1927): 275.

74. "Ideal Suburban Home in Dearborn Ford Subdivision," *Ford News* 2.9 (March 1, 1922): 3.

75. Taylor, *Satellite Cities*; Douglass, *The Suburban Trend*; McKenzie, *Metropolitan Community*; Harris, "Suburbs"; US Bureau of the Census, Clarence Batschelet, ed., *Metropolitan Districts: Population and Area* (Washington, DC: GPO, 1932); US Bureau of the Census, *Fourteenth Census of the United States: Population, 1920, Composition and Characteristics of the Population* (Washington, DC: GPO, 1921); US Bureau of the Census, *Fifteenth Census of the United States, 1930*; US Bureau of the Census, *Sixteenth Census of the United States, 1940*.

76. Aronovici, "Suburban Development."

77. Bailey, "The Twentieth Century City," 142–43.

78. Gries and Ford, *Slums, Large-Scale Housing*, 197–98.

79. US National Resources Committee, Research Committee on Urbanism, *Our Cities: Their Role in the National Economy* (Washington, DC: GPO, 1937), viii.

80. M. L. Wilson, in *Proceedings, National Conference on City Planning* (Boston: National Conference on City Planning, 1934), 141–42.

81. George B. Ford, "Proceedings of the Fifteenth National Conference on City Planning," Baltimore, MD: Conference publication, 1923, 13–14.

82. Taylor, *Satellite Cities*, 91–92.

83. George B. Ford, "Proceedings of the Fifteenth National Conference," 13–14.

84. Taylor, *Satellite Cities*, 91–92.

85. Ibid., 105–6.

86. George B. Ford, "Proceedings of the Fifteenth National Conference," 13–14.

87. Taylor, *Satellite Cities*, 126.

88. President's Research Committee on Social Trends, *Recent Social Trends in the United States* (New York: McGraw-Hill, 1933), xxii.

89. Carol Aronovici, "Let the Cities Perish," *Survey* 68 (Oct. 1, 1932): 439.

Chapter 3: The Automobile and Urban Growth

1. Harold S. Buttenheim, "Urban Planning and Land Policies," in US National Resources Committee, Research Committee on Urbanism, *Supplementary Report of the Urbanism Committee to the National Resources Committee* 2 (Washington, DC: GPO, 1939), 217.

2. Player, "Essence of America," 274.

3. Harvey Whipple, "City Plan Commission Begins Its Great Task of Bringing Order out of Detroit's Chaos," *Detroit Saturday Night*, May 3, 1919, 2.

4. Ibid.

5. "Record Construction to Continue: Building Head Urges Creation of Central Body to Control Future Problems," *Fordson Independent*, June 4, 1926.

6. "Favors Plan for Creation of Metropolitan Area," *Detroit Times*, Oct. 30, 1922; "Ford May Help Metropolitan Growth: Appointment of His Engineer to Development Committee Called Significant," *Detroit Times*, Jan. 31, 1923; "The Detroit Metropolitan Area," report (Detroit Bureau of Governmental Research, 1924); Erley, "Enlargement of Dearborn," 9–13; "About the Fourth City," *Just a Minute*, no. 16 (July 15, 1929): 1–2.

7. "About City Streets and Country Roads," *Just a Minute*, no. 46 (Feb. 10, 1930): 1.

8. Peterson, *American Automobile Workers*, 5.

9. "An Ideal Realized," *Ford Times* 6, no. 9 (June 1913): 366.

10. For more on transit history, see Robert Fogelson, *Downtown: Its Rise and Fall, 1880–1950* (New Haven: Yale University Press, 2001); Edward Weiner, *Urban Transportation Planning: An Historical Overview* (Westport: Praeger, 1999); A. Victoria Bloomfield and Richard Harris, "The Journey to Work: A Historical Methodology," *Historical Methods* 30.2 (1997): 97–109; Josef Konvitz, Mark H. Rose, and Joel Tarr, "Technology and the City," *Technology and Culture* 31 (1990): 284–94; Stanley Mallach, "The Origins of the Decline of Urban Mass Transportation in the United States, 1890–1930," *Urbanism Past and Present* (Summer 1989): 1–15. See also Davis, *Conspicuous Production*, for the chapter on transit in Detroit.

11. For more on the location of Ford Motor Company workers, see "5,000 Workers Petition for Northwest Belt Line," *Detroit News*, Jan. 25, 1925; clippings, "D.S.R. Making Oakman Study," *Detroit News*, Feb. 1925; "Figures Show Where Ford's West Side Workers Live," *Detroit News*, April 1925 (clipbook, BFRC); "New D.S.R. Line Nearly Done," *Detroit News*, March 8, 1925; "Northwestern and Other Lines to Open May 1," *Detroit News*, no month or date, 1925.

12. Donald F. Davis, "The City Remodelled: The Limits of Automotive Industry Leadership in Detroit, 1910–1929," *Histoire Sociale—Social History* 13.26 (November 1980): 473.

13. Clipping, *Detroit News*, July 13, 1915 (clipbook, BFRC).

14. Close to half (47 percent) of the Ford workers owned automobiles, but only 12 percent of them used cars to commute. "Standard of Living of Employees of Ford Motor Company in Detroit," *Monthly Labor Review* 30.6 (June 1930): 49–50.

15. In reference to the Oakman car line opening for passenger service between Highland Park and Springwells: "Industrial Sites Are Turned into Homes," *Springwells Independent*, June 26, 1925.

16. "Standard of Living of Employees of Ford Motor Company in Detroit," *Monthly Labor Review* 30.6 (June 1930): 44.

17. Helen Hall, "When Detroit's Out of Gear," *Survey* 64 (April 1, 1930): 10; William Foster and Waddill Catchings, "How Far Can Ford Go?" *World's Work* 53 (Feb. 1927): 437–44.

18. John Dancy, *Sand against the Wind* (memoir; Detroit: Wayne State University Press, 1966), 219.

19. Chester Kuta, oral history (DHM), 27–28.

20. Charles Denby, *Indignant Heart* (Detroit: Wayne State University Press, 1989), 35.

21. B. C. Forbes, "Slave-Driving in Ford Factories," *Forbes* (May 1, 1927): 19.

22. "About Ford's Investment in Men," *Pipps Weekly*, April 28, 1923, 2.

23. "Housing Facilities Are Lacking," *Dearborn Press*, June 14, 1918.

24. Gries and Ford, *Slums, Large-Scale Housing*, 213.

25. Myron Watkins, "The Labor Situation in Detroit," *Journal of Political Economics* 28 (1920): 850–51.

26. Webb Waldron, "Where Is America Going? Industrial Conditions in Detroit," *Century* 100 (May 1920): 61.

27. Bryan, *Beyond the Model T*, 38.

28. Clipping, *Dearborn Press*, June 14, 1918 (clipbook, BFRC).

29. Ford Motor Company directors' minutes, Aug. 26, 1918 (BFRC).

30. Clippings, "Ford Discusses New Car Line," *Detroit Times*, Jan. 1923; "Ford Trolley Line Plan Reported," *Detroit Times*, Jan. 1923 (clipbook, BFRC); "Ford May Help Build Car Lines for Workmen," *Detroit Free Press*, Jan. 20, 1923; "Ford to Meet with Mayor on River Car Line," *Detroit News*, June 30, 1923.

31. "5,000 Workers Petition for Northwest Belt Line," *Detroit News*, Jan. 25, 1925.

32. "New DSR Line Nearly Done," *Detroit News*, March 8, 1925.

33. "Oakman Offer Made to City," *Detroit News*, June 27, 1923.

34. Clipping, "Oakman Car Line Pact Near," Dec. 30, 1924 (clipbook, BFRC); "City Agrees to Rent Ford Plant Street Car Line," *Detroit Times*, Jan. 6, 1925; "Oakman Line Deal Approved," *Detroit News*, Jan. 22, 1925; Jack Schramm, William Henning, and Thomas Dworman, *Detroit's Street Railways, 1922-1956* (Chicago: Central Electric Railfans' Association, 1980), 40, 121.

35. Clippings, "Link Ford Would Build," Dec. 1924; "Ford Offers to Build Car Line to Rouge," Dec. 31, 1924 (clipbook, BFRC); "Ford Plans to Extend DSR," *Detroit Times*, Jan. 2, 1925; "Delay Action on Ford Offer," *Detroit Free Press*, Jan. 14, 1925; "Ford Car Line Offer Up Again," *Detroit News*, Jan. 18, 1925.

36. Clipping, "New DSR Line Nearly Done," March 8, 1925 (clipbook, BFRC); "Car Service for Employees at Rouge," *Ford News* 4.16 (June 15, 1925): 8; "Car Line Opened Last Week," *Springwells Independent*, June 19, 1925; Schramm et al., *Detroit's Street Railways*, 121; Jack Schramm, "Detroit's DSR, part 1," *Motor Coach Age* 42.1-2 (January–February 1991): 24; "Car Line Gives 6 Min. Service; Busses 21," *Springwells Independent*, July 10, 1925. For construction of the extension on Schaefer alone, Ford lent $341,175 to the DSR. Schramm et al., *Detroit's Street Railways*, 121.

37. It is possible there was a pedestrian underpass at these tracks, although I doubt it. Mention is made of its proposal in 1918, but in discussions of a street railway underpass developed there in 1927, it sounds like the walkway was never built. For instance, one article describes the street railway underpass as eliminating the "danger hazard" for employees unloading at the Eagle Loop. "DUR to Build Rouge Car Line," *Dearborn Press*, June

14, 1918; "Underpass Completed," *Ford News* 7.14 (May 15, 1927): 1; "Street Car Service Greatly Increased in 1929," *Dearborn Independent*, April 30, 1930.

38. "DUR to Build Rouge Car Line," *Dearborn Press*, June 14, 1918; "Underpass Completed," *Ford News* 7.14 (May 15, 1927): 1; Schramm et al., *Detroit's Street Railways*, 125–28.

39. Schramm et al., *Detroit's Street Railways*, 128.

40. Davis, *Conspicuous Production*, 163.

41. Bryan, *Beyond the Model T*, 71.

42. Schramm, "Detroit's DSR, part 1," *Motor Coach Age* 42.1–2 (January–February 1991): 6.

43. Davis, *Conspicuous Production*, 167.

44. Schramm et al., *Detroit's Street Railways*, 9; Schramm, "Detroit's DSR," 7.

45. Davis, *Conspicuous Production*, 164.

46. Graeme O'Geran, *A History of the Detroit Street Railways* (Detroit: Conover, 1931), 362.

47. "M.O. Plans Told by Mayo," *Detroit Times*, Dec. 12, 1922; clipping, "Expert Aid Offer Is Accepted," *Detroit Times*, c. Dec. 1922 (clipbook, BFRC).

48. Clipping, "Expert Aid Offer Is Accepted," *Detroit Times*, c. Dec. 1922 (clipbook, BFRC); "M.O. Plans Told by Mayo," *Detroit Times*, Dec. 12, 1922.

49. Davis, *Conspicuous Production*, 169.

50. Schramm et al., *Detroit's Street Railways*, 9, 11, 17.

51. Sidney Fine, *Frank Murphy: The Detroit Years* (Ann Arbor: University of Michigan Press, 1975), 422.

52. "Three Years of Municipal Railway Operation in Detroit," *American City* 33.1 (July 1925): 28.

53. Nevins and Hill, *Expansion and Challenge*, 687.

54. For a detailed account of the superhighway and other transit proposals in Detroit, see Davis, "The City Remodelled," 451–86; Schramm et al., *Detroit's Street Railways*.

55. Waldon quoted in Mark S. Foster, "From Streetcar to Superhighway: American City Planners and Urban Transportation, 1900–1940" (Philadelphia: Temple University Press, 1981), 74.

56. See Rapid Transit Commission (RTC), "Proposed Super-Highway Plan for Greater Detroit" (Detroit: RTC, 1924), "Proposed Financial Plan for a Rapid Transit System for the City of Detroit" (Detroit: RTC, 1923), "Rapid Transit System for the City of Detroit" (Detroit: RTC, 1926), "Report of the Rapid Transit Commission to the Mayor's Finance Committee" (Detroit: RTC, 1926), "The Relation of Individual to Collective Transportation" (Detroit: Heitman-Garand, 1928), "Rapid Transit System and Plan Recommended for Detroit and the Metropolitan Area, Preliminary Report to the Mayor and Common Council"(Detroit: RTC, 1958); Street Railway Commission, "Report of the Street Railway Commission and the Rapid Transit Commission to Hon. John C. Lodge, Mayor and the Honorable the Common Council on a Rapid Transit System for the City of Detroit" (Detroit: City of Detroit, 1929); Rapid Transit Commission, with Conway Corporation, "Rapid Transit Plan for Metropolitan Detroit, with a Suggested Plan for Financing Expressways and Rapid Transit, 1949" (Detroit: RTC, 1949).

57. Davis, "The City Remodelled," 468–69.

58. Rapid Transit Commission, "Proposed Financial Plan"; Rapid Transit Commission, "Report . . . to the Mayor's Finance Committee."

59. Davis, "The City Remodelled," 469.

60. Ibid., 471–72.

61. "The Vernor-Mack rapid transit line will serve about 22 per cent of the residential population of the city within a service area of one-half mile each side of the lines. It will serve about 30 per cent of the industrial population. That is, 30 per cent of the 540,000 workers in 1934 will be employed in plants within the service area." Rapid Transit Commission, "Questions and Answers on Subway Proposition," *Detroit News*, March 25, 1929.

62. "[The subway would serve] almost 50 per cent of all the activities in Detroit: Mack avenue factories and also Charlevoix-Mack avenue base ball park, Grand Trunk Gratiot avenue R.R. station, Eastern market, municipal center just south of Gratiot avenue, on St. Antoine; the downtown mercantile establishments, big league base ball park, Michigan Central R.R. station, big west side industries such as the Cadillac, Buhl Stamping Co., etc.; west side market, Baby Creek park, Woodmere Cemetery, River Rouge plant of Ford Motor and Dearborn. I know of no other route in Detroit that would accommodate so many activities at one time." Wendell Morris, letter to the editor, *Detroit News*, March 31, 1929.

63. "Voters, Attention," *Detroit News*, March 27, 1929.

64. Street Railway Commission, "Report of the Street Railway Commission and the Rapid Transit Commission to Hon. John C. Lodge, Mayor and the Honorable Common Council on a Rapid Transit System for the City of Detroit" (Detroit: City of Detroit, 1929).

65. "Transit Talks Sway Council," *Detroit News*, Feb. 9, 1929.

66. Rapid Transit Commission, "Questions and Answers on Subway Proposition," *Detroit News*, March 24, 1929.

67. Ibid., March 17, 1929.

68. John Gorman of the Street Railway Commission quoted in "Experts Plead Rapid Transit," *Detroit News*, March 24, 1929.

69. C. W. Hubbell quoted in "Subway Seen as Necessity," *Detroit News*, March 17, 1929.

70. "Transit Talks Sway Council," *Detroit News*, Feb. 9, 1929.

71. Albert Loosli, letter to the editor, *Detroit News*, March 10, 1929.

72. Ronald Wilson, letter to the editor, *Detroit News*, March 10, 1929.

73. "Transit Talks Sway Council," *Detroit News*, Feb. 9, 1929.

74. S. J. Egelston, letter to the editor, *Detroit News*, March 31, 1929.

75. Henry Regan, letter to the editor, *Detroit News*, March 31, 1929.

76. "Plain Talk," letter to the editor, *Detroit News*, March 31, 1929.

77. H. A. Wheeler, letter to the editor, *Detroit News*, March 31, 1929.

78. "A Taxpayer," letter to the editor, *Detroit News*, March 31, 1929.

79. E. M. Mearse, letter to the editor, *Detroit News*, March 24, 1929.

80. "Transit Talks Sway Council," *Detroit News*, Feb. 9, 1929.

81. "Taxpayers' Fear of Heavy Assessments Cited as Reason for Defeat," *Detroit News*, April 3, 1929.

82. Sources are unclear as to why the PWA rejected the grant, but the official reason put forth is that the application submitted by the state was considered "deficient." See Fogelson, *Downtown: Its Rise and Fall*, 309–12; Mark S. Foster, "From Streetcar to Superhighway," 154–56, 165–67.

83. Here New York and Chicago, which have thriving transit systems, are exceptions. New York was able to support transit because a turn-of-the-century consolidation of its five boroughs created a tax structure that was on a metropolitan scale. Meanwhile, Chicago in

the late 1930s was able to add a subway to its elevated lines because of New Deal money that made the local tax structure less relevant. See Brian J. Cudahy, *A Century of Subways: Celebrating 100 Years of New York's Underground Railways* (New York: Fordham University Press, 2003); Peter Derrick, *Tunneling to the Future: The Story of the Great Subway Expansion that Saved New York* (New York: New York University Press, 2001); David M. Young, *Chicago Transit: An Illustrated History* (DeKalb: Northern Illinois University Press, 1998); Bruce Moffat, *The "L": The Development of Chicago's Rapid Transit System, 1888–1932*, Bulletin of Central Electric Railfans' Association no. 131 (Chicago: Central Electric Railfans' Association, 1995).

84. "No Street Cars in 10 Years, Says Ford," *Boston American*, Nov. 22, 1919.

85. "Automobile Used More for Business than for Pleasure," *Ford News* 2.11 (April 1, 1922): 2.

86. "If Detroit Built Subways . . . ," *Detroit Times*, Dec. 16, 1923.

87. Ibid.

88. Carl Wells, *Proposals for Downtown Detroit* (Washington, DC: Urban Land Institute, 1942); Reid, *Industrial Decentralization*; Egbert Wengert, *Financial Problems of the City of Detroit in the Depression*, Detroit Bureau of Governmental Research, report no. 151 (Detroit Bureau of Governmental Research, 1939).

Chapter 4: Rising Standards in the Suburbs

1. Nevins and Hill, *Expansion and Challenge*, 332.

2. Samuel Marquis, *Henry Ford: An Interpretation* (Boston: Little, Brown, 1923), in *Henry Ford*, ed. John B. Rae (Englewood Cliffs: Prentice-Hall, 1969), 82.

3. Ford, with Crowther, *My Life and Work*, 126–28.

4. "Ford Teaches Citizenship to His Employees," *Cincinnati Post*, June 29, 1914.

5. Clipping, "Henry Ford's Troubles," Portland, OR, April 30, 1914 (clipbook, BFRC).

6. "The American Workman," *Ford News* 3.19 (Aug. 1, 1923): 2.

7. For more on welfare capitalism, see Jacoby, *Masters to Managers*; Mandell, *The Corporation as Family*; Eisner, *From Warfare State to Welfare State*; Marchand, *Creating the Corporate Soul*; Tone, *The Business of Benevolence*; Gitelman, "Welfare Capitalism Reconsidered."

8. Ford, with Crowther, *My Life and Work*, 130.

9. Clipping, "Detroit Has Strangest School in the World, Ford Runs It—Teaches Working Folks How to Spend More Money for Good Things," June 1914 (clipbook, BFRC).

10. Tone, *The Business of Benevolence*, 52.

11. Henry Ford, with Samuel Crowther, *Today and Tomorrow* (Garden City: Doubleday, 1926), 165.

12. Ford, *Ford Ideals*, 424.

13. Ibid., 293–94.

14. *Ford Man* (Sept. 20, 1917): 2–3, in "Men and Monotony: Fraternalism as a Managerial Strategy at the Ford Motor Company," Wayne Lewchuk, *Journal of Economic History* 53.4 (Dec. 1993): 842.

15. E. A. Rumely, "Mr. Ford's Plan to Share Profits," *World's Work* 27 (1914): 664–69, in ibid., 852.

16. For more on masculinity, see Roger Horowitz, ed., *Boys and Their Toys? Masculinity, Technology, and Class in America* (New York: Routledge, 2001); Paul Michel Taillon, "What We Want Is Good, Sober Men: Masculinity, Respectability, and Temperance in the Railroad Brotherhoods, c. 1870–1910," *Journal of Social History* 36.2 (2002): 319–38; Thomas Winter, *Making Men, Making Class: The YMCA and Workingmen, 1877–1920* (Chicago: University of Chicago Press, 2002).

17. Ford, *Ford Ideals*, 293.

18. Ibid., 293.

19. Ibid., 260.

20. "Citizenship," *Ford News* 3.3 (Dec. 1, 1922): 2.

21. "What You Will See When Going through Dearborn," *Ford News* 2.9 (March 1, 1922): 7.

22. Ford, *Ford Ideals*, 145, 254.

23. Ibid., 407–8.

24. Ford, with Crowther, *Moving Forward*, 113–14.

25. "Let's Have a Garden," *Ford News* 2.14 (May 15, 1922): 6, 8.

26. Ford Motor Company, *Helpful Hints and Advice to Ford Employees* (Detroit: Ford Motor Company, 1915), 13, 31–32.

27. Clipping, "Housing an Important Problem," *Automotive Industries*, April 10, 1919 (clipbook, BFRC).

28. US Bureau of the Census, *Fifteenth Census of the United States, 1930*. This is a term used by the census.

29. "Wonderful Period for Auto Industry in the Near Future," *Ford News* 1.7 (Feb. 1, 1921): 4.

30. "A Nation Turns Out-of-Doors," advertisement (file M–N, 1925, box 4, acc. 19, BFRC).

31. "Economical Transportation for All the People," advertisement (E, 1929, box 6, acc. 19, BFRC).

32. Henry Ford, with Fay Leone Faurote, *My Philosophy of Industry* (New York, Coward-McCann, 1929), 46–47.

33. Ibid., 18–19.

34. "What I Have Learned from My Work—Prize-Winning Essays," *Ford News* 6.18 (July 15, 1926): 7.

35. Ford, with Faurote, *My Philosophy of Industry*, 14–17.

36. "Mr. Ford Explains the Five-Day Week," *Ford News* 6.24 (Oct. 15, 1926): 2.

37. Ford, with Crowther, *Today and Tomorrow*, 154.

38. Ford, *Ford Ideals*, 250; "Mr. Ford Explains the Five-Day Week," *Ford News* 6.24 (Oct. 15, 1926): 2.

39. "Living Standards of Ford Men Improving with Profit Sharing," *Detroit News Tribune*, March 23, 1914.

40. Levine, *Internal Combustion*, 23.

41. Wyndham Mortimer, *Organize! My Life as a Union Man* (Boston: Beacon, 1971), 43.

42. Watkins, "The Labor Situation in Detroit," 845.

43. Thomas Wright, "Why Ford's Men Strike," *Christian Century* 50 (Nov. 29, 1933): 1502–3.

44. Player, "Essence of America," 272–73.

45. Waldron, "Where Is America Going?" 62.

46. Pound, *Dynamic City*, 306–7.

47. William Trufant Foster and Waddill Catchings, "How Far Can Ford Go?" *World's Work* 53 (Feb. 1927): 439.

48. Waldron, "Where Is America Going?" 62, 64.

49. Detroit Mayor's Inter-Racial Committee, *The Negro in Detroit* 5 (Detroit Bureau of Government Research, 1926), 22.

50. Chen-Nan Li, "A Summer in the Ford Works," *Personnel Journal* 7 (June 1928): 18–32; "Standard of Living of Employees of Ford Motor Company in Detroit," *Monthly Labor Review* 30.6 (June 1930): 11–54.

51. Li, "A Summer in the Ford Works," 29–30.

52. Ibid., 29, 30

53. "Standard of Living of Employees of Ford Motor Company in Detroit," *Monthly Labor Review* 30.6 (June 1930): 37–40.

54. Ibid., 50.

55. Li, "A Summer in the Ford Works," 29.

56. "Standard of Living of Employees of Ford Motor Company in Detroit," *Monthly Labor Review* 30.6 (June 1930):13.

57. Ibid.

58. See Whaples, "Winning the Eight-Hour Day"; Roediger and Foner, *Our Own Time*, 9; May, "Bread before Roses."

59. Gertrude Beeks, welfare worker, "Welfare Work May Conquer Great Labor Problems," *New York Times*, November 17, 1912, quoted in Tone, *The Business of Benevolence*, 209.

60. "The American Workman," *Ford News* 3.19 (Aug. 1, 1923): 2.

61. John Martin, "Home, Sweet Home!" *The Auto Worker* 1.2 (June 1919): 9.

62. "The Living Wage," *The Auto Worker* 4.12 (Dec. 1922): 5.

63. "Wage Workers' Pay," *John Swinton's Paper*, March 26, 1887, 12, quoted in Lawrence Glickman, "Inventing the 'American Standard of Living': Gender, Race and Working-Class Identity, 1880–1925," *Labor History* 34.2-3 (1993): 226.

64. "Bosses 'Americanism' to Be Revived," *The Ford Worker* 2.8 (July 15, 1927): 4.

65. L. L. Johnson, "Automobile Workers' Standard of Living," *The Auto Worker* 6.2 (Feb. 1924): 6.

66. John Martin, "Home, Sweet Home!" *The Auto Worker* 1.2 (June 1919): 9.

67. Faye Elizabeth Smith, "Jobless Men Lose Life Savings, Homes, Furniture," *The Auto Worker* 5 (May 1921): 8.

68. Arthur Rohan, "Welfare and Helfare," *The Auto Worker* 2.7 (July 1920): 12.

69. John Martin, "Home, Sweet Home!" *The Auto Worker* 1.2 (June 1919): 9.

70. "Auto Bosses Join 'Welfare Offensive,'" *Auto Workers News* 2.4 (August 1928): 4.

Chapter 5: The Lives of Automobile Workers

1. "Ford Profit Scheme Romance of the Trade," *New York Journal of Commerce*, Jan. 9, 1914.

2. Ford, with Faurote, *My Philosophy*, 14–16. "The abolition of the commercialized liquor trade in this country is as final as the abolition of slavery," Ford claimed. "These are

the two great reforms to which moral America committed itself from the beginning of its history."

3. For more on the radical potential of the 1920s, see David J. Goldberg, *Discontented America: The United States in the 1920s* (Baltimore: Johns Hopkins University Press, 1999); William Maxwell, *New Negro, Old Left: African American Writing and Communism between the Wars* (New York: Columbia University Press, 1999); Gareth Canaan, "'Part of the Loaf': Economic Conditions of Chicago's African American Working Class during the 1920s," *Journal of Social History* 35.1 (2001): 147–74; Daniel T. Rodgers, *Atlantic Crossings: Social Politics in a Progressive Age* (Cambridge: Belknap, 1998); James R. Barrett and David Roediger, "Inbetween Peoples: Race, Nationality, and the 'New Immigrant' Working Class," *Journal of American Ethnic History* 16.3 (1997): 3–44; Michael Denning, *The Cultural Front: The Laboring of American Culture in the Twentieth Century* (London: Verso, 1996); Kristi Andersen, *After Suffrage: Women in Partisan and Electoral Politics before the New Deal* (Chicago: University of Chicago Press, 1996); Stanley Coben, *Rebellion against Victorianism: The Impetus for Cultural Change in 1920s America* (New York: Oxford University Press, 1991).

4. Ticknor, "Motor City," 237–39, 190–97.

5. Thomas, *Life for Us Is What We Make It*, 90–92.

6. Myron Adams, "Detroit—A City Awake," *Survey*, Aug. 5, 1911, 666–71, cited in *Detroit Perspectives: Crossroads and Turning Points*, ed. Wilma Wood Henrickson (Detroit: Wayne State University Press, 1991), 290.

7. Detroit Mayor's Inter-Racial Committee, *The Negro in Detroit* 5, p. 1.

8. Editorial, *The Detroiter*, Dec. 15, 1919.

9. Len Shaw, *Detroit Free Press*, June 3, 1917.

10. Pound, *Dynamic City*, 250.

11. Clipping, "Wave of Population Growth Rolls West from Detroit," Nov. 30, 1924 (clipbook, BFRC).

12. Zunz, *Changing Face of Inequality*, 327–28.

13. By the mid-1920s, virtually all new subdivisions in Dearborn had some form of restrictions attached. This is based on a random sample taken from the Wayne County Registry of Deeds. For more on racial restrictions in Detroit, see Harold Black, "Restrictive Covenants in Relation to Segregated Negro Housing in Detroit" (master's thesis, Wayne State University, 1947). See also Wendy Plotkin, "Deeds of Mistrust: Race, Housing, and Restrictive Covenants in Chicago, 1900–1953" (PhD diss., University of Illinois–Chicago, 2000); Michael Jones-Correa, "The Origins and Diffusion of Racial Restrictive Covenants," *Political Science Quarterly* 115.4 (2000–2001): 541–68; Kevin Gotham, "Urban Space, Restrictive Covenants, and the Origin of Racial Residential Segregation in a U.S. City, 1900–1950," *International Journal of Urban and Regional Research* 24.3 (Summer 2000): 616–33; Joe Darden, "Black Residential Segregation since the 1948 Shelley v. Kraemer Decision," *Journal of Black Studies* 25.6 (1995): 680–91.

14. Ticknor, "Motor City," 234.

15. In the early 1920s, when the Ford Homes were developed, deed restrictions were not as common as they would be later in the decade.

16. The 1930 manuscript census.

17. Joyce Shaw Peterson, "Black Automobile Workers in Detroit, 1910–1930," *Journal of Negro History* 64.3 (1979): 177–90.

18. "The Negro," *Dearborn Independent* 26.4 (Nov. 14, 1925): 11.

19. "Facing the Race Issue," *Dearborn Independent* 22.7 (Dec. 10, 1921): 2.

20. "The Negro," *Dearborn Independent* 26.4 (Nov. 14, 1925): 11.

21. "Mr. Ford's Page," *Dearborn Independent* 22.52 (Oct. 21, 1922): 5.

22. John Barnard, *Walter Reuther and the Rise of the Auto Workers* (Boston: Little, Brown, 1983), 21.

23. For more on the experience of Great Migration blacks in Detroit, see Thomas, *Life for Us Is What We Make It*; Wiese, *Places of Their Own*; Victoria Wolcott, *Remaking Respectability: African American Women in Interwar Detroit* (Chapel Hill: University of North Carolina Press, 2001); John Brueggemann, "The Power and Collapse of Paternalism: The Ford Motor Company and Black Workers, 1937–1941," *Social Problems* 47.2 (2000): 220–40; Sidney Fine, *"Expanding the Frontiers of Civil Rights": Michigan, 1948–1968* (Detroit: Wayne State University Press, 2000); Thomas Maloney and Warren Whatley, "Making the Effort: The Contours of Racial Discrimination in Detroit's Labor Markets, 1920–1940," *Journal of Economic History* 55.3 (1995): 465–93; Elizabeth Anne Martin, *Detroit and the Great Migration, 1916–1929* (Ann Arbor: Bentley Historical Library, 1993); Howard Lindsey, "Fields to Fords, Feds to Franchise: African American Empowerment in Inkster, Michigan" (PhD diss., University of Michigan, 1993); Black, "Restrictive Covenants."

24. Clipping, Walter White, "Negro Segregation Comes North," *The Nation* 121.3146 (Oct. 1925): 458 (clipbook, BFRC).

25. *Michigan Chronicle*, Aug. 25, 1945, in Black, "Restrictive Covenants," 16.

26. Levine, *Internal Combustion*, 160–61.

27. Clipping, Walter White, "Negro Segregation Comes North," *The Nation* 121.3146 (Oct. 1925): 458 (clipbook, BFRC).

28. "Mayor's Open Letter," *Detroit Free Press*, Sept. 13, 1925.

29. Detroit Mayor's Inter-Racial Committee, *The Negro in Detroit*. In Dancy, *Sand against the Wind*, 219.

30. Secondary breadwinners were male since Henry Ford almost never hired women.

31. The 1930 manuscript census.

32. Sugrue, *Origins of the Urban Crisis*, 38. See also Thomas, *Life for Us Is What We Make It*.

33. Detroit Mayor's Inter-Racial Committee, *The Negro in Detroit* 5, 10–11.

34. Film documentary, "Remembering Detroit's Old West Side, 1920–1950" (Royal Oak: Captured Live Productions, 1997).

35. Dancy, *Sand against the Wind*, 58. In fact, Inkster Gardens was about equally distant (seven miles or so) from the Rouge as downtown Detroit.

36. Clipping, "Inkster Gardens, Detroit's Foremost Colored Community," real estate advertisement, *Pipp's Weekly*, Aug. 8, 1925 (clipbook, BFRC).

37. The 1930 manuscript census.

38. US Bureau of the Census, *Sixteenth Census of the United States, 1940*.

39. Marvel Daines, *Be It Ever So Tumbled: The Story of a Suburban Slum* (Detroit, 1940), 3, cited in "Places of Our Own: Suburban Black Towns before 1960," Andrew Wiese, *Journal of Urban History* 19.3 (May 1993): 43.

40. Ford, *Ford Ideals*, 311.

41. Henry Ford's testimony to the Congressional Committee on Industrial Relations (1915), 7628, cited in "The Historical Problem of the Family Wage: The Ford Motor Company and the Five Dollar Day," Martha May, *Feminist Studies* 8.2 (Summer 1982): 114.

42. Clipping, "Detroit Has Strangest School in the World; Ford Runs It—Teaches Working Folks How to Spend More Money for Good Things," 1916 (clipbook, BFRC).

43. "Mr. Ford Explains the Five-Day Week," 2.

44. Ford, with Crowther, *My Life and Work*, 123.

45. Ford, with Faurote, *My Philosophy*, 6.

46. "Should Married Women Work?" in *Ford Ideals*, Ford, 309–12.

47. Kate Richards O'Hare, "Has Henry Ford Made Good?" *The National Rip-Saw*, Jan. 1916, 6.

48. Clipping, "Ford Assailed by Women, Indignant at His Reason for Discriminating," Jan. 1913 (clipbook, BFRC); "Ford Gives Women Same Pay as Men, to Receive $5 for an Eight-Hour Day," *New York Evening Post*, Oct. 25, 1916.

49. For women in the auto industry, see Martha May, "Bread before Roses"; Bruce Pietrykowski, "Gendered Employment in the U.S. Auto Industry: A Case Study of the Ford Motor Co. Phoenix Plant, 1922-1940," *Review of Radical Political Economics* 27.3 (1995): 39–48; Elaine Tyler May, "Rosie the Riveter Gets Married," *Mid-America* 75.3 (1993): 269–82; Sherrie A. Kossoudji and Laura J. Dresser, "The End of a Riveting Experience: Occupational Shifts at Ford after World War II," *American Economic Review* 82.2 (1992): 519–25; Nancy Gabin, *Feminism in the Labor Movement: Women and the United Auto Workers, 1935-1975* (Ithaca: Cornell University Press, 1990); Judith N. McArthur, "From Rosie the Riveter to the Feminist Mystique: An Historiographical Survey of American Women and World War II," *Bulletin of Bibliography* 44.1 (1987): 10–18.

50. Li, "A Summer in the Ford Works," 27, 29.

51. The 1930 manuscript census.

52. Henry Ford was not alone in this effort, as it was a popular cause among reformers to eliminate boarding. See Richard Harris, "The End Justified the Means," *Journal of Social History* 26.2 (Winter 1992): 331–60.

53. Ford, with Crowther, *My Life and Work*, 128.

54. Irene Young Marinovich, oral history (Archives of Labor and Urban Affairs, Reuther Library, Wayne State University), 17.

55. Andrew Parlogean and Nellie Parlogean, oral history (DHM), 29; also Marinovich, oral history, 16.

56. Marinovich, oral history, 16.

57. Ibid., 10, 35 (side by side), 3 (hands).

58. Ibid., 12 (triple jobs), 10 (shifts), 3 (pinch).

59. Ibid., 8–9. Overall, 90 percent were in favor of the union, which indicates a notably high amount of solidarity.

60. Ibid., 5. Like any autoworker, Marinovich worked the circuit of plants in the Detroit metropolis, switching jobs at will or compelled by layoffs to move on.

61. Karmann, oral history, 12–13.

62. ". . . Big Raid in South End," *Dearborn Press*, July 21, 1932.

63. Becker, oral history, 150.

64. Ibid., 150–51. See also Kuta, oral history, 25.

65. Li, "A Summer in the Ford Works," 30–31.

66. William Henson, oral history (DHM), 11.

67. "Presence of Blind Pigs Here Is Admitted by Henry Ford," *Dearborn Star*, March 25, 1930; "Blind Pig Operators Arraigned," *Dearborn Independent*, May 2, 1930.

68. "Blind Pigs Have Gone Say Police," *Dearborn Press*, June 12, 1930.

69. "Henry Ford in 'War' on Jazz Dancing," *Herald*, July 10, 1925.

70. "Waxed Dance Floor Playground of Henry Ford," *Detroit Free Press*, Aug. 2, 1925.

71. "Old Dances for New," *Boston Traveler*, Aug. 5, 1925.

72. Edmund Wilson, "Despot of Dearborn," 34. "On a polished hardwood floor in the engineering laboratories, between a collection of antique girandoles and lustres and a glossy, gleaming row of new car models, Ford amuses himself by giving balls for the purpose of reviving the schottische and the polka—occasions at which he personally instructs the new generation of those older pre-automobile Detroit families who twenty or twenty-five years ago were still laughing at him as a yokel and an upstart."

73. "Graces of Yesterday Revived by Henry Ford," *Ford News* 8.5 (Jan. 15, 1928): 3; "May Queen Crowned at Festival on Village Green," *Ford News* 10.12 (June 16, 1930): 137.

74. Barbara Stoney, *Henry Ford: The Motorman* (London: Hodder and Stoughton, 1981), 90.

75. For the rise of commercial entertainment and issues of working-class leisure, see Richard Butsch, ed., *For Fun and Profit: The Transformation of Leisure into Consumption* (Philadelphia: Temple University Press, 1990); Alexis McCrossen, *Holy Day, Holiday: The American Sunday* (Ithaca: Cornell University Press, 2000); Randy McBee, *Dance Hall Days: Intimacy and Leisure among Working-Class Immigrants in the United States* (New York: New York University Press, 2000); Madelon Powers, *Faces along the Bar: Lore and Order in the Workingman's Saloon, 1870-1920* (Chicago: University of Chicago Press, 1999); David Nasaw, *Going Out: The Rise and Fall of Public Amusements* (New York: Basic Books, 1993); Douglas Gomery, *Shared Pleasures: A History of Movie Presentation in the United States* (Madison: University of Wisconsin Press, 1992); Steven Riess, *City Games: The Evolution of American Urban Society and the Rise of Sports* (Urbana: University of Illinois Press, 1989).

76. Li, "A Summer in the Ford Works," 30–31.

77. Ammerman, "Sociological Survey of Dearborn," 56–57.

78. Peterson, *American Automobile Workers*, 91–92.

79. Henson, oral history, 8.

80. Becker, oral history, 151–52.

81. Adray, oral history, 4, 7.

82. Ibid.

83. Henson, oral history, 8.

Chapter 6: The Transformation of Fordism

1. "The American Workman," *Ford News* 3.19 (Aug. 1, 1923): 2. Capitalization in the original.

2. Clipping, "Detroit Has Strangest School in the World; Ford Runs It—Teaches Working Folks How to Spend More Money for Good Things," 1916 (clipbook, BFRC).

3. Pound, *Dynamic City*, 299. "By suddenly lifting minimum wages in his plant to five dollars a day, Ford initiated a rise in basic wages the country over. . . . Other companies . . . followed him; had to, in order to keep their best men. . . . Coal-miners now drawing six dollars a day [in 1940] perhaps have Henry Ford to thank for that no less [than] their own leaders."

4. Charles Walker, "Down and Out in Detroit," *The Forum* 86 (Sept. 1931): 128–36, in Charles Beard, *America Faces the Future* (Boston, Houghton Mifflin 1932), 71.

5. For more about the unionization of automobile workers, see Nelson Lichtenstein, "Life at the Rouge: A Cycle of Workers' Control," in *Life and Labor: Dimensions of American*

Working-Class History, eds. Charles Stephenson and Robert Asher (Albany: State University of New York Press, 1986); Brueggemann, "Power and Collapse of Paternalism"; Mike Smith, "Spirit of 1937," *Michigan History Magazine* 84.6 (2000): 62–69; Judith Stepan-Norris and Maurice Zeitlin, *Talking Union* (Urbana: University of Illinois Press, 1996); Kevin Boyle, "'There Are No Union Sorrows that the Union Can't Heal': The Struggle for Racial Equality in the UAW, 1940–1960," *Labor History* 35 (1995): 5–23; Gabin, *Feminism in the Labor Movement*.

6. McKenzie, *Metropolitan Community*, 69.

7. Ticknor, "Motor City," 241–42.

8. "About Going a-Borrowing," *Just a Minute*, no. 25 (Sept, 16, 1929): 1, 2.

9. "About Pay-As-You-Go," *Just a Minute*, no. 3 (April 1, 1929): 1.

10. "About No Matter Who Is Elected," *Just a Minute*, no. 30 (Sept. 21, 1929): 1, 2.

11. Pound, *Dynamic City*, 335.

12. Irving Bernstein, *The Lean Years: A History of the American Worker, 1920–1933* (Baltimore: Penguin, 1966), 300–301.

13. Sidney Glazer, *Detroit* (New York: Bookman Associates, 1965), 97–100.

14. Charles Walker, "Down and Out in Detroit," *The Forum* 86 (Sept. 1931): 128–36, in *America Faces the Future*, Charles Beard (Boston: Houghton Mifflin, 1932), 82.

15. Raymond Fragnoli, *The Transformation of Reform: Progressivism in Detroit* (New York: Garland, 1982), 360.

16. "Asks Industry to Back Relief," *Detroit News*, Feb. 10, 1931; "Seeks to Split Welfare Costs," *Detroit News*, April 21, 1931; "Murphy Asks Industry Run 'Own Welfare,'" *Detroit News*, April 26, 1931.

17. In these settings, workers were recruited to join what were known as the Unemployed Councils, advocacy groups intended to represent their interests in dealings with city hall.

18. Sidney Fine, *Frank Murphy: The Detroit Years* (Ann Arbor: University of Michigan Press, 1975), 276–81, 399–402.

19. Peterson, *American Automobile Workers*, 130–31.

20. Edmund Wilson, "Despot of Dearborn," 25.

21. "A Detroit Sample," *Survey* (April 1932): 84; "Standard of Living of Employees of Ford Motor Company in Detroit," *Monthly Labor Review* 30.6 (June 1930): 11–54.

22. "A Detroit Sample," *Survey* (April 1932): 84.

23. Thomas Wright, "Why Ford's Men Strike," *Christian Century* 50 (Nov. 29, 1933): 1503.

24. Hall, "When Detroit's Out of Gear," 9–10.

25. Peterson, *American Automobile Workers*, 130.

26. Sub-Committee of the Detroit Mayor's Unemployment Committee, *The Effects upon Detroit of the Three Years of the Depression*, 1932, in ibid., 133.

27. Mayor Clyde Ford, "Bankers . . . Report to Mayor on . . . Relief for Home-Owners," *Dearborn Press*, Aug. 25, 1932.

28. Peterson, *American Automobile Workers*, 119.

29. Dave Moore, oral history, in *Talking Union*, Stepan-Norris and Zeitlin, 43.

30. John Dos Passos, "Detroit: City of Leisure," *New Republic* (July 27, 1932): 280–81.

31. Hall, "When Detroit's Out of Gear," 10.

32. Ibid., 13–14.

33. Ibid., 13.

34. Ibid., 14, 11.

35. Barnard, *Walter Reuther*, 28.

36. Paul Betters with J. Kerwin Williams and Sherwood Reeder, *Recent Federal-City Relations* (Washington, DC: United States Conference of Mayors, 1936), 3–4.

37. Sidney Fine, *Frank Murphy: The Detroit Years*, 353.

38. "Unemployed Seek Aid," *Dearborn Independent*, Jan. 23, 1931.

39. Ibid.

40. Becker, oral history, 72–73.

41. Cardinal, speech, 16.

42. Mildred Mourer, "Welfare Workers Cope with Unusual Local Situation," *Dearbornite*, Oct. 1930, 11.

43. See also "Dearborn Citizens to Get Welfare Relief First, Others Later," *Dearborn Independent*, Sept. 16, 1932.

44. Mildred Mourer, "Welfare Workers Cope with Unusual Local Situation," *Dearbornite*, Oct. 1930, 11.

45. "City Kitchen Gives Meals to Needy," *Dearborn Star*, Jan. 27, 1931.

46. "Rapidly Rising Need for Welfare Stores," *Dearborn Press*, Sept. 29, 1932.

47. "Budget Requests Cut," *Dearborn Press*, March 10, 1932.

48. "Community Fund Is Planned for City," *Dearborn Star*, April 8, 1930; "Citizens Gifts Exceed $20,000," *Dearborn Independent*, Nov. 6, 1931.

49. "Needy to Earn Their Keep," *Dearborn Press*, Dec. 8, 1932.

50. "Bankers . . . Report to Mayor on . . . Relief for Home-Owners," *Dearborn Press*, Aug. 25, 1932; "Dearborn Takes Steps to Aid Small Home Owners; Will Petition Congress," *Dearborn Press*, Jan. 5, 1933; "Mayor Ford's Address," *Dearborn Press*, Jan. 15, 1933; "Aid Building Boom," *Dearborn Independent*, June 5, 1936.

51. "Officials Seek Washington Aid," Feb. 18, 1938; "City Is Assured Added WPA Funds," Feb. 25, 1938; "1400 Certified for WPA Work," March 25, 1938; "WPA Sponsors Open House Week May 20," May 10, 1940; all in *Dearborn Independent*.

52. Lindsey, "Fields to Fords," 37.

53. Ibid., 26–27.

54. Keith Sward, *The Legend of Henry Ford* (New York: Rinehart, 1948), 228–30; Peterson, *American Automobile Workers*, 136, 137; Stepan-Norris and Zeitlin, *Talking Union*, 5.

55. "20,000 Storm Ford Plant," *Dearborn Star*, April 1, 1930.

56. Robert Cruden, "The Great Ford Myth," *New Republic* (March 16, 1932): 117.

57. "Mayor Issues Call to Relief," Feb. 5, 1930; "Unemployed Seek Aid," Jan. 23, 1931; "Mayor Warns Agitators," Nov. 25, 1932; all in *Dearborn Independent*.

58. "Unemployed Seek Aid," *Dearborn Independent*, Jan. 23, 1931.

59. "Council Plans to Aid Single Jobless Men," *Dearborn Press*, Jan. 23, 1931.

60. "Forward . . . ," *Dearborn Independent*, June 12, 1931.

61. This fateful demonstration was later known as the "1932 Hunger March." See Sidney Fine, *Frank Murphy: The Detroit Years*; Irving Bernstein, *The Lean Years: A History of the American Worker, 1920–1933* (Baltimore: Penguin, 1966); Maurice Sugar, *The Ford Hunger March* (Berkeley: Meiklejohn Civil Liberties Institute, 1980).

62. Woodford, *This Is Detroit*, photo, 123.

63. "300 Police Hold Marchers at Line," *Dearborn Independent*, June 9, 1933. A smaller follow-up march was held a little over a year later, which was squelched by hundreds

of local, county, and state police who put up a show of force with nightsticks, revolvers, and grenades of tear gas, while two National Guard airplanes swooped by at a low altitude. One newspaper estimated that there was a ratio of one gun per marcher. The marchers camped out for many hours on the Detroit-Dearborn border before giving up around midnight.

64. Babson, *Working Detroit*, 71–75.

65. Sidney Fine, *Sit-Down: The General Motors Strike of 1936-1937* (Ann Arbor: University of Michigan Press, 1969).

66. Babson, *Working Detroit*, 75.

67. Ibid., 92–93.

68. Alfred Chandler, ed., *Giant Enterprise: Ford, General Motors, and the Automobile Industry* (New York: Harcourt Brace, 1964), 225.

69. David Nye, *Henry Ford: "Ignorant Idealist"* (Port Washington, NY: Kennikat, 1979), 50–51; Babson, *Working Detroit*, 93.

70. Carl Raushenbush, *Fordism: Ford and the Workers, Ford and the Community* (New York: League for Industrial Democracy, 1937), 39–42.

71. Cardinal, speech, 30. Actually, Ford himself had started handpicking Dearborn police officers in the early 1920s.

72. Cardinal, speech, 27.

73. Babson, *Working Detroit*, 109.

74. Ibid.; Lichtenstein, "Life at the Rouge," 241–42.

75. The right to picket was upheld in *Thornhill v. Alabama*.

76. Babson, *Working Detroit*, 109–10.

77. Lichtenstein, "Life at the Rouge," 242.

78. Babson, *Working Detroit*, photos, 94, 104, 107.

79. Letter from Walter Reuther to AFL-CIO, 1967, in *American Labor: The Twentieth Century*, Jerold Auerbach (New York: Bobbs-Merrill, 1969): 433–34.

80. Reuther from 1950, quoted in *Walter Reuther*, Barnard, 144.

81. Ford, *Ford Ideals*, 293.

82. "Dearborn Michigan Market Report," Growth and Population (VF.DHM).

Chapter 7: Detroit Metropolis after Henry Ford

1. "One-Third," from "A Fair Day's Pay for a Fair Day's Work," Roosevelt to Congress, May 24, 1937.

2. For the welfare state, see William Chafe, ed., *The Achievement of American Liberalism: The New Deal and Its Legacies* (New York: Columbia University Press, 2003); Ronald Edsforth, *The New Deal: America's Response to the Great Depression* (Malden: Blackwell, 2000); Roland Marchand, "Where Lie the Boundaries of the Corporation? Explorations in 'Corporate Responsibility' in the 1930s," *Business and Economic History* 26.1 (1997): 80–100; Alan Brinkley, *The End of Reform: New Deal Liberalism in Recession and War* (New York: Knopf, 1995); Gwendolyn Mink, *The Wages of Motherhood: Inequality in the Welfare State, 1917-1942* (Ithaca: Cornell University Press, 1995); Colin Gordon, *New Deals: Business, Labor, and Politics in America, 1920-1935* (Cambridge University Press, 1994); David Montgomery, "Labor and the Political Leadership of New Deal America," *International Review of Social History* [Great Britain] 39.3 (1994): 335–60; Lizabeth Cohen, *Making a New Deal: Industrial Workers in Chicago, 1919-1939* (Cambridge University Press, 1990.

3. Alfred Sloan, *My Years with General Motors* (Garden City: Doubleday, 1964), 402.

4. For Detroit during these years, see Sugrue, *Origins of the Urban Crisis*. For this period generally, see Lizabeth Cohen, *A Consumer's Republic: The Politics of Mass Consumption in Postwar America* (New York: Alfred A. Knopf, 2003); Martin Daunton et al., eds., *The Politics of Consumption: Material Culture and Citizenship in Europe and America* (New York: Oxford University Press, 2001); Henry Louis Gates Jr. and Cornel West, *The African American Century: How Black Americans Have Shaped Our Country* (New York: Free Press, 2000); Olivier Zunz, *Why the American Century?* (Chicago: University of Chicago Press, 1998).

5. Babson, *Working Detroit*, 133.

6. Robert Sinclair and Bryan Thompson, *Metropolitan Detroit: An Anatomy of Social Change* (Cambridge: Ballinger, 1977), 10, 30.

7. *National Observer*, July 15, 1963, in *Detroit: City of Race and Class Violence*, B. J. Widick (Chicago: Quadrangle, 1972), 156–57.

8. Babson, *Working Detroit*, 131.

9. Barnard, *Walter Reuther*, 135.

10. Babson, *Working Detroit*, 133, 131.

11. The census statisticians expanded the boundaries of the metropolitan district from its 1930 definition, when it consisted of portions within Wayne, Macomb, and Oakland Counties, to an area that now included Lapeer, Livingston, Monroe, and St. Clair Counties in addition to the original three.

12. Ticknor, "Motor City," 290.

13. Babson, *Working Detroit*, 133–34 (original italics).

14. Ibid.; David Poremba, *Detroit: A Motor City History* (Charleston: Arcadia, 2001), 129; Darden et al., *Detroit*, 81; Thomas, *Redevelopment and Race*, 73.

15. Ticknor, "Motor City," 289–90.

16. Darden et al., *Detroit*, 22, 24.

17. *Detroit Free Press*, Oct. 14, 1940, in "Detroit's DSR, part 2," Jack Schramm, *Motor Coach Age* (March–April 1992): 15–16.

18. These are all the communities with a population of four thousand or more located in Detroit's metropolitan district as defined by the 1930 census, excluding Pontiac, Highland Park, and Hamtramck.

19. Thomas, *Redevelopment and Race*, 85–87; Darden et al., *Detroit*, 80–81.

20. Darden et al., *Detroit*, 126, 129; Sinclair and Thompson, *Metropolitan Detroit*, 31.

21. Thomas, *Redevelopment and Race*, 17.

22. Darden et al., *Detroit*, 138.

23. Ibid., 68; Thomas, *Life for Us Is What We Make It*, 158; Barnard, *Walter Reuther*, 206–7; Thomas Sugrue, "The Structures of Urban Poverty," in *The "Underclass" Debate: Views from History*, ed. Michael Katz (Princeton University Press, 1993), 106; Boyle, "No Union Sorrows," 23.

24. Barnard, *Walter Reuther*, 206–7; Sugrue, "Structures of Urban Poverty," 107.

25. Sugrue, "Structures of Urban Poverty," 107–8.

26. Barnard, *Walter Reuther*, 207.

27. Darden et al., *Detroit*, 76; Sugrue, *Origins of the Urban Crisis*, 144.

28. US Bureau of the Census, *Fifteenth Census of the United States, 1930*. Refer especially to the Sanborn maps, city directories, tax assessment rolls, subdivision plats, and real estate deeds.

29. "Dearborn Michigan Market Report," Growth and Population (VF.DHM)..

30. "Ford Foundation Plans 68 Homes, Apartments," *Milwaukee Sentinel*, July 16, 1939; National Register of Historic Places, "Preliminary Questionnaire, Springwells Park," 2013. The 1939 article states the projected population to be sixteen thousand; in the end, the 2010 population was sixteen hundred. I assume the original newspaper estimate was off by one decimal, as it seems unlikely one subdivision could hold so many people.

31. Bryan, *Beyond the Model T*, 80, 83.

32. National Register of Historic Places, "Preliminary Questionnaire, Springwells Park," 2013.

33. Ibid.

34. Wayne County Registry of Deeds.

35. "Springwells Park (Springwells) neighborhood in Dearborn, Michigan (MI), 48120, 48126 detailed profile," City-Data, http://www.city-data.com/neighborhood/Springwells-Park-Dearborn-MI.html.

36. Freund, *Colored Property*.

37. "Springwells Park (Springwells) neighborhood in Dearborn, Michigan (MI), 48120, 48126 detailed profile," City-Data, http://www.city-data.com/neighborhood/Springwells-Park-Dearborn-MI.html.

38. Sarah Jo Peterson, "The Politics of Land Use and Housing in World War II Michigan: Building Bombers and Communities" (PhD diss., Yale University, 2002); International Union, United Automobile, Aircraft and Agricultural Implement Workers of America (UAW-CIO), *Memorandum on Post War Housing* (Detroit: UAW-CIO, 1944); Thomas, *Redevelopment and Race*, 30–31, 33.

39. UAW-CIO, *Memorandum on Post War Urban Housing*, 10, 21.

40. Nelson Lichtenstein, *Most Dangerous Man in Detroit: Walter Reuther and the Fate of American Labor* (New York: Basic Books, 1995), 307–8.

41. UAW-CIO, *Memorandum on Post War Urban Housing*, 9, 11, 21–22.

42. Ibid., 9.

43. Stepan-Norris and Zeitlin, *Talking Union*, 20–25; Lichtenstein, "Life at the Rouge," 252.

44. Thomas, *Redevelopment and Race*, 73; Lichtenstein, "Life at the Rouge," 252; Boyle, "No Union Sorrows," 11; Sugrue, "Inalienable Right to Work," 115.

45. Sugrue, "Inalienable Right to Work," 117; Lichtenstein, "Life at the Rouge," 252.

46. William Andrew, "Factionalism and Anti-Communism: Ford Local 600," *Labor History* 20 (Spring 1979): 245–46; Lichtenstein, *Most Dangerous Man*, 290–91; Kevin Boyle, *The UAW and the Heyday of American Liberalism, 1945–1968* (Ithaca: Cornell University Press, 1995), 76–77.

47. Sugrue, "Inalienable Right to Work," 1995, 121.

48. Ibid., 121, 112.

49. Ibid., 124.

50. Lichtenstein, *Most Dangerous Man*, 290–91.

51. Sugrue, "Inalienable Right to Work," 119.

52. See Peterson, "Politics of Land Use."

53. For failed attempts at metropolitan planning by local policy makers, see Darden et al., *Detroit*, 235–50.

54. Ticknor refers to Detroit as a "blue-collar El Dorado" ("Motor City," 149); "slippery gains" is from Thomas, *Life for Us Is What We Make It*, 314.

Discussion of Sources

This study relies on some sources never before used by professional historians, such as a cache of automobile workers' oral histories at the Dearborn Historical Museum, or never before available, such as the 1930 manuscript census released in 2002. The use of oral histories as primary source material for the history of the automobile industry is valuable for relaying firsthand accounts of conditions for workers, both on and off the factory floor, and for addressing their lives at work as well as within the wider community. The manuscript census portrays these conditions in even more minute detail, covering household formation, familial relationships, communal living, the ratio of breadwinners to dependents, levels of occupation, homeownership status, appraisal value of housing, and distance to workplace.

Also newly published here are many sources that document the Ford Motor Company's shift during the 1920s toward acculturating workers to a suburban lifestyle and the attempt to raise rates of home- and car ownership. After all, Henry Ford viewed his company as an instrument of social change, and in the tradition of welfare capitalism, he took an interest in the living conditions of his workers. He also was keenly aware of his role in promoting a new form of urbanism, the suburb for the masses. Among the communication outlets at his disposal was *Ford News*, a company newsletter for workers that ran during the 1920s. While many other publications by the Ford Motor Company (such as *Ford Times*) or by workers (such as *Ford Facts*) have been written about extensively, *Ford News* has been rather neglected. What makes it worthy of historical examination is its role as a propaganda tool in advocating suburbanization.

Rounding out this work are fresh interpretations of sources that have already been published, such as oral histories from the Archives of Labor and Urban Affairs (ALUA) at Wayne State University. In addition, Ford Motor Company workers attracted intense attention from academics, statisticians, and reformers, whose observations are rich in sociological detail. Among the more useful studies are Chen-Nan Li's "A Summer in the Ford Works" (1928) and a survey conducted by the Bureau of Labor Statistics

(1930). These sources provide a valuable amount of information about the workers, including their education, financial status, commutes, recreation, consumer goods, even what they ate and how they slept. This study also uses sources essential for any urban history, such as Sanborn maps, housing deeds, building permits, subdivision plats, architectural plans, photographs, city directories, tax rolls, government reports, real estate advertisements, promotional literature, campaign materials, transit maps and schedules, town meeting minutes, ordinances and regulations, and newspapers. While some of these sources are stored at the Dearborn Historical Museum, others are found outside of conventional historical archives, located instead at governmental offices at the local and county levels.

Newspapers referred to within this work are the *Dearborn News, Dearborn Press, Dearborn Magazine, Fordson Independent, Springwells Independent,* and *Springwells Star,* as well as Detroit papers such as the *Detroit News, Detroit Times, Detroit Free Press,* and *Michigan Chronicle.* Also used is the *Dearborn Independent,* and it is important to note that, with the exception of the period from 1919 to 1927, when it was owned by Henry Ford and circulated nationally, this functioned merely as another local paper. However, while under Ford's ownership, the *Dearborn Independent* became infamous as a vehicle for his anti-Semitic diatribes. This study uses citations from the *Dearborn Independent* in both its phases.

The definitive collection for the Ford Motor Company is the Ford Archives, housed in the new Benson Ford Research Center located at the former Henry Ford Museum, now known as "The Henry Ford." This collection consists of papers found in Henry Ford's home and papers of the Ford Motor Company donated by the Ford Motor Company Archives (FMCA) for public use. The FMCA itself is a private collection managed by the company that is not open to the public. In other words, the Ford Archives are a subset of the Ford Motor Company Archives. Within this study, sources from the Ford Archives at the Benson Ford Research Center are referred to as BFRC.

From its inception shortly after Henry Ford's death in 1947, the Ford Archives collection has been used by scholars, and it was the main source for the most encyclopedic account of the Ford Motor Company to date: the trilogy of books by Allan Nevins and Frank Ernest Hill entitled *Ford,* published in the late 1950s and early 1960s. However, some scholars, in citing the Ford Archives, have failed to differentiate between this and the FMCA. Works that refer to the Ford Archives as FMCA include Stephen Meyer's *The Five Dollar Day* (1981) and Joyce Shaw Peterson's *American Automobile*

Workers, 1900–1933 (1987). More recently, Douglas Brinkley's *Wheels for the World* (2003) made the error of referring to the Benson Ford Research Center as the "Henry Ford Museum and Library."

For the purposes of this work, the Benson Ford Research Center was a source for newspaper clippings, company newsletters, advertisements, oral histories, and memoirs.

Selected Bibliography

Abbreviations

DHM   Dearborn Historical Museum
HF   City of Dearborn, Consolidation, History File
BFRC   Benson Ford Research Center's Ford Archives at the Henry Ford Museum
ALUA   Archives of Labor and Urban Affairs in the Reuther Library at Wayne State University
GPO   Government Printing Office

Primary Sources

Firsthand Accounts

Adray, Michael. Oral history. DHM.
Becker, Iris. Oral history. DHM.
Biermann, Bob. *The Gang on Kendal Street*. Memoir. Loudon, TN: St. Ben, 1999.
Cardinal, Joseph. Speech dated February 3, 1966. DHM.
Dancy, John. *Sand against the Wind*. Memoir. Detroit: Wayne State University Press, 1966.
Denby, Charles. *Indignant Heart*. Memoir. Detroit: Wayne State University Press, 1989.
Ford, Clyde. Memoir. BFRC.
"Greater Dearborn: The Consolidation Story." Unpublished paper. HF, DHM.
Henson, William. Oral history. DHM.
Karmann, Joseph. Oral history. DHM.
Kuta, Chester. Oral history. DHM.
Lathers, Marcus. "The Rural Area around Detroit." Papers, 1945–1961. DHM.
Marinovich, Irene Young. Oral history. ALUA.
Moore, Dave. Oral history. In *Talking Union*, by Judith Stepan-Norris and Maurice Zeitlin. Documentary history. Urbana: University of Illinois Press, 1996.
Moore, Julia. "History of the Dearborn Area." Unpublished paper dated 1957, Bentley Library, University of Michigan.
Parlogean, Andrew, and Nellie Parlogean. Oral history. DHM.
Sugar, Maurice. *The Ford Hunger March*. Berkeley: Meiklejohn Civil Liberties Institute, 1980.
Vartanian, Harold. Oral history. DHM.
Wibel, A.M. Reminiscences. BFRC.

Authored or Published by Henry Ford

"An America of Homes." *Ford News* 2.6 (January 15, 1922): 2.
"The American Workman." *Ford News* 3.19 (August 1, 1923): 2.

"Builders with Brains Plus Courage Create an Ideal Colony for Workers." *Dearborn Independent*, December 6, 1919.

"Car Service for Employes at Rouge." *Ford News* 4.16 (June 15, 1925): 8.

"Citizenship." *Ford News* 3.3 (December 1, 1922): 2.

"Employees' Sales Plan Finds Favor." *Ford News* 4.9 (March 1, 1924): 1–2.

"Employes Buy Fords." *Ford News* 4.11 (April 1, 1924): 1.

"Facing the Race Issue." *Dearborn Independent* 22.7 (December 10, 1921): 2.

Ford, Henry. *Ford Ideals*. Vol. 1, *Being a Selection from "Mr. Ford's Page" in The Dearborn Independent*. Dearborn Publishing, 1926.

———. Letter to the public. *Dearborn News*, June 9, 1928.

———. "Progress Reflected by City's High Standards." *Dearborn Press*, May 21, 1931.

Ford, Henry [attributed]. *The International Jew: The World's Foremost Problem*. Reprint of articles appearing in the *Dearborn Independent*. Dearborn Publishing, 1920.

Ford, Henry, with Samuel Crowther. *Moving Forward*. Garden City: Doubleday, 1930.

———. *My Life and Work*. Garden City: Doubleday, 1922.

———. *Today and Tomorrow*. Garden City: Doubleday, 1926.

Ford, Henry, with Fay Leone Faurote. *My Philosophy of Industry*. New York: Coward-McCann, 1929.

Ford Motor Company. *Helpful Hints and Advice to Ford Employees*. Detroit: Ford Motor Company, 1915.

"Graces of Yesterday Revived by Henry Ford." *Ford News* 8.5 (January 15, 1928): 3.

"Ideal Home Not in Crowded City." *Ford News* 1.9 (March 1, 1921): 1, 8.

"Ideal Suburban Home in Dearborn Ford Subdivision." *Ford News* 2.9 (March 1, 1922): 3.

"Immigrants." *Ford News* 1.7 (February 1, 1921): 4.

"Let's Have a Garden." *Ford News* 2.14 (May 15, 1922): 6, 8.

"May Queen Crowned at Festival on Village Green." *Ford News* 10.12 (June 16, 1930): 137.

"Mr. Ford Explains the Five-Day Week." *Ford News* 6.24 (October 15, 1926): 2.

"Mr. Ford's Page." *Dearborn Independent* 22.52 (October 21, 1922): 5.

"The Negro." *Dearborn Independent* 26.4 (November 14, 1925): 11.

"Prices Cut on All Ford Houses in Dearborn." *Ford News* 1.16 (June 15, 1921): 4, 8.

"Recreation." *Ford News* 3.24 (October 15, 1923): 2.

"Underpass Completed." *Ford News* 7.14 (May 15, 1927): 1.

"What I Have Learned from My Work: Prize-Winning Essays." *Ford News* 6.18 (July 15, 1926): 7.

"What You Will See When Going through Dearborn." *Ford News* 2.9 (March 1, 1922): 7.

"Wonderful Period for Auto Industry in the Near Future." *Ford News* 1.7 (February 1, 1921): 4.

Policy Studies and Proposals

"About City Streets and Country Roads." *Just a Minute* 46 (February 10, 1930): 1.

"About Going a-Borrowing." *Just a Minute* 25 (September 16, 1929): 1.

"About No Matter Who Is Elected." *Just a Minute* 30 (September 21, 1929): 1, 2.

"About Pay-as-You-Go." *Just a Minute* 3 (April 1, 1929): 1.

"About the Fourth City." *Just a Minute* 16 (July 15, 1929): 1–2.

Betters, Paul, with J. Kerwin Williams and Sherwood Reeder. *Recent Federal-City Relations*. Washington, DC: US Conference of Mayors, 1936.

Buttenheim, Harold S. "Urban Planning and Land Policies." In US National Resources Committee, Research Committee on Urbanism, *Supplementary Report of the Urbanism Committee to the National Resources Committee, Part III, Section I.* Washington, DC: GPO, 1939.

Consolidated Cities Association. Pamphlet. HF, DHM.

Detroit Housing Commission. "The Detroit Plan: A Program for Blight Elimination." Detroit: Housing Commission, 1946.

Detroit Mayor's Inter-Racial Committee. *The Negro in Detroit.* Detroit: Bureau of Government Research, 1926.

"The Detroit Metropolitan Area." Report. Detroit: Bureau of Governmental Research, 1924.

Douglass, Harlan. *The Suburban Trend.* New York: The Century, 1925.

Federal Writers' Program, Works Progress Administration (WPA). *Michigan: A Guide to the Wolverine State.* New York: Oxford, 1941.

Fordson Board of Commerce. "Fordson, Michigan: Western Gateway to Detroit." Report. City of Fordson. HF, DHM, 1927.

Glover Watson Organization. "Dearborn Facts and Figures." Pamphlet. City of Dearborn. HF, DHM, 1927.

Gries, John, and James Ford, eds. *Slums, Large-Scale Housing, and Decentralization.* Washington, DC: President's Conference of Home Building and Home Ownership, 1932.

Harris, Chauncy. "Suburbs." *American Journal of Sociology* 49.1 (July 1943): 1–13.

Li, Chen-Nan. "A Summer in the Ford Works." *Personnel Journal* 7 (June 1928): 18–32.

McKenzie, Roderick. *Metropolitan Community.* New York: McGraw-Hill, 1933.

Munger, Thomas. *Detroit Today.* Detroit: Board of Commerce, 1921.

Peddicord, Donley. "Henry Ford and His Home Town." Pamphlet. Henry Ford. HF, DHM, 1924.

Pound, Arthur. *Detroit: Dynamic City.* New York: D. Appleton-Century, 1940.

Rapid Transit Commission. "Proposed Financial Plan for a Rapid Transit System for the City of Detroit." Detroit: Rapid Transit Commission, 1923.

———. "Report of the Rapid Transit Commission to the Mayor's Finance Committee." Detroit: Rapid Transit Commission, 1926.

Reid, Paul. *Industrial Decentralization, Detroit Region, 1940–1950 (Projection to 1970).* Detroit: Metropolitan Area Regional Planning Commission, 1951.

"Standard of Living of Employees of Ford Motor Company in Detroit." *Monthly Labor Review* 30.6 (June 1930): 11–54.

Taylor, Graham. *Satellite Cities.* 1915. New York: Arno, 1970.

US Bureau of the Census. *Fourteenth Census of the United States: Population, 1920. Composition and Characteristics of the Population.* Washington, DC: GPO, 1921.

———. *Fifteenth Census of the United States, 1930: Population.* Washington, DC: GPO, 1931–1933.

———. *Sixteenth Census of the United States, 1940: Population.* Washington, DC: GPO, 1942–1943.

———. *Metropolitan Districts: Population and Area.* Clarence Batschelet, ed. Washington, DC: GPO, 1932.

US Bureau of the Census with Warren Thompson. *Population: The Growth of Metropolitan Districts, 1900–1940.* Washington, DC: GPO, 1947.

US National Resources Committee, Research Committee on Urbanism. *Our Cities: Their Role in the National Economy.* Washington, DC: GPO, 1937.

Wells, Carl. *Proposals for Downtown Detroit*. Washington, DC: Urban Land Institute, 1942.

Wengert, Egbert. *Financial Problems of the City of Detroit in the Depression*. Detroit Bureau of Governmental Research, Report No. 151. Detroit: Bureau of Governmental Research, 1939.

Wirth, Louis. "Urbanism as a Way of Life." *American Journal of Sociology* 44 (July 1938): 1–24.

Magazine Articles

Arnold, Marion. "Dearborn, Child of Destiny and Fate." *Dearborn Magazine* 1.1 (1926): 2.

Aronovici, Carol. "Let the Cities Perish." *Survey* 68 (October 1, 1932): 437–40.

———. "Suburban Development." In *Housing and Town Planning*, ed. Carol Aronovici. *Annals of the American Academy of Political and Social Science* 51. Philadelphia: American Academy of Political and Social Science, 1914.

Bailey, William. "The Twentieth-Century City." *American City* 31.2 (August 1924): 142–43.

Clyde, Walt. "Henry Ford's Home Town." *Dearborn Magazine* 1.1 (1926): 2.

Commons, John R. "Henry Ford, Miracle Maker." *The Independent* 102.3720 (May 1, 1920): 160–61, 189–91.

Cummings, Edith Mae. "The Reason for My Faith in Dearborn." *Pipp's Weekly* (August 8, 1925): 27.

Dos Passos, John. "Detroit: City of Leisure." *New Republic*, July 27, 1932, 280–82.

Duffus, Robert. "Detroit: Utopia on Wheels." *Harper's* 162 (December 1930): 50–51.

Erley, Robert. "The Enlargement of Dearborn." *City Manager Magazine* 8.7 (July 1926): 9–13.

Foster, William Trufant, and Waddill Catchings. "How Far Can Ford Go?" *World's Work* 53 (February 1927): 437–44.

Fowler, Charles. "Detroit's Struggle with the Traffic Problem." *American City* 30.6 (June 1924): 612–13.

Hall, Helen. "When Detroit's Out of Gear." *Survey Graphic* 64 (April 1, 1930): 9–14, 51–54.

"Housing an Important Problem." *Automotive Industries*, April 10, 1919. Clipbook, BFRC.

"The Inside Story of Henry Ford." *Dearborn Magazine* 1.1 (1926): 3.

Josephson, Matthew. "Detroit: City of Tomorrow." *Outlook* 151 (February 13, 1929): 243–78.

Kellor, Frances. "The Application of Americanization to Housing." *Architectural Review* 5.1 (January 1917): 2.

Lee, John R. "So Called Profit Sharing System in the Ford Plant." *Annals of the American Academy of Political and Social Science* 65 (May 1916): 297–310.

Levin, Samuel. "End of Ford Profit Sharing." *Personnel Journal* (October 1927): 161–70.

———. "Ford Profit Sharing, 1914–1920." *Personnel Journal* (October 1927): 75–86.

"Living on Ford's $7 a Day." *Literary Digest*, August 2, 1930, 8–9.

MacKaye, Benton, and Lewis Mumford. "The Townless Highways for the Motorist: A Proposal for the Automobile Age." *Harper's* 163 (August 1931): 347–56.

Morse, Mary. Letter to the editor. *New Republic*, August 31, 1927, 46.

Mumford, Lewis. "The Fourth Migration." *Survey Graphic*, special issue, 54.3 (May 1, 1925): 130–33.

———. "Regions—To Live In." *Survey Graphic* 54.3 (May 1, 1925): 152.

Nimmo, H.M. "Detroit." *American Magazine* 84 (December 1917): 36–65.

Pearson, Drew. "Ford Predicts the Passing of Big Cities and Decentralizing of Industry." *Motor World* 80 (August 28, 1924): 9.
Player, Cyril Arthur. "Detroit: Essence of America." *New Republic* (August 3, 1927): 272–75.
Strother, French. "What Kind of Pittsburgh Is Detroit?" *World's Work*, October 1926, 636.
Tarbell, Ida. "Every Man a Trade and a Farm." *McCall's* (July 1927): 5, 79–80.
"Three Years of Municipal Railway Operation in Detroit." *American City* 33.1 (July 1925): 28.
Van Cleef, Eugene. "The World's Greatest Migration." *American City* 39.3 (September 1928): 154.
Waldron, Webb. "Where Is America Going? Industrial Conditions in Detroit." *Century* 100 (May 1920): 61–62.
Walker, Charles. "Down and Out in Detroit." *The Forum* 86 (September 1931): 128–36.
Welliver, Judson. "Detroit, the Motor-Car Metropolis." *Munsey's* 67 (1919): 655.
Wilson, Edmund. "The Despot of Dearborn." *Scribner's* 90 (July 1931): 25–34.
———. "Detroit Paradoxes." *New Republic*, July 12, 1933, 232.

Newspaper Articles

"Asks Industry to Back Relief." *Detroit News*, February 10, 1931.
"Auto Builders Don't Sanction Profit Sharing." *Moline Mail*, January 9, 1914.
". . . Big Raid in South End." *Dearborn Press*, July 21, 1932.
"Blind Pigs Have Gone Say Police." *Dearborn Press*, June 12, 1930.
"Blind Pig Operators Arraigned." *Dearborn Independent*, May 2, 1930.
"Building Activities Are Being Rushed; Hundreds of Apartments and Homes under Construction." *Springwells Independent*, October 2, 1925.
"C. W. Treadwell O.K.'s Building of Small Homes." *Springwells Independent*, June 13, 1924.
"Calls Gifts Hush Money." No name of newspaper, January 19, 1914. Clipbook, BFRC.
"City Agrees to Rent Ford Plant Street Car Line." *Detroit Times*, January 6, 1925.
"City of Shacks or Fine Homes?" *Springwells Independent*, March 27, 1925.
"City's Growth Is in Suburbs." *Springwells Independent*, July 4, 1924.
"Consolidation Committee . . ." *Fordson Independent*, September 2, 1927.
"Construction Here during Year Exceeds $8,000,000." *Dearborn Independent*, June 12, 1931.
"Dearborn Again Tops Metropolitan Cities." *Dearborn Independent*, June 13, 1930.
"Dearborn Is Called Smiling, Happy City." *Detroit News*, October 6, 1923.
"Dearborn Is Cynosure of National Interest." *Grand Rapids Press*, September 23, 1923.
"Dearborn Is 27th in U.S. in Building." *Dearborn Star*, August 9, 1929.
"Dearborn Throbs, but without Smoke, Noise." *Detroit Free Press*, November 25, 1923.
"Delay Action on Ford Offer." *Detroit Free Press*, January 14, 1925.
"Detroit Has Strangest School in the World; Ford Runs It—Teaches Working Folks How to Spend More Money for Good Things." 1916. Clipbook, BFRC.
"DUR to Build Rouge Car Line." *Dearborn Press*, June 14, 1918.
Egelston, S.J. Letter to the editor. *Detroit News*, March 31, 1929.
"Expert Aid Offer Is Accepted." *Detroit Times*, December 1922. Clipbook, BFRC.
"Favors Plan for Creation of Metropolitan Area." *Detroit Times*, October 30, 1922.
"5,000 Workers Petition for Northwest Belt Line." *Detroit News*, January 25, 1925.
"Ford Assailed by Women, Indignant at His Reason for Discriminating." N.p., January 1913. Clipbook, BFRC.

"Ford Car Line Offer Up Again." *Detroit News*, January 18, 1925.
"Ford Discusses New Car Line." *Detroit Times*, January 1923. Clipbook, BFRC.
"Ford Foundation Plans 68 Homes, Apartments." *Milwaukee Sentinel*, July 16, 1939.
"Ford Gift Praised in Many Sermons." *Detroit News*, January 1914. Clipbook, BFRC.
"Ford Gives Women Same Pay as Men, to Receive $5 for an Eight-Hour Day." *New York Evening Post*, October 25, 1916.
"Ford May Help Build Car Lines for Workmen." *Detroit Free Press*, January 20, 1923.
"Ford May Help Metropolitan Growth: Appointment of His Engineer to Development Committee Called Significant." *Detroit Times*, January 31, 1923.
"Ford Offers to Build Car Line to Rouge." No name of newspaper, December 31, 1924. Clipbook, BFRC.
"Ford Plans to Extend DSR." *Detroit Times*, January 2, 1925.
"Ford Praised by Labor Men." *Springfield, Illinois, News*, January 8, 1914.
"Ford System Is Given Praise by Housing Expert." *Detroit News Tribune*, February 4, 1917.
"Ford Teaches Citizenship to His Employees." *Cincinnati Post*, June 29, 1914.
"Ford to Meet with Mayor on River Car Line." *Detroit News*, June 30, 1923.
"Ford Trolley Line Plan Reported." *Detroit Times*, January 1923. Clipbook, BFRC.
"Fordson and the City Beautiful." *Fordson Independent*, November 18, 1927.
Haigh, Henry. "Future Given in Address." *Dearborn Press*, May 21, 1931.
"Henry Ford in 'War' on Jazz Dancing." *Herald*, July 10, 1925.
"Henry Ford's Troubles." No name of newspaper, Portland, OR, April 30, 1914. Clipbook, BFRC.
"Housing Facilities Are Lacking." *Dearborn Press*, June 14, 1918.
"Illinois Labor Unions Rejoice at Precedent of Ford People." *Joliet Herald*, January 8, 1914.
"Industrial Sites Are Turned into Homes." *Springwells Independent*, June 26, 1925.
"An Interview with Henry Ford." *Chicago Daily Tribune*, July 12, 1935.
"Jo Labadie Praises Ford for Gift to Men." *Detroit Times*, January 8, 1914.
"Joy Reigns Supreme among Ford Employees." *Detroit Times*, January 1914. Clipbook, BFRC.
"The Joys, Pleasure, and Profits of Home Ownership in Springwells." *Springwells Independent*, June 13, 1924.
"The Labor World Is Startled." *Des Moines Capital*, January 18, 1914.
"Link Ford Would Build." N.p., December 1924. Clipbook, BFRC.
"Living Standards of Ford Men Improving with Profit Sharing." *Detroit News Tribune*, March 23, 1914.
Loosli, Albert. Letter to the editor. *Detroit News*, March 10, 1929.
"Mayor's Open Letter." *Detroit Free Press*, September 13, 1925.
McLauchlin, R. J. "Dearborn Sighs and Lays Away Dream of Industrial Greatness." *Detroit Saturday Night*, October 29, 1921.
Mearse, E. M. Letter to the editor. *Detroit News*, March 24, 1929.
"M.O. Plans Told by Mayo." *Detroit Times*, December 12, 1922.
"Move Out in Ozone District." *Springwells Independent*, July 4, 1924.
"Murphy Asks Industry Run 'Own Welfare.'" *Detroit News*, April 26, 1931.
"New DSR Line Nearly Done." *Detroit News*, March 8, 1925.
"No Street Cars in 10 Years, Says Ford." *American*, Boston, November 22, 1919.
"Oakman Car Line Pact Near." No name of newspaper, December 30, 1924. Clipbook, BFRC.

"Oakman Line Deal Approved." *Detroit News*, January 22, 1925.
"Oakman Offer Made to City." *Detroit News*, June 27, 1923.
"Old Dances for New." *Traveler*, Boston, August 5, 1925.
"Philanthropist Ford." *Monitor*, Wankato, KS, April 30, 1914.
"Plain Talk." Letter to the editor. *Detroit News*, March 31, 1929.
"Presence of Blind Pigs Here Is Admitted by Henry Ford." *Dearborn Star*, March 25, 1930.
"Professors Interested in Expenditures of $10 Million." *Muskegon Times*, January 8, 1914.
"Realtors Pledge Aid for Better Homes." *Springwells Independent*, July 3, 1925.
"Record Construction to Continue: Building Head Urges Creation of Central Body to Control Future Problems." *Fordson Independent*, June 4, 1926.
Regan, Henry. Letter to the editor. *Detroit News*, March 31, 1929.
"Salaries and Marriages." *St. Paul Dispatch*, January 28, 1914.
Save Dearborn Association. Editorial. *Dearborn Press*, May 17, 1928.
"Seeks to Split Welfare Costs." *Detroit News*, April 21, 1931.
"Storm Factory for Ford Jobs." *La Crosse Tribune*, January 12, 1914.
"Street Car Service Greatly Increased in 1929." *Dearborn Independent*, April 30, 1930.
"A Taxpayer." Letter to the editor. *Detroit News*, March 31, 1929.
"10 Million Ford Gives to Employees Will Be Spent by Individual Families Question Interesting U. of M. Sociologists." *Detroit Tribune*, January 7, 1914.
"They Know How to Get Along." *Dearborn Independent*, May 10, 1940.
"300 Police Hold Marchers at Line." *Dearborn Independent*, June 9, 1933.
"Wave of Population Growth Rolls West from Detroit." N.p., November 30, 1924. Clipbook, BFRC.
"Waxed Dance Floor Playground of Henry Ford." *Detroit Free Press*, August 2, 1925.
Wheeler, H. A. Letter to the editor. *Detroit News*, March 31, 1929.
Whipple, Harvey. "City Plan Commission Begins Its Great Task of Bringing Order out of Detroit's Chaos." *Detroit Saturday Night*, May 3, 1919.
Wilson, Ronald. Letter to the editor. *Detroit News*, March 10, 1929.
"Workers' Prosperity Key to City's Success." *Detroit Free Press*, January 25, 1925.

Secondary Sources

Ammerman, Albert. "A Sociological Survey of Dearborn." Master's thesis, University of Michigan Press, 1940.
Asher, Robert, and Ronald Edsforth, eds. *Autowork*. Albany: State University of New York Press, 1995.
Asher, Robert, and Charles Stephenson, eds. *Labor Divided: Race and Ethnicity in United States Labor Struggles, 1835–1960*. Albany: State University of New York Press, 1990.
Babson, Steve. "Class, Craft, and Culture: Tool and Die Makers and the Organization of the UAW." *Michigan Historical Review* 14.1 (1988): 33–55.
———. *Working Detroit: The Making of a Union Town*. New York: Adama, 1984.
Bak, Richard. *Detroit: Across Three Centuries*. Ann Arbor, MI: Sleeping Bear Press, 2001.
———. *Henry and Edsel: The Creation of the Ford Empire*. Hoboken, NJ: Wiley and Sons, 2003.
Barnard, John. *American Vanguard: The United Auto Workers During the Reuther Years, 1935–1970*. Detroit: Wayne State University Press, 2004.

────. *Walter Reuther and the Rise of the Auto Workers*. Boston: Little, Brown, 1983.

Baron, Ava, ed. *Work Engendered: Towards a New History of American Labor*. Ithaca: Cornell University Press, 1991.

Barrett, James R. "Americanization from the Bottom Up: Immigration and the Remaking of the Working Class in the United States, 1880–1930." *Journal of American History* 79 (1992): 996–1020.

Barrett, James R., and David Roediger. "Inbetween Peoples: Race, Nationality, and the 'New Immigrant' Working Class." *Journal of American Ethnic History* 16.3 (1997): 3–44.

Black, Harold. "Restrictive Covenants in Relation to Segregated Negro Housing in Detroit." Master's thesis, Wayne State University Press, 1947.

Borchert, James. "Cities in the Suburbs: Heterogeneous Communities on the U.S. Urban Fringe, 1920–1960." *Urban History* [Great Britain] 23.2 (1996): 211–27.

Boyle, Kevin. *Arc of Justice: A Saga of Race, Civil Rights, and Murder in the Jazz Age*. New York: Holt, 2004.

────. "The Ruins of Detroit: Exploring the Urban Crisis in the Motor City." *Michigan Historical Review* 27.1 (2001): 109–27.

────. "'There Are No Union Sorrows that the Union Can't Heal': The Struggle for Racial Equality in the UAW, 1940–1960." *Labor History* 35 (1995): 5–23.

────. *The UAW and the Heyday of American Liberalism, 1945–1968*. Ithaca: Cornell University Press, 1995.

Brinkley, Alan. *The End of Reform: New Deal Liberalism in Recession and War*. New York: Alfred A. Knopf, 1995.

Brinkley, Douglas. *Wheels for the World*. New York: Viking, 2003.

Brody, David. "Reconciling the Old Labor History and the New." *Pacific Historical Review* 62.1 (1993): 1–18.

Brogger, Fredrik. "Grinding the Gears of Production and Consumption: Representational versus Nonrepresentational Advertising for Automobiles in the Mid-1920s." *Prospects* 15 (1990): 197–224.

Brown, Clair. *American Standards of Living, 1918–1988*. Cambridge: Blackwell, 1994.

Brown, Michael K. "Bargaining for Social Rights: Unions and the Reemergence of Welfare Capitalism, 1945–1952." *Political Science Quarterly* 112.4 (1997–1998): 645–74.

Brueggemann, John. "The Power and Collapse of Paternalism: The Ford Motor Company and Black Workers, 1937–1941." *Social Problems* 47.2 (2000): 220–40.

Bruegmann, Robert. *Sprawl: A Compact History*. Chicago: University of Chicago Press, 2005.

Brunk, Thomas. *Leonard B. Willeke: Excellence in Architecture and Design*. Detroit: University of Detroit Press, 1986.

Bryan, Ford. *Beyond the Model T: The Other Ventures of Henry Ford*. Detroit: Wayne State University Press, 1990.

Canaan, Gareth. "'Part of the Loaf': Economic Conditions of Chicago's African American Working Class during the 1920s." *Journal of Social History* 35.1 (2001): 147–74.

Cleven, Brian. "Henry Ford's 'Tasty Little Town': Life and Logging in Pequaming." *Michigan History* 83.1 (1999): 18–23.

Coben, Stanley. *Rebellion against Victorianism: The Impetus for Cultural Change in 1920s America*. New York: Oxford University Press, 1991.

Cohen, Lizabeth. *A Consumer's Republic: The Politics of Mass Consumption in Postwar America*. New York: Alfred A. Knopf, 2003.

———. *Making a New Deal: Industrial Workers in Chicago, 1919–1939.* Cambridge University Press, 1990.

Cowie, Jefferson, and Joseph Heathcott, eds. *Beyond the Ruins: The Meanings of Deindustrialization.* Ithaca: ILR Press, 2003.

Crawford, Margaret. *Building the Workingman's Paradise: The Design of American Company Towns.* London: Verso, 1995.

Cullen, Jim. *The American Dream: A Short History of an Idea That Shaped a Nation.* New York: Oxford University Press, 2003.

Darden, Joe, et al. *Detroit: Race and Uneven Development.* Philadelphia: Temple University Press, 1987.

Daunton, Martin, and Matthew Hilton, eds. *The Politics of Consumption: Material Culture and Citizenship in Europe and America.* New York: Oxford University Press, 2001.

Davis, Donald F. "The City Remodelled: The Limits of Automotive Industry Leadership in Detroit, 1910–1929." *Histoire Sociale—Social History* 13.26 (November 1980): 451–86.

———. *Conspicuous Production: Automobiles and Elites in Detroit, 1899–1933.* Philadelphia: Temple University Press, 1988.

Dempsey, Mary. "Fordlandia." *Michigan History* 78.4 (1994): 24–33.

Denning, Michael. *The Cultural Front: The Laboring of American Culture in the Twentieth Century.* London: Verso, 1996.

Eckert, Kathryn Bishop. *Buildings of Michigan.* New York: Oxford University Press, 1993.

Edsforth, Ronald. *Class Conflict and Cultural Consensus: The Making of a Mass Consumer Society in Flint, Michigan.* New Brunswick: Rutgers University Press, 1987.

Farber, David. *Sloan Rules: Alfred P. Sloan and the Triumph of General Motors.* Chicago: University of Chicago Press, 2002.

Fine, Sidney. *Violence in the Model City: The Cavanaugh Administration, Race Relations, and the Detroit Riot of 1967.* Ann Arbor: University of Michigan Press, 1989.

Fishman, Robert. "The Metropolitan Tradition in American Planning." In *The American Planning Tradition,* ed. Robert Fishman. Baltimore: Johns Hopkins University Press, 2000.

Fogelson, Robert. *Bourgeois Nightmares: Suburbia, 1870–1930.* New Haven: Yale University Press, 2005.

Foster, Mark S. "From Streetcar to Superhighway: American City Planners and Urban Transportation, 1900–1940." Philadelphia: Temple University Press, 1981.

Freidmann, John, and Robin Bloch. "American Exceptionalism in Regional Planning, 1933–2000." *International Journal of Urban and Regional Research* 14.4 (December 1990): 576–601.

Freund, David. *Colored Property: State Policy and White Racial Politics in Suburban America.* Chicago: University of Chicago Press, 2007.

Gabin, Nancy. *Feminism in the Labor Movement: Women and the United Auto Workers, 1935–1975.* Ithaca: Cornell University Press, 1990.

Gitelman, H. M. "Welfare Capitalism Reconsidered." *Labor History* 33.1 (1992): 5–31.

Goings, Kenneth, and Raymond Mohl, eds. *The New African American Urban History.* Thousand Oaks: Sage, 1996.

Goldberg, David. *Discontented America: The United States in the 1920s.* Baltimore: Johns Hopkins University Press, 1999.

Grandin, Greg. *Fordlandia: The Rise and Fall of Henry Ford's Forgotten Jungle City.* New York: Metropolitan Books, 2009.

Green, William C., and Ernest J. Yanarella, eds. *North American Auto Unions in Crisis: Lean Production as Contested Terrain.* Albany: State University of New York Press, 1996.

Harris, Richard. *Creeping Conformity: How Canada Became Suburban, 1900–1960.* Toronto: University of Toronto Press, 2004.

Harris, Richard, and Robert Lewis. "The Geography of North American Cities and Suburbs, 1900–1950: A New Synthesis." *Journal of Urban History* 27.3 (March 2001): 262–93.

Harvey, David. *The Condition of Postmodernity.* Oxford: Blackwell, 1989.

Henrickson, Wilma Wood, ed. *Detroit Perspectives: Crossroads and Turning Points.* Detroit: Wayne State University Press, 1991.

Hirsch, Arnold. "With or Without Jim Crow: Black Residential Segregation in the United States." In *Urban Policy in Twentieth-Century America,* edited by Arnold Hirsch and Raymond Mohl. New Brunswick: Rutgers University Press, 1993.

Hise, Greg. "Homebuilding and Industrial Decentralization in Los Angeles: The Roots of the Post–World War II Urban Region." In *Planning the Twentieth-Century American City,* edited by Mary Corbin Sies and Christopher Silver. Baltimore: Johns Hopkins University Press, 1996.

Hooker, Clarence. *Life in the Shadows of the Crystal Palace, 1910–1927: Ford Workers in the Model T Era.* Bowling Green: Bowling Green State University Press, 1997.

Hounshell, David. *From the American System to Mass Production.* Baltimore: Johns Hopkins University Press, 1984.

Jacoby, Sanford. *Masters to Managers.* New York: Columbia University Press, 1991.

Jones, Jacqueline. *The Dispossessed: America's Underclasses from the Civil War to the Present.* New York: Basic Books, 1992.

Katz, Michael, ed. *The Underclass Debate: Views from History.* Princeton, NJ: Princeton University Press, 1993.

Kay, Jane Holtz. *Asphalt Nation: How the Automobile Took Over America, and How We Can Take It Back.* New York: Crown, 1997.

Kruse, Kevin. *White Flight: Atlanta and the Making of Modern Conservatism.* Princeton, NJ: Princeton University Press, 2005.

Kruse, Kevin, and Thomas Sugrue, eds. *The New Suburban History.* Chicago: University of Chicago Press, 2006.

Kusmer, Kenneth. "African Americans in the City since World War II: From the Industrial City to the Post Industrial Era." *Journal of Urban History* 21 (1995): 458–504.

Lassiter, Matthew. *The Silent Majority: Suburban Politics in the Sunbelt South.* Princeton, NJ: Princeton University Press, 2006.

Levine, David Allan. *Internal Combustion: The Races in Detroit, 1915–1926.* Westport: Greenwood Press, 1976.

Lewchuk, Wayne. "Men and Monotony: Fraternalism as a Managerial Strategy at the Ford Motor Company." *Journal of Economic History* 53.4 (December 1993): 824–56.

Lewis, David. "The Rise and Fall of Old Henry's Northern Empire." *Cars and Parts* (December 1973): 90–97.

Lewis, Robert, ed. *Manufacturing Suburbs.* Philadelphia: Temple University Press, 2004.

Lichtenstein, Nelson. "Life at the Rouge: A Cycle of Workers' Control." In *Life and Labor: Dimensions of American Working-Class History,* edited by Charles Stephenson and Robert Asher (Albany: State University of New York Press, 1986).

———. *Most Dangerous Man in Detroit: Walter Reuther and the Fate of American Labor.* New York: Basic Books, 1995.

Lindsey, Howard. "Fields to Fords, Feds to Franchise: African American Empowerment in Inkster, Michigan." PhD diss., University of Michigan, 1993.

Littmann, William. "Designing Obedience: The Architecture and Landscape of Welfare Capitalism, 1880–1930." *International Labor and Working-Class History* 53 (1998): 88–114.

Loeb, Carolyn. "Entrepreneurial Vernacular: Developers' Subdivisions in the 1920s." PhD diss., City University of New York, 1990.

Maloney, Thomas N., and Warren C. Whatley. "Making the Effort: The Contours of Racial Discrimination in Detroit's Labor Markets, 1920–1940." *Journal of Economic History* 55.3 (1995): 465–93.

Mandell, Nikki. *The Corporation as Family: The Gendering of Corporate Welfare, 1890–1930*. Chapel Hill: University of North Carolina Press, 2002.

Martin, Elizabeth Anne. *Detroit and the Great Migration, 1916–1929*. Ann Arbor: Bentley Historical Library, 1993.

Massey, Douglas, and Nancy Denton. *American Apartheid: Segregation and the Making of the Underclass*. Cambridge: Harvard University Press, 1993.

May, Martha. "Bread before Roses: American Workingmen, Labor Unions, and the Family Wage." In *Women, Work and Protest*, edited by Ruth Milkman. London: Routledge, 1985.

McShane, Clay. *Down the Asphalt Path*. New York: Columbia University Press, 1994.

Mendel, Ronald. "Industrial Unionism in the American Automobile Industry during the Post-World War I Era, 1918–1923." *Labour History Review* [Great Britain] 67.1 (2002): 49–63.

Montgomery, David. "Labor and the Political Leadership of New Deal America." *International Review of Social History* [Great Britain] 39.3 (1994): 335–60.

Mullin, John. "Henry Ford Field and Factory: An Analysis of the Ford Sponsored Village Industries Experiment in Michigan, 1918–1941." *Journal of the American Planning Association* 48.4 (1982): 419–31.

Murage, Njeru. "Making Migrants an Asset: The Detroit Urban League-Employers Alliance in Wartime Detroit, 1916–1919." *Michigan Historical Review* 26.1 (2000): 66–93.

Nelson, Bruce. "Class, Race and Democracy in the CIO: The 'New' Labor History Meets the 'Wages of Whiteness.'" *International Review of Social History* [Great Britain] 41.3 (1996): 351–74.

Nevins, Allan, and Frank Ernest Hill. *Ford: Decline and Rebirth, 1933–1962*. New York: Scribner, 1963.

———. *Ford: Expansion and Challenge, 1915–1933*. New York: Scribner, 1957.

———. *Ford: The Times, the Man, the Company*. New York: Scribner, 1954.

Nicolaides, Becky. *My Blue Heaven: Life and Politics in the Working-Class Suburbs of Los Angeles, 1920–1965*. Chicago: University of Chicago Press, 2002.

Nicolaides, Becky, and Andrew Wiese, eds. *The Suburb Reader*. New York: Routledge, 2006.

Peterson, Joyce Shaw. *American Automobile Workers, 1900–1933*. Albany: State University of New York Press, 1987.

Peterson, Sarah Jo. "The Politics of Land Use and Housing in World War II Michigan: Building Bombers and Communities." PhD diss., Yale University, 2002.

Pietrykowski, Bruce. "Gendered Employment in the U.S. Auto Industry: A Case Study of the Ford Motor Co. Phoenix Plant, 1922–1940." *Review of Radical Political Economics* 27.3 (1995): 39–48.

Piore, Michael J., and Charles F. Sabel. *The Second Industrial Divide*. New York: Basic Books, 1984.

Poremba, David. *Detroit: A Motor City History*. Charleston: Arcadia, 2001.

Radford, Gail. *Modern Housing for America*. Chicago: University of Chicago Press, 1996.

Roediger, David. "The Limits of Corporate Reform: Fordism, Taylorism, and the Working Class in the United States, 1914–1929." In *Worktime and Industrialization*, edited by Gary Cross. Philadelphia: Temple University Press, 1988.

———. "What If Labor Were Not White and Male? Recentering Working-Class History and Reconstructing Debate on the Unions and Race." *International Labor and Working-Class History* 51 (1997): 72–95.

Roediger, David, and Philip S. Foner. *Our Own Time: A History of American Labor and the Working Day*. New York: Greenwood Press, 1989.

Rubenstein, James M. *Making and Selling Cars: Innovation and Change in the U.S. Automotive Industry*. Baltimore: Johns Hopkins University Press, 2001.

Rupert, Mark. *Producing Hegemony: The Politics of Mass Production and American Global Power*. Cambridge University Press, 1995.

Sharoff, Robert. *American City: Detroit Architecture, 1845–2005*. Detroit: Wayne State University Press, 2005.

Schramm, Jack. "Detroit's DSR, Part 1." *Motor Coach Age* 42.1–2 (January–February 1991): 24.

———. "Detroit's DSR, Part 2." *Motor Coach Age* (March–April 1992): 15–16.

Schramm, Jack, William Henning, and Thomas Dworman. *Detroit's Street Railways, 1922–1956*. Chicago: Central Electric Railfans' Association, 1980.

Segal, Howard P. "'Little Plants in the Country': Henry Ford's Village Industries and the Beginning of Decentralized Technology in Modern America." *Prospects* 13 (1988): 181–223.

———. *Recasting the Machine Age: Henry Ford's Village Industries*. Amherst: University of Massachusetts Press, 2005.

Smith, Mike. "'Let's Make Detroit a Union Town': The History of Labor and the Working Class in the Motor City." *Michigan Historical Review* 27.2 (2001): 157–73.

Smith, Terry. *Making the Modern*. Chicago: University of Chicago Press, 1993.

Stepan-Norris, Judith, and Maurice Zeitlin. *Talking Union*. Urbana: University of Illinois Press, 1996.

Stevenson, Heon. *Selling the Dream: Advertising the American Automobile, 1930–1980*. London: Academy, 1995.

Stilgoe, John. *Borderland: Origins of the American Suburb, 1820–1939*. New Haven: Yale University Press, 1988.

Sugrue, Thomas. "Crabgrass-Roots Politics: Race, Rights, and the Reaction against Liberalism in the Urban North, 1940–1964." *Journal of American History* 82.2 (September 1995): 551–78.

———. "'Forget about Your Inalienable Right to Work': Deindustrialization and Its Discontents at Ford, 1950–1953." *International Labor and Working-Class History* 48 (1995): 112–30.

———. *Origins of the Urban Crisis: Race and Inequality in Postwar Detroit*. Princeton, NJ: Princeton University Press, 1996.

———. "Segmented Work, Race-Conscious Workers: Structure, Agency and Division in the CIO Era." *International Review of Social History* [Great Britain] 41.3 (1996): 389–406.

———. "The Structures of Urban Poverty." In *The "Underclass" Debate: Views from History*, edited by Michael Katz. Princeton, NJ: Princeton University Press, 1993.

Taylor, Henry, and Walter Hill, eds. *Historical Roots of the Urban Crisis: African Americans in the Industrial City, 1900–1950*. New York: Garland, 2000.

Teaford, Jon C. *Cities of the Heartland: The Rise and Fall of the Industrial Midwest*. Bloomington: Indiana University Press, 1993.

Thomas, June Manning. *Redevelopment and Race: Planning a Finer City in Postwar Detroit*. Baltimore: Johns Hopkins University Press, 1997.

Thomas, Richard W. *Life for Us Is What We Make It: Building Black Community in Detroit, 1915–1945*. Bloomington: Indiana University Press, 1992.

Thompson, Heather. *Whose Detroit? Politics, Labor, and Race in a Modern American City*. Ithaca: Cornell University Press, 2001.

Ticknor, Thomas. "Motor City: The Impact of the Automobile Industry upon Detroit, 1900–1975." PhD diss., University of Michigan, 1978.

Tobey, Ronald, Charles Wetherell, and Jay Brigham. "Moving Out and Settling In: Residential Mobility, Home Owning and the Public Enframing of Citizenship, 1921–1950." *American Historical Review* 95 (1990): 1395–422.

Tone, Andrea. *The Business of Benevolence: Industrial Paternalism in Progressive America*. Ithaca: Cornell University Press, 1997.

Walker, Richard, and Robert Lewis. "Beyond the Crabgrass Frontier: Industry and the Spread of North American Cities, 1850–1950." *Journal of Historical Geography* [Great Britain] 27.1 (2001): 3–19.

Watkins, Myron. "The Labor Situation in Detroit." *Journal of Political Economics* 28 (1920): 845–51.

Watts, Steven. *The People's Tycoon: Henry Ford and the American Century*. New York: Alfred A. Knopf, 2005.

Whaples, Robert. "Winning the Eight-Hour Day, 1909–1919." *Journal of Economic History* 50.2 (June 1990): 393–406.

Wiese, Andrew. *Places of Their Own: African-American Suburbanization in the Twentieth Century*. Chicago: University of Chicago Press, 2004.

Wolcott, Victoria W. *Remaking Respectability: African American Women in Interwar Detroit*. Chapel Hill: University of North Carolina Press, 2001.

Woodford, Arthur. *This Is Detroit, 1701–2001*. Detroit: Wayne State University Press, 2001.

Wunsch, James. "The Suburban Cliché." *Journal of Social History* 28 (1995): 643–58.

Zunz, Olivier. *The Changing Face of Inequality: Urbanization, Industrial Development, and Immigrants in Detroit, 1880–1920*. Chicago: University of Chicago Press, 1982.

Index